THE
EVERYTHING®
Organic Cooking
for Baby & Toddler
Book

Dear Reader,

Like you, we are parents trying to take the best possible care of our children. In our quest to help guide our children to good health, we have found organic cooking to be an important part of our family life. Our children come into this world all-natural, and we are trying our best to keep them that way.

We also believe that, as parents, we have a responsibility to protect our planet for our children and their children. Organic farming and food production contribute to that goal. Rather than putting toxic chemicals into the air, soil, and water, organic farming uses natural solutions to food-production challenges. Organics are not just better for our families and our planet, but they are also better for the people who work hard to bring food to our tables, because they are not exposed to dangerous chemicals.

The organic lifestyle helps us to be better parents, better members of the world community, and better advocates for the future of the planet. Thank you for joining us in this endeavor.

Good eating,

Megan and *Kim*

Welcome to the EVERYTHING® Series!

These handy, accessible books give you all you need to tackle a difficult project, gain a new hobby, comprehend a fascinating topic, prepare for an exam, or even brush up on something you learned back in school but have since forgotten.

You can choose to read an *Everything*® book from cover to cover or just pick out the information you want from our four useful boxes: e-questions, e-facts, e-alerts, and e-ssentials.

We give you everything you need to know on the subject, but throw in a lot of fun stuff along the way, too.

We now have more than 400 *Everything*® books in print, spanning such wide-ranging categories as weddings, pregnancy, cooking, music instruction, foreign language, crafts, pets, New Age, and so much more. When you're done reading them all, you can finally say you know *Everything*®!

QUESTION?
Answers to
common questions

FACTS
Important snippets
of information

ALERTS!
Urgent
warnings

ESSENTIALS
Quick
handy tips

PUBLISHER Karen Cooper

DIRECTOR OF ACQUISITIONS AND INNOVATION Paula Munier

MANAGING EDITOR, EVERYTHING SERIES Lisa Laing

COPY CHIEF Casey Ebert

ACQUISITIONS EDITOR Katie McDonough

DEVELOPMENT EDITOR Brett Palana-Shanahan

EDITORIAL ASSISTANT Hillary Thompson

Visit the entire Everything® series at *www.everything.com*

THE EVERYTHING® ORGANIC COOKING FOR BABY & TODDLER BOOK

300 naturally delicious recipes to
get your child off to a healthy start

Kim Lutz and Megan Hart, MS, RD

A adamsmedia

Avon, Massachusetts

An Everything® Series Book.
Everything® and everything.com® are registered trademarks of F+W Publications, Inc.

Published by Adams Media, an F+W Publications Company
57 Littlefield Street, Avon, MA 02322. U.S.A.
www.adamsmedia.com

ISBN 10: 1-59869-926-1
ISBN 13: 978-1-59869-926-5

Printed in the United States of America.

J I H G F E D C B A

Library of Congress Cataloging-in-Publication Data
available from the publisher.

This publication is designed to provide accurate and authoritative information with regard to the subject matter covered. It is sold with the understanding that the publisher is not engaged in rendering legal, accounting, or other professional advice. If legal advice or other expert assistance is required, the services of a competent professional person should be sought.
—From a *Declaration of Principles* jointly adopted by a Committee of the American Bar Association and a Committee of Publishers and Associations

Many of the designations used by manufacturers and sellers to distinguish their products are claimed as trademarks. Where those designations appear in this book and Adams Media was aware of a trademark claim, the designations have been printed with initial capital letters.

This book is available at quantity discounts for bulk purchases.
For information, please call 1-800-289-0963.

Dedication

This book is dedicated to our loving and supportive families—Andy and Mason, Steve, Casey, and Evan.

Acknowledgments

Thanks to everyone who helped us with this project. Humongous thanks go to Andy and Steve. Andy packed up the house, acted as Super Dad, washed dishes, walked the dog, and was an all-around good guy. Steve tasted about a million dishes, entertained and distracted the children, and tried to maintain some order in the house. Our children kept us as level-headed as possible, laughing in the midst of all the chaos. Immense gratitude goes to our parents and siblings who supported us and believed in us. Thanks to our many friends who provided us with invaluable support, taste testing, child care, and input during the creation of this book. Thank you also to Gina, who brought us this great opportunity.

Contents

Introduction   ix

1   **Why Organic?**   1
What Is Organic?   2
Why Is Organic Important?   3
Top Twenty Heroic Organic Foods   4
How to Create a Healthy Organic Table   6
Fresh, Frozen, or Canned? What to Choose   7

2   **Introduction to Feeding**   11
Breast Milk: The Ultimate Organic Food   12
When Formula Is Best   14
When Is My Baby Ready for Solids?   16
How Much Food Should I Offer My Child?   18
How Do I Safely Feed My Child?   22
Kitchen Equipment, Tools, and Gadgets   27
The Organic Family Pantry   28

3   **Four to Six Months**   31

4   **Six to Nine Months**   55

5   **Nine to Twelve Months**   83

6   **Twelve to Eighteen Months**   119

7   **Eighteen to Twenty-Four Months**   153

8   **Twenty-Four to Thirty-Six Months**   195

Appendix A: Weekly Organic Menus for Each Age Group   235
Appendix B: Resources for More Information   247
Appendix C: Nutritional Information for Common Baby Foods   251
Appendix D: Glossary of Basic Cooking Terms   257

Index   269

Introduction

New parents are faced with what seems like a million decisions to make. The choices surrounding how and what to feed your baby or toddler are some of the most important decisions that you will make. The foods that you choose to provide will help your child's body and mind grow and develop to their fullest potential. How those foods came from the farm to the table will greatly impact not only the health of your baby, but also the health of our planet. Choosing to feed your baby and toddler organic food is one choice that is good for your child, your family, and your world.

Luckily, this serious decision is also delicious! *The Everything® Organic Cooking for Baby & Toddler Book* contains more than 300 recipes that will delight your baby from first foods to organic family dining. How can preparing Pear Apple Crisp, Blueberry Pancakes, and Pineapple Coconut Rice Pudding help save the world? As this book explains, organic farming is better for the environment. Organic farmers do not use toxic pesticides, insecticides, and synthetic fertilizers. Instead, organic farmers use natural methods—including crop rotation, natural fertilizers, and letting fields lie fallow—to allow nature's bounty to shine through. Organic livestock are given access to fresh air, fresh water, and a healthy diet; they are not given routine doses of antibiotics or warehoused in cramped quarters. Organic farming contributes to cleaner air, water, and soil. The simple act of choosing organic means that you are also helping to ensure that the natural environment is protected.

Since the vast majority of a baby's nutrition in the first year of life comes from breast milk or formula, babies have the opportunity to learn about different tastes and textures during their early experiences with food. This cookbook provides recipes for those basic purées and sets the groundwork for introducing a variety of tastes, flavors, and combinations to help babies develop into healthy eaters as they grow.

These recipes emphasize natural sweeteners and seasonings rather than relying on refined sugars and salt. Developing good eating habits begins right from your baby's first experience with food. Your baby will come to know food with its true flavors shining through rather than being masked by unhealthy additives.

The recipes in *The Everything® Organic Cooking for Baby & Toddler Book* emphasize a variety of fruits, vegetables, grains, and proteins. You will discover a few surprises tucked in among the healthy, organic versions of long-time favorites. Comfort foods like pot pies, lasagnas, and soups are scrumptious when given an organic makeover. By introducing your toddler and your other family members to tastes from around the world, for example—Tabouli Salad, Caribbean Baked Risotto, and Baked Honey Pescado—you might discover some new favorites and lay the groundwork for a lifetime of delicious and healthy culinary possibilities.

Many children go through phases where their palates become more limited. For pickier little ones, there are a variety of options that provide sound nutrition in the guise of a treat. There are cool sorbets, fruity smoothies, and fun dips to enchant even the most reluctant eater. Even birthday cakes are given the organic once-over in this family-friendly cookbook.

This cookbook can help you set the table for healthy eating habits that will last a lifetime. Organic eating can also help you contribute to a healthier planet. Enjoy watching your baby grow into a healthy, happy, organic child!

In closing here is one important note: When reading the recipes in this book please remember that while each individual ingredient does not have the word "organic" before it, it is assumed that you will be using only organic foods for these recipes.

Chapter 1

Why Organic?

With so many choices facing new parents, why is it important to consider feeding your baby and toddler organic food? Because your child will undergo so many significant changes during the first three years of life, it is imperative that he receive the best tools to grow and develop. Food that has been organically grown and produced provides just what your baby needs to grow from a tiny, smiling bundle to an active, engaged toddler without any dangerous chemicals to get in the way of that healthy development.

What Is Organic?

At its core, organic food is food that has been grown and produced as close as possible to the way that nature intended. Organic produce is grown without the aid of pesticides, herbicides, or synthetic fertilizers. Because organic livestock does not receive routine doses of antibiotics, the animals have living conditions that promote good health, including adequate space, fresh air, fresh water, and healthy feed. Furthermore, genetically modified organisms (GMOs), synthetic hormones, and irradiation are not allowed in organic agricultural products. Not only is organic food grown in accordance with organic practices, but the organic commitment also continues all the way from field to store.

Since 2002, the United States Department of Agriculture (USDA) has overseen the national organic program in the United States. The USDA has instituted an extensive set of rules that dictate what is allowable and what is prohibited in organic agricultural products for food and nonfood use. The USDA also oversees third-party certifiers, which ensure that the rules are followed by organic producers. There are three levels to the USDA organic labeling program.

- Products labeled "100 Percent Organic" are made entirely from organic ingredients or components.
- Products that are made up of at least 95 percent organic ingredients or components, and have remaining ingredients that are approved for use in organic products, can display the "USDA Organic" seal.
- Products that are made up of at least 70 percent organic ingredients or components can list "organic" before those ingredients on their ingredient lists.

ALERT!

The USDA does not require third-party certification of organic products from farmers or distributors who sell less than $5,000 of goods per year. However, if these exempt producers attempt to misuse the "organic" label, and are caught, they are subject to a significant penalty.

Why Is Organic Important?

As a new parent, there is nothing as important as taking good care of your child. There are many ways to ensure your child's good health, happiness, and safety. Buying and preparing organic foods contributes to these goals in several ways.

Organics Are Good for Your Baby's Body

A variety of wholesome, nutritious foods is what your baby needs to develop in both body and mind. Chemicals, in the form of added artificial flavorings, dyes, pesticide and herbicide residues, and hydrogenated fats, do nothing to promote good health, and can even detract from it. Organically grown and produced food is free of these chemicals, leaving only the good taste and nutrition that nature intended.

Babies and children who are fed an organic diet are not overexposed to antibiotic residue in their food, either. Animals are healthier when farmed organically, because they have adequate access to fresh air, appropriate diet, and outdoor space. Therefore, the need for antibiotic overuse is eliminated. (According to USDA rules, organic meat must be antibiotic-free.)

Organics Are Better for the Planet

Taking care of the world that your baby will inherit is also good parenting. Organic farming is based on keeping the soil healthy through natural means like rotating crops, letting fields lie fallow, and using natural fertilizing methods rather than spraying on toxic pesticides and herbicides that can run off into water supplies and contaminate the soil.

Organic livestock farms provide adequate room for the animals and do not rely on factory-farm overcrowding and the waste-disposal issues that accompany it. Because organic livestock is fed an organic diet, that also means fewer synthetic pesticides and herbicides are used in the crops that are dedicated for their feed.

Increased soil fertility is another bonus of organic farming. Organic farmers use natural methods to replenish the soil so they don't strip the earth of its nutrients by overfarming. Conscientious stewardship of the soil is a hallmark of organic farming as it is the only way for the organic farmer to reap another year's yield.

Top Twenty Heroic Organic Foods

Although the ideal is to provide your baby with a completely organic diet, there are several reasons why that might not be possible all the time. For one, organics can be more expensive than conventional foods, and some family budgets cannot support buying all organic all the time. Another reason is that, depending on the season, fresh, locally grown organic produce might not be available.

Choosing Pesticide-Free Organic Produce

When deciding which organics to choose, the relative pesticide load of each conventionally grown produce variety should be factored into the decision. The Environmental Working Group ranks produce based on its pesticide load. The fruits and vegetables at the top of the list are those that, when produced conventionally, carry the heaviest load of pesticides. The following list includes the twenty fruits and vegetables for which it is most important to buy organic. To see an updated list, visit the Environmental Working Group's website, *www.foodnews.org*.

1. Peaches
2. Apples
3. Sweet bell peppers
4. Celery
5. Nectarines
6. Strawberries
7. Cherries
8. Lettuce
9. Grapes
10. Pears
11. Spinach
12. Potatoes
13. Carrots
14. Green beans
15. Hot peppers
16. Cucumbers
17. Raspberries
18. Plums
19. Oranges
20. Cauliflower

Even though most people wash their produce before eating or cooking, some pesticide residue can remain. This list considers common washing practices and the residue that remains after washing.

Milk

USDA-certified milk is produced at farms that follow all of the rules and regulations for organic dairy farming. These rules include feeding the cows an organic diet, using organic fertilizer, allowing the cows adequate space and access to fresh air, and restricting medications. Depending on economic circumstances, milk can cost up to twice as much as conventional milk. If that extra expense puts buying milk out of reach for your family 100 percent of the time, there are other options.

FACT

Some milk is fortified with Omega-3 fatty acids. Omega-3 is an essential fatty acid that is required for healthy growth. Regular intake of Omega-3 can protect you from various diseases and helps you reduce incidences of heart disease, certain types of cancer, and arthritis.

Hormone-free milk is a category that falls somewhere between organic and conventional milk. The hormone rBGH (recombinant bovine growth hormone) is a substance that is given to cows to increase their milk production. It can, however, increase the chance of infection and other health problems in the cows that receive it. The idea behind rBGH-free or hormone-free milk is that cows are healthier without the hormone, and therefore require less medical care. Specifically, it is believed that these cows will need fewer antibiotics, and therefore there will be less chance of antibiotic residue in the milk supply from rBGH-free cows. For more information on rBGH or other synthetic hormones, visit *www.organicconsumers.org* or *www.centerforfoodsafety.org*.

Genetically Modified Organisms

The term genetically modified organism (GMO) is usually applied to food crops that have had their genetic material engineered to incorporate the genetic material of another species. Farmers have always taken advantage of cross-breeding, creating hybrids within a species and taking advantage of genetic mutations. The navel orange, for instance, is a mutation that has been commercially farmed for generations. However, there is some controversy over whether introducing the genetic material of different species into seeds or plants is safe. Studies are currently underway to help us better understand whether GMOs are safe for the human body and/or the environment.

All organics are GMO-free, but so are many conventional fruits and vegetables. If you are trying to buy GMO-free, look for a label stating that the product doesn't use any genetically modified ingredients. According to the USDA, three crops make up the majority of GMOs in the United States:

- Corn
- Cotton
- Soybeans

For more detailed information, visit *www.ers.usda.gov/Data/BiotechCrops.*

Choosing to buy food products that are formulated with the organic versions of these ingredients, or that avoid using these ingredients, will greatly decrease the occurrence of GMOs in your diet. For example, a juice drink that is free of corn syrup is much more likely to be free of GMOs than one that contains corn syrup.

How to Create a Healthy Organic Table

As with most everything, in feeding your family variety is the spice of life. Serving seasonal produce in a variety of colors with a wide range of whole grains and protein sources ensures that your family receives the full spectrum of nutrients that bodies need to function at their best. The USDA's *Dietary Guidelines for Americans 2005* emphasizes this variety by recommending that Americans over age two follow the food pyramid guidelines.

These recommendations emphasize:

- Eating a variety of fruits, vegetables, and legumes in a variety of colors
- Eating a variety of whole-grain products
- Consuming low-fat or fat-free dairy products or equivalent milk products (Remember, these recommendations are for people over age two. Until age two, children should be fed whole milk.)
- Limiting added sugar, salt, and saturated fat, and avoiding trans fats

For a personal food pyramid, visit *www.MyPyramid.gov.*

Fresh, Frozen, or Canned? What to Choose?

The decision to promote your baby's good health and development by providing organic food is a great first step on the road to healthy eating for your family and better health for the planet. More decisions await, however. Is it always best to choose fresh produce? The answer to that is—it depends.

Fresh, Seasonal Produce

The ideal would be to be able to have a wide variety of fresh, organic produce available at an affordable price all year long. There are a number of avenues to procure fresh, organic produce. One is your local farmers' market or farm stand. In rural communities, farm stands on the side of the road sell the fresh-picked fruits and vegetables that were growing on the farm just that morning. Some farms even offer you-pick-it opportunities to bring the consumer closer to the land. Nothing could be fresher than picking a bushel of apples off the tree and bringing them home to eat and cook right away. In urban communities around the country, the farm comes to them. Farmers awaken in the pre-dawn hours to bring fresh-picked produce to urban neighborhoods for same-day purchase. Not only does the farmers' market shopper get the chance to purchase fresh, in-season produce, but she also gets the chance to ask questions directly to the farmer about growing practices, thereby getting the best information about possible chemical exposure or organic status.

Another option that is gaining popularity is community-supported agriculture (CSA). The basic idea behind a CSA is that the consumer helps support the costs of growing the fruits and vegetables. Consumers purchase a "share" or membership in the CSA, and then pay either by the week or by the growing season in order to receive a box or bag of fresh fruits and vegetables. The CSA model has helped many small farmers to continue to farm. The revenue gained from the membership or share fees goes toward buying seed and the initial costs of planting, so the farmer does not have to wait for the harvest to collect money. This model allows the consumer to play a more active role in the food-production process. An interesting facet of the CSA idea is that usually you will receive a box or bag of produce, but won't know beforehand what you are going to get. This element of surprise can keep cooking exciting when you receive a previously unknown root vegetable or variety of green.

Organic produce is becoming increasingly available at well-stocked grocery stores. Demand dictates what grocery stores stock, so if you want to see more organics at your local market, be sure to ask the manager. By letting management know that organics will be purchased and not go to waste, you are likely to see a positive response to your requests.

Organic produce can be as close as your own backyard. Growing organic fruits and vegetables can be as easy as setting up some pots with organic soil and seed on your balcony or in your backyard. This can be an inexpensive option to ensure that the organic tomatoes you love are readily at hand. You can also turn an area of your yard into an organic garden plot. This can take longer, as you often have to remedy past soil contamination problems, but can be well worth the effort if you have the space and the inclination. The Internet, libraries, and bookstores are full of resources to help the interested gardener. For instance, check out *www.organichomegardener.com* and *Organic Gardener* magazine. Don't be afraid to ask for help at your local gardening center, either.

It can be difficult to know what produce is in season in each region of the country. The National Resources Defense Council has made it much easier to figure out when to expect Brussels sprouts in your community. Visit *www .nrdc.org* and check out the "What's Fresh Near You" service. It lets you know what's growing in your region of the country.

Fabulous Frozen Food

One of the best ways to take advantage of each growing season is to freeze extra fruits or vegetables for later use. Whether you cook up an extra-large batch of purées, or you wash and freeze an extra quart of blueberries, you will be happy to have the taste of late summer when the leaves are falling off the trees. Frozen fruits and vegetables can be used for up to six months, and meats can be used for up to three months. That means that May's plums can still be enjoyed in October. Freezing can allow you to store extra produce for future use, extending the life of fruits and vegetables that would otherwise go to waste. If you have five very ripe bananas, but will only be able to eat one in the next day, peel the others and freeze them for use in smoothies later.

Most vegetables and fruits are picked, packaged, and frozen within six hours of being harvested. These frozen vegetables can have more of certain vitamins than the fresh ones that you buy at your grocery store, as that produce may have been harvested five or more days before it reached you.

Because most commercially frozen organic produce is flash frozen immediately after picking, most of the nutrients are preserved. Although your supermarket might have fresh organic berries in December, they could have traveled halfway around the world before they came to your community. Buying frozen fruit that was grown and frozen in your state will have used considerably fewer resources than the out-of-season fresh option. You can use these frozen fruits and vegetables to add variety when there are only limited fresh choices available in your region of the country.

What about Canned?

Canned beans, fruits, and vegetables can provide convenience and nutrition. Although dry beans can be an extremely affordable protein source, sometimes busy parents don't have the time necessary to soak and cook the beans before preparing them in their dinner entrée. Canned beans are a good source of protein, iron, and fiber. They also only require draining and rinsing before they're ready to incorporate in a salad, soup, or casserole.

FACT

Canned tomatoes and tomato sauces are among the best sources of lycopene. Lycopene, found in red-pigmented fruits and vegetables like tomatoes, may help prevent certain cancers. The heat from the canning process allows the lycopene in the tomatoes to be better absorbed in the body.

Many canned fruits, like pineapple, mandarin oranges, and tomato products, are good sources of vitamin C. They are great to have on hand to use in a wide range of recipes. Canned tomatoes and tomato sauces are also a great source of lycopene, an antioxidant. Using canned pumpkin instead of cooking a whole pumpkin can mean the difference between having quick, nutrition-packed muffins or doing without. The important thing is to ensure that your family is eating a diet rich in a variety of fruits and vegetables. Using a combination of fresh, frozen, and canned can help promote your family's good health.

Chapter 2

Introduction to Feeding

You are starting on the path to feeding your child organically. Where do you begin? This chapter takes you through the first few years of feeding your child. You will learn about breastfeeding and formula feeding your infant, how to determine when your child is ready for solid foods, and how to gradually introduce foods to your child in a safe manner. This chapter will also help you to stock your kitchen and pantry so you are ready to prepare fun and healthful organic meals and snacks for your child.

Breast Milk: The Ultimate Organic Food

As a parent, you have the privilege of feeding your child. There are many choices that a parent has in feeding their family and at times it can be overwhelming. Breastfeeding is one choice that parents may make to help their child get started on the organic eating path. Overall, the number of mothers choosing to breastfeed is on the rise.

Although breastfeeding is wonderful and natural, breastfeeding successfully can be hard. Many people struggle with achieving a solid breastfeeding schedule. Gather people around you who support breastfeeding and expect to need their help in order to be successful. Contact the local chapter of La Leche League early in your pregnancy to begin to develop your support system for breastfeeding.

The Gold Standard

The benefits of breastfeeding are thoroughly researched and well known in the medical community. There are emotional, physical, and cognitive benefits to breastfeeding. Breastfeeding promotes infant-maternal bonding through close contact and changes to a mother's hormone levels during breastfeeding. There is very little that compares to the feeling of nurturing your child through breastfeeding. The convenience and low cost of breastfeeding is also a plus for many mothers.

Breast milk has many fantastic health benefits. The nutritional composition of breast milk is superior to formula. Breast milk is the ultimate "gold standard" for infant feeding. Commercially available infant formulas all strive to be as close to breast milk as possible. However, there are many reasons why breast milk is the best choice for infant nutrition. First, the composition of breast milk is very easy for your infant to digest and absorb. The protein available in breast milk is easily and readily utilized by growing infants. Additionally, the calcium and phosphorous in breast milk is easily used by your infant's rapidly growing bones.

Beyond Nutrition

Beyond nutrition, breast milk has other benefits for your child. Breast milk contains antibodies. Antibodies are molecules in the immune system that help children fight infections. In developed countries, the effects on the immune system from these antibodies might be seen in the following ways: lower rates of diarrhea, lower rates of infections in the lungs and respiratory system, and lower rates of ear and urinary tract infections. There is also some evidence to suggest that breastfeeding improves cognitive development in infants. This information does not mean that your breastfed infant will not have any of these problems; however, the risk of them is less. If they do occur, they might be less severe.

FACT

There is some research that indicates that your child may have a lower risk of chronic diseases if they are breastfed as infants. It is possible that breastfeeding can lower your child's risk of certain gastrointestinal diseases, certain lymphomas, and some types of diabetes.

It is recommended that breast milk be the sole source of nutrition until six months of age and be offered in addition to solid food until at least the age of one year. Breast milk provides all the nutrients, vitamins, minerals, and fluids that your young infant needs to grow and develop. However, there are a few exceptions to this rule. Most babies receive a single dose of vitamin K at birth to help with blood clotting. According to the American Academy of Pediatrics, most exclusively breastfed infants also need an additional 200–400 international units of vitamin D. Recommendations about iron and fluoride are specific to your individual feeding plan and water source for your family. Please discuss the vitamins that your child may benefit from adding to their diet with your pediatrician or dietitian and decide what is right for your baby.

When Formula Is Best

There are many situations in life that prevent families from being able to choose breastfeeding as their child's primary source of nutrition. Many times, parents choose to feed their infant with commercially prepared infant formulas due to certain medical and social situations. Parents should not feel guilty about this decision. It is important for each family to make the best decision for their own unique needs. Fortunately, there are many excellent options for feeding your child.

QUESTION?

What formula should you choose?
Going into the formula aisle can be overwhelming. There are so many types of formulas all made by different companies. How do you choose? It is important to know that all commercially prepared infant formulas must meet basic federal guidelines regarding composition. They vary slightly in how they achieve these guidelines but all formulas—except low-iron formulas—are adequate to support the growth and development of infants.

Types of Formula

Most commercially prepared infant formulas are split into three general categories based on the type of protein that is in the formula. The categories are whole protein formula, partially digested protein formula, and free amino acid based formula.

What does this mean? Proteins are made up of many small amino acids. Protein helps your baby to grow. The type of protein can make a formula easier or harder for your baby to digest. Most infants tolerate whole proteins without problems and grow nicely on a standard cow's milk based infant formula. There are different medical situations that would make a child need a protein that is easier to digest. In the partially digested or free amino acid formulas, the protein is partially or completely broken down for your child.

These formulas tend to be easier to digest, but not every baby needs these special formulas. This book will focus on the use of standard whole protein formulas since these are the most common. Talk with your pediatrician or dietitian about the possibility that your child may need a more specialized formula, such as a partially digested formula or a free amino acid formula.

Standard Infant Formulas

The most common and widely used formula is a standard infant formula with iron. These formulas have been made with whole proteins that have not been broken down or predigested for your child. They are typically made from protein derived from cow's milk or from soy protein. Certain formulas indicate that they are made from "comfort proteins" and these are also included in this class of standard infant formulas. These formulas process their protein a little differently, but they are still whole protein sources.

Cow's milk protein infant formulas with iron are the most widely used formulas overall. The cow's milk protein in infant formulas is not the same thing as whole milk. It has been altered by adding vegetable oils and carbohydrate sources to provide balanced and age-appropriate nutrition for your infant. This protein blend is readily bioavailable to your child, meaning that your child can absorb this protein better for growth and development.

Soy Protein Formulas

Soy protein formulas with iron use the protein from a soy-protein-isolate that is fortified with different amino acids and iron. Soy formulas differ slightly from the standard cow's milk protein formula. It is rare that children need a soy-based formula. Soy formulas meet all the federal guidelines for infant formulas; however, the nutrients are not always in the most bioavailable form for your child.

There are certain medical conditions that require an infant to need a soy formula. Notably, if you suspect that your child has an allergy to cow's milk protein, the recommendation is to *not* change them to a soy protein formula. If your child is allergic to cow's milk protein, there is a high chance that they could be allergic to soy formula as well. The current recommendation from the American Academy of Pediatrics is to change a child with cow's milk protein allergy to a special protein made from free amino acids. This means the formula is totally predigested for your child. These are highly specialized formulas and only available by prescription.

Organic Formula

The demand for organic products continues to increase. This has also led to an increased demand for organic infant formulas. Many formula companies are now producing infant formulas made from organic materials. Organic formulas are available in both cow's milk protein formula and soy-based formulas.

These formulas are typically certified organic in accordance with USDA regulations. To be certified USDA Organic and display the USDA Organic seal, a product must contain at least 95 percent organic ingredients by weight. Moreover, they are often certified organic by Quality Assurance International (QAI). The ingredients in these infant formulas are produced without using pesticides, added growth hormones, or antibiotics. These formulas meet the same standards as other formula for infant nutrition. They include all the components that a young infant needs to grow and thrive.

When Is My Baby Ready for Solids?

It is recommended that breast milk or infant formula with iron be the sole source of nutrition until age six months. However, some people feel that their baby is ready to start solids as early as four months. Discuss your baby's feeding plan with your pediatrician or dietitian before starting solids.

The rule of thumb in deciding if your child is ready for solids is to watch your baby, not the calendar. Your baby will let you know when she is ready for solids with some simple cues. Feeding before these cues are shown can lead to overfeeding and obesity.

Watch Your Baby, Not the Calendar

Your baby will give the following cues to show you she is ready for solids:

- Baby can hold her neck steady
- Baby can sit with support
- Baby can swallow nonliquid foods
- She opens her mouth for food
- She leans forward to indicate hunger
- She leans back to show that she is satisfied
- She can draw in her lip as the spoon is removed from her mouth
- She can move food from the front to the back of the mouth

If your baby is showing the above signs, he or she is ready to begin taking solids.

As your child moves through the next six months of the first year, you will have the joy of teaching your child how to eat independently. Get your bibs and washcloths or drop cloths ready! Watching your child begin to experience food is a fun time.

Advancing Your Baby's Diet

As you child becomes more comfortable with being fed, you can start teaching him to self-feed. Here are some skills to work on the next six months of your child's life:

- Self-feeding with easy, soft finger foods
- Trying to use a sippy cup at six to eight months
- Holding his own bottle or cup
- Exposing him to different textures and flavors

Feeding your child is a wonderful way to bond with him and teach him all about flavor and textures. Never force feed your child. Your job as a parent is to provide healthful options at meal and snack times. Allow your child to determine how much to eat of the foods that you offer.

How Much Food Should I Offer My Child?

Every baby is unique. Each child advances at his or her own pace and time. Pay attention to your child's developmental stages and feed according to those skills. The amounts of food to offer your child given in this chapter are just a guide; each baby is different and your child may eat more or less than these recommended servings. Your job as a parent is only to offer the foods to your child. Pay attention to your child's feeding cues to know if she is finished eating or wants to continue to eat. Here is a guide for feeding advancement for the first year through toddler eating.

Birth to Four Months

Your baby should have a rooting reflex which means that he turns his head toward you to eat. Your baby should also be able to suck and swallow liquids. Babies at this age should only be taking breast milk or iron-fortified infant formula. His schedule will be sporadic but overall his daily intake of breast milk or iron-fortified infant formula should be 21 to 24 ounces. Your infant does not need any additional water or juice—these are not needed in the first year of life. Breast milk or formula can provide all the hydration that your infant needs under age one.

Five Months

Your baby can hold her neck up and begin to sit with support. At this age, babies should be drinking only breast milk or iron-fortified infant formula. She will begin to spread out her feeding and feed about four to six times per day. The overall goal amount of breast milk or iron-fortified infant formula is about 24 to 34 ounces per day.

Six to Seven Months

Your baby is starting to reach and grasp for objects. He has also been experimenting with moving his jaw up and down. Your infant should continue to drink 24 to 34 ounces of breast milk or iron-fortified infant formula per day, but this is the appropriate time to introduce iron-fortified rice cereal in addition to breast milk or formula. Your baby may eat about 4 tablespoons per day of cereal. Only introduce rice cereal with a spoon, as it is not appropriate to put rice cereal in a baby's bottle. You can also begin to introduce 4 tablespoons of vegetables and 4 tablespoons of fruits per day. Only introduce one new food at a time and wait four to seven days between each new food to monitor your child for potential allergies.

Eight to Nine Months

Your baby can now sit alone without support. She is also developing her pincher grasp and can pick up small items with her thumb and finger. She is getting better at chewing so you can begin to move away from all-puréed foods to a more mashed food consistency. She should drink 24 to 34 ounces of breast milk or iron-fortified infant formula per day. She can continue with the grain cereals, fruits, and vegetables and may take about ¼ to ½ cup of each of these per day. It is now appropriate to begin to introduce some soft meat purées. If her pincher grasp is ready, go ahead and give her some soft finger foods such as soft crackers, toast, cereal Os, or teething biscuits.

Ten to Twelve Months

Time to work on independent feeding! Your baby can now begin to hold a cup and will be interested in playing with food and self-feeding. He should still continue to drink 24 to 34 ounces of breast milk or iron-fortified infant formula per day. You can begin to offer small amounts of these in a sippy cup. Fruit juice can also be offered but your child should only have 4 ounces of juice per day. Juice can contribute to overfeeding and obesity so be careful not to offer more than the recommended amount. Continue to expand the variety of cereals, fruits, vegetables, meats, soft breads, and finger foods. Babies will take about ¼- to ½-cup servings of each of these per day at this age.

Over Twelve Months

Your child has now been introduced to all the types of food groups. The goal is to continue to offer your child and your family a wide variety of textures, tastes, and food experiences. Playing with food is a normal and developmentally appropriate way to learn to accept new and different foods. Encourage playing with food.

Specific amounts of food that your child should eat are hard to prescribe. Toddlers' eating is sporadic and unpredictable. Children have days that they eat large amounts and days that they just pick at food. This is normal. Over time, your child will get the nutrients that she needs to grow.

Toddler and Preschool Patterns and Portions

Here are some guidelines on toddler eating portions, but keep in mind that every child is different. Notice that their serving sizes are much smaller than adult portions.

- **GRAINS AND BREADS: 6 servings per day**
  Serving size: ¼ to ½ slice of bread or ½ cup of grain
  Example: 1 to 2 slices of bread + 1 cup of cereal per day
  Recipes: Blueberry Pancakes (page 129) and Quinoa Bean Salad (page 124)

- **VEGETABLES: 3 servings per day**
  Serving size: ¼ to ⅓ of a cup
  Example: ½ cup cooked vegetables + ¼ cup of beans
  Recipes: Roasted Carrots (page 170) and Grilled Summer Vegetables (page 222)

- **FRUITS: 2 servings per day**
  Serving size: ⅓ of a cup
  Example: ⅓ cup of apple + ½ a banana
  Recipes: Carrot Pineapple Salad (page 199) and Blueberry Sorbet (page 232)

- **MILK: 2 servings per day**
  Serving size: 8 ounces of milk or 1 cup yogurt
  Example: 8 ounces whole milk + 1 (8 ounce) yogurt
  Recipes: Banana Yogurt Milkshake (page 133) and Pink Milk
                    (page 152)

The goal is to transition to whole milk at one year old. Toddlers should stay on whole milk until the age of two and then can be switched to a lower-fat milk. Toddlers need two servings of dairy per day, or about 16 ounces. If your child cannot tolerate dairy, they should eat two servings of calcium- and vitamin D–fortified dairy substitute.

- **PROTEIN: 2 servings per day**
  Serving size: 1 to 2 ounces meat, 1 egg, ½ cup beans or tofu
  Example: 1 egg + 2 tablespoons tofu at lunch + 2 tablespoons
                    meat at dinner
  Recipes: Tofu-Stuffed Shells (page 225) and Barbecue Meatloaf
                    Muffins (page 182)

Children also need adequate amounts of zinc and protein in their diet. These nutrients can be obtained from two servings per day of meat, bean, or legume protein sources. Serving sizes for this age group are about 1 to 4 tablespoons of meat, and ½ cup of beans or legumes.

Children under the age of two need to get a high percentage of their calories from fat for adequate brain development. For this reason, you should not limit the fat your child consumes under the age of two. Choose healthy fats from avocados, olive oil, and canola oil. For children over the age of two, you can begin to lower fat in the diet but children should never be on an extremely low-fat diet.

How Do I Safely Feed My Child?

When your child is showing all the developmental signs that he is ready for feeding, it is time to begin. It is such an exciting time in your child's life. You, as a parent, get to introduce them to a whole new part of life—eating solid food. It is important that you do this in a safe manner.

Choking

Choking is a concern for every parent, but there are steps that you can take to prevent choking. Always watch your child when he is eating or playing around food. Do not allow your child to run around with food in his mouth. Your child should be seated and supervised for all meals and snacks. Make sure all items that your child could choke on are out of reach. And, most important, learn how to help your child if he is choking. Most community hospitals teach parents' first aid and CPR classes.

According to the Center for Disease Control and Prevention, thousands of children visit the emergency each year due to choking. In fact, in the year 2000, there were 17,500 visits to the emergency room due to choking. Sixty percent of those visits were caused by children choking on food.

There are a handful of foods that are dangerous due to the high likelihood that your child could choke on them. The American Academy of Pediatrics recommends that all children under the age of four years old should avoid the following food items:

- Hot dogs
- Nuts and seeds (they recommend children be seven years old for nuts)
- Chunks of meat or cheese
- Whole grapes

- Hard, gooey, or sticky candy
- Popcorn
- Chunks of peanut butter
- Raw vegetables
- Raisins
- Chewing gum

Allergy Prevention

A food allergy is a reaction by your body's immune system to a food that it thinks is a threat. It is an "overreaction" of the immune system. The specific reactions range from rashes or hives to trouble breathing.

Research presented in the *Journal of Pediatrics* indicates that 4 to 6 percent of children have documented food allergies. Food allergies appear to be on the rise. More and more families are adjusting their dietary habits due to food allergies. These changes can be minor inconveniences or major life changes depending on the number and severity of food allergies.

The eight most common food allergies are milk, egg, peanut, wheat, soy, tree nuts, fish, and shellfish. Some people have allergies to more than one of these top allergens. It is possible for your child to outgrow their allergies by the age of three. The only preventive measure to take for food allergies is total avoidance of the allergen; the only treatment is medication to help if a child is accidentally exposed to allergenic food.

There are steps that you can take to potentially decrease the chance that your child will develop food allergies. The current recommendation from the American Academy of Pediatrics is to exclusively breastfeed for the first six months of life to decrease their exposure to allergens. If breastfeeding is not possible, the recommendation is to exclusively formula feed and delay introduction of solids until the age of six months. In addition, it is recommended to not introduce cow's milk or egg yolks before the age of one year. If there is a family history of food allergies or atopic disease (e.g., hay fever, asthma, eczema) the recommendation is to further delay the introduction of eggs until the age of two and to wait until the age of three to introduce peanuts, tree nuts, fish, and seafood.

QUESTION?

I think my child has a food allergy. What should I do?
You and your pediatrician will need to decide how you are going to limit your child's exposure to high-allergen foods. If you suspect allergies in your child, see a pediatric allergist who is trained to identify true food allergies in your child.

Some families, after consulting with their pediatrician, will begin to introduce solids to their infant as early as four months of age. This cookbook does include recipes for infants at this age to show how to introduce solids appropriately. If you start solids at this age, your child should be meeting the developmental milestones to support taking in solid foods. Take your time introducing food to your child. Eating is a new experience and there is no need to rush into offering a huge variety of foods to a very young infant.

Your child's first food should be a prepared iron-fortified infant rice cereal. This is a very hypoallergenic food. Take your time introducing new foods to look for signs of a food allergy. It is important to only introduce one new food at a time. It is recommended that you wait four to seven days after introducing one food before you introduce another. In those four to seven days, you should be watching your child for signs of food allergies. Look for signs such as itching, burning around mouth, runny nose, skin rash, hives, diarrhea, vomiting, and trouble breathing. Once your child has tolerated a food, it is then acceptable to mix that food with another food that has also been established to be tolerated.

Nitrates

What are nitrates? Nitrates are molecules that are comprised of nitrogen and oxygen. They are naturally found in the produce and in the water that people drink. As part of a balanced diet in adults, these products are not harmful. Nitrates can be harmful to young infants. The American Academy of Pediatrics (AAP) cautions parents about the risks of nitrate poisoning in infants.

Nitrate poisoning causes your baby to have high levels of methemoglobin in their bodies. Why is this a problem? If there is too much methemoglobin in the blood, oxygen has a hard time reaching your baby's cells. Cells need oxygen to function. This syndrome is sometimes called "blue baby" syndrome since baby's skin turns slightly blue due to lack of oxygen. Although rare, this can be a serious and life-threatening condition.

The highest risk for babies to develop nitrate poisoning is from well water with high levels of nitrates. Do not use well water unless it has been tested for nitrates. The concentration should be should be less than 10 parts per million (ppm). Another risk factor involves certain types of produce that can be high in nitrates due to the soil that they are grown in. These vegetables are spinach, beets, broccoli, and carrots. The AAP cautions parents against making their own baby food using these vegetables for infants under six months of age. Many commercial makers of baby food voluntarily screen their vegetables for nitrates to ensure the supply is safe. If you are feeding any of these higher-risk vegetables to an infant under six months, it is safest to purchase commercially prepared and screened infant food. Infants over six months should be able to tolerate the nitrates that might be in these vegetables.

Food Safety

In the first few months of your baby's life, it is important to sterilize items that may come in contact with her in order to minimize her exposure to bacteria and viruses. However, once your baby is a little mobile and begins to explore the world with her mouth, it is not necessary to sterilize everything in her environment except bottles and nipples.

The most important way to decrease the risk of a food-borne illness is follow safe food handling practices. Safe food handling practices for infants and children are no different than for adults. Hand washing is the first step to every adventure in the kitchen. Here are some quick tips for food safety from the United States Department of Agriculture Food Safety and Inspection:

- Frequently clean the areas where you prepare food.
- Separate meat and poultry from other foods; do not cross contaminate.
- Always cook food to proper temperatures.
- Refrigerate your food right away so bacteria cannot grow on it.

Cooking and preparing food safely involves following guidelines that help decrease the chance that bacteria can grow in your food. These recommendations help ensure that your baby will not get food poisoning due to unsafe kitchen practices.

Once you purchase or cook your food, you need to safely store it. The rule is to always put perishable food in the refrigerator within two hours. If you live in a hot climate or the temperature is over 90 degrees, that time decreases to only one hour. Cook or freeze chicken, fish, or ground meat within two days. If it is heartier meat like beef, veal, lamb, or pork you can wait three to five days before freezing. Store your uncooked poultry, fish, or meat separately from fruit, vegetables, or any other raw food to help stop cross contamination. Refrigerators should be at 40° F or below, and freezers should be at 0°F.

In food preparation, use separate cutting boards for raw meats so that they won't contaminate the fruits and vegetables that you are preparing. Wash cutting boards thoroughly in hot, soapy water after each use. There are three ways to thaw frozen meats. You can place them in the refrigerator to thaw; you can submerge the meats in cold water in the sink and change the water every thirty minutes; or you can use the microwave to thaw frozen items. It is not safe to thaw foods on the counter at room temperature. Letting meat sit out at room temperature allows bacteria to grow on the food.

Once food is thawed, it is possible to refreeze it without cooking it first, but only if you thawed it in the refrigerator. If you thaw it in the microwave or in cold water, you need to cook the food and then refreeze it. It is recommended that you go through this cycle only once and not continue to freeze and thaw the same food over and over again.

When cooking foods, make sure that you cook meats to the proper temperature. Use a meat thermometer to tell if the food has reached the proper temperature. Beef, veal, lamb, roasts, and chops all need to reach 145°F. Pork and ground meat (beef, veal, and lamb) need to reach 160°F. Poultry, such as chicken and turkey, needs to reach 165°F.

Kitchen Equipment, Tools, and Gadgets

If you go into any kitchen supply store you will find a gadget for everything. This can be overwhelming; however, you do not have to buy all these gadgets to be a successful cook. Do you need fancy equipment to make your own baby food and cook healthy organic food for your family? No! Most people have everything that they need to get started making their own organic baby food. Here is a list of some of the basics to make sure you have on hand:

1. **Food processor or blender:** The size of the processor or blender needed depends on how much puréeing you want to do at one time. If you are planning to prepare large batches of purées at one time, a large processor will be helpful. Most people will be successful with puréeing in a simple blender or mini processor.

2. **Sieve or strainer:** Your pasta colander is not sufficient for straining purées for your infant. A small metal strainer is needed to catch the fine seeds and fibers that did not get puréed fine enough. Make sure that this item is in good condition with no rust on the strainer.

3. **Steamer:** A small metal collapsible steamer that fits inside your saucepan is fine for steaming small batches. If you plan on steaming large batches, you might want to invest in a combined rice and vegetable steamer. This is a nice addition to your kitchen for more than just purées. You can continue to use this to cook rice and steam vegetables perfectly without having to watch the stove constantly.

4. **Ice cube trays or small glass containers:** This is the easiest way to store your prepared purées. Once your foods are puréed, you can pour them into ice cube trays and freeze. Once frozen, you pop them out and into storage containers for your freezer. Each ice cube–sized portion is about a 2-tablespoon portion of baby food, or about 1 ounce. As your child gets older, it might be helpful to use small glass containers for freezing larger portions. Then these containers can go right from the freezer to the microwave. Be sure to label and date your containers so you know how long the purées have been in storage.

5. **Appliances:** A microwave is wonderful for thawing or heating up purées and toddler meals for your child. Make sure to always microwave in glass containers or on plates. Microwaving in plastics can make the plastics

unstable and may not be healthy for your family in the long term. Microwaves often heat foods unevenly, so be sure to test the temperature of the food. There could be very hot spots in the food that can burn your baby. Stir food well after heating and always test the temperature before feeding your baby.

6. **Handy helpers:** Some items to keep handy in your kitchen drawers that are helpful for making organic foods for your child include the following: vegetable peeler, assortment of different-sized knifes, wet and dry measuring cups, measuring spoons, kitchen timer, spatula, whisk, kitchen scissors, small hand grater, meat thermometer, and wooden spoons.

7. **Feeding supplies:** A small bowl, a few shallow plastic spoons, and a bib are all that you need to start. Be sure to test the temperature of the food yourself. Do not rely on the spoons and bowls that change color if the food is too hot.

8. **High chair:** Your baby should be able to sit in the high chair to start taking some of his first solids. Initially, it might make your child more comfortable with this new experience for you to hold him. Be careful not to continue this past the first couple of feeds. You want your child to learn that eating is done in the high chair. This helps establish a regular eating pattern with your child from the beginning.

As you can see, a few small investments are all that you need to begin cooking and preparing healthful organic food for your baby and family. Organizing and equipping your kitchen is fun way to start off this adventure in organic cooking!

The Organic Family Pantry

If you are new to organic cooking, choosing and purchasing organic products for your kitchen can be overwhelming. Restocking your kitchen pantry can be a fun way to jump-start your family on the path to organic eating. Here is a list of some common organic ingredients that are used in this cookbook; having these items on hand will make sure that you are prepared. With a well-stocked pantry and some good recipe ideas, you will always be able to answer the question "What's for dinner?"

Staples in an Organic Family Pantry

GRAINS AND DRIED BEANS	PRODUCE	OILS, SAUCES, AND SEASONINGS	BAKING GOODS
Brown rice	In-season fresh produce	Olive oil	Whole wheat pastry flour
Arborio rice	Onions	Canola oil	All-purpose flour
Barley	Garlic	Vegetable bouillon	Brown sugar
Quinoa	Avocado	Chicken bouillon	Baking powder
Oatmeal	Banana	Chicken broth	Baking salt
Kasha	Dried blueberries	Beef broth	Old-fashioned oats
Grits	Lemons	Barbecue sauce	Corn starch
Lentils	Limes	Light agave nectar	White whole wheat flour
Black Beans		Wildflower honey	
Pinto Beans		Rice wine vinegar	
Wheat germ		Red wine vinegar	
Flaxseed meal		White wine vinegar	
Whole Flaxseed		Dijon mustard	
		Vegenaise	
		Pure maple syrup	

CANNED GOODS	FROZEN FOODS	BREADS/CEREALS	DAIRY PRODUCTS
Beans: black, pinto, cannellini, kidney	Frozen berries	Whole-wheat bread	Milk
Diced tomatoes	Frozen mangos	Whole-wheat tortillas	Sour cream
Sunflower nut butter	Frozen spinach	Corn tortillas	Greek yogurt
Canned pineapple	Frozen broccoli	Whole-wheat cereal	Shredded cheese
Canned pumpkins	Frozen mixed vegetables	Whole-wheat English muffins	Cream cheese
Light coconut milk	Frozen chicken breasts	Whole-wheat pizza crust	Omega-3 fortified eggs
Marinara sauce	Frozen fish portions	Whole-wheat croutons	Butter
Applesauce	Apple juice concentrate	Whole-wheat pasta	

Take your time shopping when you are new to cooking. Stroll the store aisles, read the labels, and talk to the farmers at the market. You can learn so many tips and tricks by spending time with people who enjoy cooking with organic foods. You will see new and exciting foods each time that you go organic grocery shopping. New foods help add variety to your family's meals. Variety in your diet helps you stay adventurous and healthy.

Chapter 3

Four to Six Months

Baby's First Rice Cereal   32

Sweet Pea Purée   32

Green Bean Purée   33

Squash Purée   34

Sweet Potato Purée   34

Apple Purée   35

Avocado Mash   35

Banana Mash   36

Pear Purée   36

Dried Plum Purée   37

Papaya Purée   37

Peach Purée   38

Apricot Purée   38

Mango Purée   39

Pumpkin Pear Rice Cereal   39

Green Beans & Rice Cereal   40

Mango, Peach, & Rice Cereal   40

Green Beans, Mango, & Rice Cereal   41

Banana, Sweet Pea, & Rice Cereal   41

Banana & Oatmeal Cereal   42

Papaya, Pear, & Oatmeal Cereal   42

Banana, Apricot, & Oatmeal Cereal   43

Apple & Oatmeal Cereal   43

Pumpkin, Peach, & Oatmeal Cereal   44

Papaya, Apple, & Oatmeal Cereal   44

Avocado & Barley Cereal   45

Dried Plum & Barley Cereal   45

Apricot, Dried Plum, & Barley Cereal   46

Apple, Pumpkin, & Barley Cereal   46

Avocado Banana Mash   47

Pear Mango Purée   47

Papaya & Banana Mash   48

Apricot Pear Purée   48

Sweet Pea & Apple Purée   49

Peach & Avocado Mash   49

Mango & Apricot Purée   50

Avocado Pumpkin Mash   50

Dried Plum & Pear Purée   51

Peach Pear Purée   51

Banana Pumpkin Mash   52

Green Beans & Avocado Mash   53

Sweet Pea & Mango Purée   53

Pumpkin Purée   54

Baby's First Rice Cereal

Mix all ingredients together. Consistency should be equal
to or only slightly thicker than breast milk or formula.

First Taste—Get Your Camera!

Your baby's first taste of infant rice cereal may be more exciting for you
than for her! She may make funny faces, be disinterested, or dribble it
all over herself. Or, she may look at you like you have been holding out
on her and gobble it all up. Enjoy this moment and each opportunity you
have to feed your child. They are a gift.

Yields 1 serving

INGREDIENTS:

1 tablespoon iron-fortified prepared rice cereal

4–5 tablespoons expressed breast milk or formula

Sweet Pea Purée

Sweet peas are often a child's first vegetable.
If he does not like the first taste, continue to offer this periodically.
It can take many tries for a child to accept new foods!

1. Steam the peas in the water. Save water when done steaming.

2. Put peas in food processor or blender. Process on and off until desired consistency reached (for ages 4–6 months, consistency should be equal to or only slightly thicker than breast milk or formula). Use a small amount of the cooking liquid to thin the final product if necessary. Work the pulp through a strong strainer to remove any fibrous material.

Freezing Tips

If you are planning on making a large batch of vegetables to freeze, use
water to thin out the purée, if needed. Breast milk and formula do not
freeze well in purées.

Yields 16 tablespoons

INGREDIENTS:

1 cup sweet peas

1–2 tablespoons water

Green Bean Purée

Snap the beans! Remove both ends of the beans by either snapping them off or cutting them with a knife or kitchen scissors.

1. Steam the green beans in the water. Save water when done steaming.

2. Put beans in food processor or blender. Process on and off until desired consistency reached (for ages 4–6 months, consistency should be equal to or only slightly thicker than breast milk or formula). Use a small amount of the cooking liquid to thin the final product if necessary. If you plan to freeze the final product, do not thin with breast milk or formula. Work the pulp through a strong strainer to remove fibrous materials.

Snapping the Beans

Snapping the beans is an easy way to engage your older children in preparing foods and they will be more likely to accept the dish.

Yields 16 tablespoons

INGREDIENTS:

1 cup green beans

1–2 tablespoons water

Squash Purée

Most babies love the sweet, smooth consistency of puréed squash.
Acorn and butternut are two of the main varieties.

Yields 16 tablespoons

INGREDIENTS:

16 tablespoons of squash
(variety of your choice)
½ cup water

1. Peel, seed, and chop squash. Steam in steamer with water for 7–10 minutes.

2. Put squash in food processor or blender. Process on and off until desired consistency reached. Use a small amount of the cooking liquid to thin the final product if necessary. If you plan to freeze the final product, do not thin with breast milk or formula. Work the pulp through a strong strainer to remove any fibrous materials.

Sweet Potato Purée

Sweet potatoes are easy for most babies to digest, and are a favorite first food.
They are also easy to keep on hand, because they last longer than fruit and other
vegetables.

Yields 12 tablespoons

INGREDIENTS:

1 medium sweet potato
3 cups of water

1. Peel and chop potato into small pieces that are all about the same size. In a medium-sized pan, bring water to a boil. Place potato in water. Cover and cook for about 10 minutes, until tender. Drain.

2. Place potato in a food processor or blender. Process on and off until desired consistency reached. Use a small amount of the cooking liquid to thin the final product if necessary. If you plan to freeze the final product, do not thin with breast milk or formula.

Apple Purée

Red Delicious, Braeburn, and Gala apples make particularly good apple purée, though almost any variety can be used.

1. Peel fruit and chop apples into small pieces that are all about the same size. In a medium-sized pan, combine the fruit and water. Cover and cook for about 10 minutes until tender.

2. In food processor or blender, combine all ingredients. Process on and off until desired consistency is reached. If you plan to freeze the final product, do not thin with breast milk or formula.

Apple Pops
Freeze your purées in ice cube trays. Put the purée in ice cube trays and cover with plastic wrap and freeze. Pop out a cube when you are ready to use! Each cube is about 2 tablespoons of food.

Yields 12 tablespoons

INGREDIENTS:
2 medium apples (variety of your choice)
1–2 tablespoons water

Avocado Mash

Avocado is a great first food. It's loaded with monosaturated fat (the good fat), folate, potassium, and fiber. Avocados do have more calories than other fruits and vegetables, so use in moderation.

1. Slice avocado around the outside lengthwise. Twist both sides off the seed of the avocado. Scoop out flesh from one side of the avocado. Mash until desired consistency reached.

2. Wrap remaining avocado with the seed in it with plastic wrap and store in the refrigerator.

Can You Freeze an Avocado?
Avocados do not freeze well due to their consistency. You can use lemon juice on the avocado to help prevent browning; however, your baby is not ready for citrus until closer to one year old, so only cut the amount of avocado that you can use in that day. Or, make the family guacamole and pull some plain avocado out for your baby.

Yields 6 tablespoons

INGREDIENTS:
1 ripe avocado

Banana Mash

Yields 6 tablespoons

INGREDIENTS:

½ ripe banana

Bananas do not freeze well so only prepare the amount that you can use for 1–2 feedings. Bananas are an excellent source of potassium.

1. Cut banana in half and peel one half, removing any strings.
2. Place banana flesh in bowl.
3. Mash with a fork until desired consistency is reached.

The Perfect Food

Bananas are often called the "perfect food." Bananas are an excellent source of potassium, which is helpful for controlling blood pressure. In addition, each banana contains 4 grams of fiber and 2 grams of protein.

Pear Purée

Yields 12 tablespoons

INGREDIENTS:

2 medium pears
1–2 tablespoons water

Pears are very sweet, and most babies like them right away. Look for a ripe pear with a good fragrance that yields just slightly to the touch.

1. Peel and chop fruit into small pieces that are all about the same size.
2. In a medium-sized pan, combine the fruit and water.
3. Cover and cook for about 4–6 minutes, until tender.
4. Place the cooked mixture into a food processor or blender. Process on and off until desired consistency is reached. If you plan to freeze the final product, do not thin with breast milk or formula.

Dried Plum Purée

*It is possible to also use whole fresh plums to make a purée.
Follow the recipe for Peach Purée found on page 38 but substitute plums. They may
need additional straining due to their fibrous skin!*

1. In food processor or blender, combine plums (or prunes) and water.

2. Process on and off until desired consistency is reached. If the mixture
   is still too coarse, pass it through a fine strainer.

Regular Old Prunes
Prunes contain 2 grams of fiber per ounce. Your child needs fiber to
help maintain a healthy gastrointestinal tract and regular bowel move-
ments. Adding prunes to your child's diet can help keep them regular.

Yields 8 tablespoons

INGREDIENTS:

⅔ cup (4 ounces) pitted
dried plums or prunes

3 tablespoons water

Papaya Purée

*Papaya is a fruit that does not freeze well. It is recommended to
only make what you can use fresh. It does keep for a few days
nicely in the fridge and continues to soften over time.*

1. Cut papaya in half lengthwise; scrape out the seeds and discard them.

2. Scoop out the flesh of ½ the papaya and put in bowl.

3. Add formula or breast milk to papaya and mash with fork.

4. Mash until desired consistency reached.

How Do You Know if a Papaya Is Ripe?
You want to buy a papaya when it is almost ripe and is half-green and
half-yellow. It will take two to four days to ripen from this stage. You can
begin to smell the papaya as it ripens, and you can tell it's ripe when it is
slightly sensitive to pressure.

Yields 12 tablespoons

INGREDIENTS:

½ medium papaya

1–2 tablespoons formula
or breast milk

Peach Purée

Yields 12 tablespoons

INGREDIENTS:

2 medium peaches

1–2 tablespoons water

If peaches are not in season, buy frozen unsweetened peaches, thaw, and use to purée for your baby. Frozen fruit and vegetables is a great way to get produce out of season.

1. Cut peaches in half lengthwise and twist off of pit.

2. In food processor or blender, combine peaches and water. Process on and off until desired consistency is reached.

Apricot Purée

Yields 12 tablespoons

INGREDIENTS:

4 medium apricots

1–2 tablespoons water

If fresh apricots are not available, buy dried apricots. Simmer the dried apricots on the stove in water for about 8–10 minutes until tender and then purée.

1. Cut apricots in half lengthwise and twist off of pit.

2. In food processor or blender, combine apricots and water. Process on and off until desired consistency is reached. Work the pulp through a strong strainer to remove any fibrous materials.

Move Over, Carrots

Carrots are not the only foods that are an excellent source of vitamin A! Apricots are excellent sources of vitamin A, beta carotene, lycopene, and fiber. Vitamin A, beta carotene, and lycopene all help protect eye function and are great sources of antioxidants. The fiber in apricots is good for your cholesterol level and can help maintain regularity.

Mango Purée

Frozen mango slices can also work as a purée.
Just thaw and then purée according to these directions.

1. Remove flesh from mango.

2. In food processor or blender, combine mango and water. Process on and off until desired consistency is reached. Work the pulp through a strong strainer to remove any fibrous materials.

How Do You Cut a Mango?

There are two flat sides to a mango and a large square pit in the middle. Cut off the two flat sides. Take a knife and make lengthwise and cross-wise scores in the mango but do not cut thru the skin. Take your thumbs and turn this "inside out." Slice the mango pieces off the skin. Repeat around the whole mango.

Yields 12 tablespoons

INGREDIENTS:

2 medium mangos

1–2 tablespoons water

Pumpkin Pear Rice Cereal

Use whatever variety of pear is fresh at your grocery store or farmers' market for this dish. Good choices include Bartlett, D'Anjou, and Bosc.

Combine all ingredients.

Yields 6 tablespoons

INGREDIENTS:

2 tablespoons prepared iron-fortified rice cereal (with either breast milk or formula)

2 tablespoons Pumpkin Purée (page 54)

2 tablespoons Pear Purée (page 36)

Green Beans & Rice Cereal

Yields 4 tablespoons

INGREDIENTS:

2 tablespoons prepared iron-fortified rice cereal (with either breast milk or formula)

2 tablespoons Green Bean Purée (page 33)

This is a traditional baby-food combination.

Combine all ingredients.

Mango, Peach, & Rice Cereal

Yields 6 tablespoons

INGREDIENTS:

2 tablespoons prepared iron-fortified rice cereal (with either breast milk or formula)

2 tablespoons Mango Purée (page 39)

2 tablespoons Peach Purée (page 38)

These two fruits complement each other with their sweet tanginess.

Combine all ingredients.

Green Beans, Mango, & Rice Cereal

Although to adults this combination might seem unconventional, babies are just learning about different food tastes and textures. Babies should not be limited by an adult palate.

Combine all ingredients.

Hot-Blooded Mangos

Since mango trees cannot tolerate cool weather, they are not locally available in many parts of the United States. However, frozen organic mango is available in many well-stocked supermarkets.

Yields 6 tablespoons

INGREDIENTS:

2 tablespoons prepared iron-fortified rice cereal (with either breast milk or formula)

2 tablespoons Green Bean Purée (page 33)

2 tablespoons Mango Purée (page 39)

Banana, Sweet Pea, & Rice Cereal

If you're child doesn't like sweet peas on their own, this combination might do the trick.

Combine all ingredients.

Yields 6 tablespoons

INGREDIENTS:

2 tablespoons prepared iron-fortified rice cereal (with either breast milk or formula)

2 tablespoons Banana Mash (page 36)

2 tablespoons Sweet Pea Purée (page 32)

Banana & Oatmeal Cereal

Remember that bananas tend to constipate babies so use this recipe only occasionally.

Combine all ingredients.

Yields 4 tablespoons

INGREDIENTS:

2 tablespoons prepared iron-fortified oatmeal cereal (with either breast milk or formula)

2 tablespoons Banana Mash (page 36)

Papaya, Pear, & Oatmeal Cereal

Jarred pear sauce can be used in place of the Pear Purée.

Combine all ingredients.

Yields 6 tablespoons

INGREDIENTS:

2 tablespoons prepared iron-fortified oatmeal cereal (with either breast milk or formula)

2 tablespoons Papaya Purée (page 37)

2 tablespoons Pear Purée (page 36)

Banana, Apricot, & Oatmeal Cereal

*This combination includes lots of nutrients that a
growing baby needs, including potassium, iron, and vitamin A.*

Combine all ingredients.

Yields 6 tablespoons

INGREDIENTS:

*2 tablespoons prepared
iron-fortified oatmeal
cereal (with either breast
milk or formula)*

*2 tablespoons Banana
Mash (page 36)*

*2 tablespoons Apricot
Purée (page 38)*

Apple & Oatmeal Cereal

This combination is an almost universal baby-pleaser.

Combine all ingredients.

Apples, the Local Option
Although crabapples are the only apple that is native to North America,
apples today are grown in all fifty states. Look for locally grown organic
apples at the farmers' market in the fall.

Yields 4 tablespoons

INGREDIENTS:

*2 tablespoons prepared
iron-fortified oatmeal
cereal (with either breast
milk or formula)*

*2 tablespoons Apple
Purée (page 35)*

Pumpkin, Peach, & Oatmeal Cereal

The combination of pumpkin and peach will result in a vibrant orange color.

Combine all ingredients.

Yields 6 tablespoons

INGREDIENTS:

2 tablespoons prepared iron-fortified oatmeal cereal (with either breast milk or formula)

2 tablespoons Pumpkin Purée (page 54)

2 tablespoons Peach Purée (page 38)

Papaya, Apple, & Oatmeal Cereal

This combination is a sweet and yummy way to start the day.

Combine all ingredients.

Amazing Apple Juice
Between 20,000 and 40,000 tons of apples are converted into apple juice every year. Due to the demand for organics, the share of organic apple juice is steadily increasing. Although apples are converted to juice only during the fall (typically in October) thanks to sterile storing and packaging, apple juice can be enjoyed throughout the year.

Yields 6 tablespoons

INGREDIENTS:

2 tablespoons prepared iron-fortified oatmeal cereal (with either breast milk or formula)

2 tablespoons Papaya Purée (page 37)

2 tablespoons Apple Purée (page 35)

Avocado & Barley Cereal

When making a salad for the whole family, set aside some of the avocado and mash it up for the youngest family member.

Combine all ingredients.

Avocados, a Native Fruit

Avocados are native to North America, originating in Central America and Mexico thousands of years ago. Today, more than 90 percent of the avocados at the supermarket come from California.

Yields 4 tablespoons

INGREDIENTS:

2 tablespoons prepared iron-fortified barley cereal (with either breast milk or formula)

2 tablespoons Avocado Mash (page 35)

Dried Plum & Barley Cereal

The same process used to make the Dried Plum Purée can be used to turn dried apricots into an apricot purée.

Combine all ingredients.

Yields 4 tablespoons

INGREDIENTS:

2 tablespoons prepared iron-fortified barley cereal (with either breast milk or formula)

2 tablespoons Dried Plum Purée (page 37)

Apricot, Dried Plum, & Barley Cereal

This dish is the perfect choice for a constipated baby.

Combine all ingredients.

Yummy Cousins

Apricots and plums are part of the same family "tree." Both are part of the plant family genus *Plumus*. Like their cousin, apricots are delicious fresh, but they are also nutritious and delicious when dried.

Apple, Pumpkin, & Barley Cereal

Pumpkin Purée adds a creamy texture to this combination.

Combine all ingredients.

Organic Jarred Applesauce

Organic applesauce is readily available. Keep a jar or two on hand for days when life gets in the way of cooking. It can be combined with cereal and breast milk or formula, mixed with a vegetable purée or just served on its own. Most commercially available brands have a very smooth consistency that works well with even beginning eaters. Remember to make sure that there is no added sugar. If the texture is lumpy, you should still purée it for baby.

Yields 6 tablespoons

INGREDIENTS:

2 tablespoons prepared iron-fortified barley cereal (with either breast milk or formula)

2 tablespoons Apple Purée (page 35)

2 tablespoons Pumpkin Purée (page 54)

Avocado Banana Mash

These two buttery items make such a great combination for your baby.
Both have similar textures and blend together nicely!

Combine all ingredients and mash with a fork until desired consistency.

Bananas Not Ripe?

If your bananas are not quite ripe, heat them in the microwave for a few seconds to soften to the correct consistency for mashing. Another way to ripen bananas is to place them in a brown bag. This will speed up the process.

Yields 4 tablespoons

INGREDIENTS:

2 tablespoons Avocado Mash (page 35)

2 tablespoons Banana Mash (page 36)

Pear Mango Purée

Cantaloupe can also be used as a substitute for either of these ingredients and makes a nice purée as well. All these orange fruits together help provide your baby with vitamin A!

Combine all ingredients.

Yields 4 tablespoons

INGREDIENTS:

2 tablespoons Pear Purée (page 36)

2 tablespoons Mango Purée (page 39)

Papaya & Banana Mash

A nickname for the papaya is the "tree melon."

Combine all ingredients.

Yields 4 tablespoons

INGREDIENTS:

2 tablespoons Papaya Purée (page 37)

2 tablespoons Banana Mash (page 36)

Apricot Pear Purée

There are 6 grams of fiber in a medium pear! These can be used as well as prunes to help with your baby's stool pattern.

Combine all ingredients.

Yields 4 tablespoons

INGREDIENTS:

2 tablespoons Apricot Purée (page 38)

2 tablespoons Pear Purée (page 36)

Sweet Pea & Apple Purée

If your baby did not like plain sweet peas, try this mixture with apples. The sweet taste of the apples may help your baby to accept the peas in disguise.

Combine all ingredients.

Are Peas a Vegetable?

You may be surprised to learn that peas are a legume or bean. A legume is a plant that bears fruits in the form of pods. These pods grow and then hold the seeds that we know as peas or beans. Sweet peas are actually a legume.

Yields 4 tablespoons

INGREDIENTS:

2 tablespoons Sweet Pea Purée (page 32)

2 tablespoons Apple Purée (page 35)

Peach & Avocado Mash

In the summer, many local nurseries allow you to go and pick your own peaches. Make this a fun family activity with your children as they grow.

Combine all ingredients and mash with a fork until desired consistency.

Yields 4 tablespoons

INGREDIENTS:

2 tablespoons Peach Purée (page 38)

2 tablespoons Avocado Mash (page 35)

Mango & Apricot Purée

Once you try a fruit or vegetable and your child has no reaction after four to seven days, try combining different items for new flavors.

Combine all ingredients.

Are Unusual Combinations Okay?

Babies are developing their taste buds. Try unusual combinations of fruits and vegetables, even if they sound strange to you. Your child may love a combination of plums and sweet peas even if it does not sound good to you. Experiment and have fun with feeding your child.

INGREDIENTS:

2 tablespoons Mango Purée (page 39)

2 tablespoons Apricot Purée (page 38)

Avocado Pumpkin Mash

The color of this combination might not be appealing to an adult, but this won't be a problem for your baby.

Combine all ingredients.

INGREDIENTS:

2 tablespoons Avocado Mash (page 35)

2 tablespoons Pumpkin Purée (page 54)

Dried Plum & Pear Purée

You can use fresh plums in season in place of dried plums in this yummy purée.

Combine all ingredients.

Yields 4 tablespoons

INGREDIENTS:

2 tablespoons Dried Plum Purée (page 37)

2 tablespoons Pear Purée (page 36)

Peach Pear Purée

Different varieties of pears are available all throughout the year.

Combine all ingredients.

Baked Pears
Another delicious way to enjoy fresh pears is to bake them. First preheat oven to 350°F. Then cut pears into chunks. Cover and bake 40–60 minutes. Purée baby's portion, and serve the larger chunks to the rest of the family.

Yields 4 tablespoons

INGREDIENTS:

2 tablespoons Peach Purée (page 38)

2 tablespoons Pear Purée (page 36)

INGREDIENTS:

2 tablespoons Banana Mash (page 36)

2 tablespoons Pumpkin Purée (page 54)

Banana Pumpkin Mash

Mix this purée with 1 teaspoon sunflower seed butter for a yummy spread for toast or muffins when your baby is a little older.

Combine all ingredients.

Sunflower Seed Butter

Since peanut butter is off-limits due to potential food allergies for little children, sunflower seed butter steps in to create delicious recipes. Due to its peanut-butter–like consistency, it shouldn't be given to children under three years on its own, but it can be baked up in muffins or blended in smoothies and dips. Sunflower seed butter is available commercially or you can make your own by tossing roasted sunflower seeds (without the shells) in the food processor with a little canola oil. Process until smooth.

Green Beans & Avocado Mash

*Green beans are loaded with vitamins and minerals,
including K, C, potassium, and iron.*

Combine all ingredients.

Yields 4 tablespoons

INGREDIENTS:

*2 tablespoons Green
Bean Purée (page 33)*

*2 tablespoons Avocado
Mash (page 35)*

Sweet Pea & Mango Purée

Frozen organic sweet peas are readily available and relatively inexpensive.

Combine all ingredients.

Yields 4 tablespoons

INGREDIENTS:

*2 tablespoons Sweet Pea
Purée (page 32)*

*2 tablespoons Mango
Purée (page 39)*

Pumpkin Purée

Yields 16 tablespoons

INGREDIENTS:

½ small pumpkin
(approximately 8 ounces)

½ cup water

*For a shortcut, use a can of plain, organic pumpkin—
just open the can and serve. Make sure to buy plain
pumpkin with no added spices, sugars, or dairy products.*

1. Peel, seed, and chop pumpkin. Steam in steamer with water for 7–10 minutes.

2. Put pumpkin in food processor or blender. Process on and off until desired consistency reached. Use a small amount of the cooking water to thin the final product if necessary. If you plan to freeze the final product, do not thin with breast milk or formula. Work the pulp through a strong strainer to remove any fibrous materials.

Pumpkins Are Not Just for Halloween

Choose a "pie pumpkin" to make this purée. Wash the outside of the pumpkin, cut in half, and scrape out the seeds. Remove the stem, put in microwaveable bowl and add 2"–3" of water, and cover. Cook on high for 15 minutes and check to see if the pumpkin is tender. Cook another 15 minutes on high until done. The pumpkin is done when it is tender enough to scrape out with a fork. Scrape flesh out and purée.

Chapter 4

Six to Nine Months

Brown Rice   **56**

Basic Barley   **56**

Quinoa   **57**

Oatmeal   **57**

Kasha (Roasted Buckwheat)   **58**

Basic Grits   **58**

Lentils   **59**

Split Peas   **59**

Black Bean Mash   **60**

Refried Pinto Beans   **60**

Apple & Pear Purée   **61**

Apricot, Pear, & Barley Cereal   **61**

Apple, Sweet Potato, & Cinnamon Purée   **62**

Banana & Blueberry Purée   **62**

Butternut Squash & Corn Purée   **63**

Fall Harvest Purée   **63**

Homemade Applesauce   **64**

Apple & Carrot Mash   **64**

Mango Banana Purée   **65**

Two-Potato Mash   **65**

Papaya & Banana Mash   **66**

Peach Raspberry Purée   **66**

Potato & Plum Purée   **67**

Pumpkin & Parsnip Purée   **67**

Rutabaga & Pear Purée   **68**

Spinach & Potato Purée   **68**

Sweet Potato & Carrot Purée   **69**

Apricot & Banana Mash   **69**

Apricot & Apple Purée   **70**

Apple & Plum Compote   **70**

Butternut Squash with Apples & Pears   **71**

Butternut Squash with Carrots   **71**

Mashed Turnip & Sweet Potato   **72**

Peaches & Quinoa   **72**

Avocado & Black Beans   **73**

Orzo & Sweet Pea Purée   **73**

Zucchini & Rice Cereal   **74**

Rice Cereal & Peach Purée   **74**

Apple & Banana Oatmeal Cereal   **75**

Pinto Beans & Brown Rice   **75**

Pinto Beans, Apples, & Barley   **76**

Island Breakfast Cereal   **76**

Kasha with Peach & Pear Purée   **77**

Chicken with Cherries & Brown Rice   **77**

Chicken & Mango Purée   **78**

Chicken, Banana, & Coconut   **78**

Chicken, Papaya, & Nutmeg Mash   **79**

Chicken & Parsnip Purée   **79**

Chicken, Carrot, & Sweet Onion Mash   **80**

Beef Stew Mash   **80**

Beef & Barley   **81**

Minced Pork Chop with Applesauce   **81**

Poached Fish & Carrots   **82**

Lamb & Pumpkin Mash   **82**

Brown Rice

Brown rice is a tender, delicious whole grain.

1. Combine brown rice and water in a small saucepan.
2. Bring to a boil.
3. Cover, reduce heat, and simmer 40 minutes or until water is absorbed.
4. Remove saucepan from heat, and let sit covered for 5 minutes.
5. Fluff and serve.

Yields 2 cups

INGREDIENTS:

1 cup brown rice
2 cups water

Basic Barley

Barley is an easy and delicious grain that is as versatile as rice.

1. In a small saucepan, combine barley and water.
2. Cover saucepan.
3. Simmer 45–55 minutes, or until barley is tender.

Yields 3½ cups

INGREDIENTS:

1 cup pearled barley
3 cups water

Quinoa

Not only is quinoa high in protein, but it is also high in fiber and essential amino acids. Make sure your child tolerates rice, oatmeal, and barley before introducing quinoa.

1. Thoroughly rinse quinoa under running water.
2. Combine quinoa and the 2 cups of water in a medium saucepan.
3. Bring to a boil.
4. Reduce heat, cover, and simmer for 15 minutes or until the outer ring of each grain separates.
5. Fluff before serving.

Yields 2 cups

INGREDIENTS:

1 cup quinoa

2 cups water

Oatmeal

Oatmeal is a high-protein, high-fiber whole grain.

1. Bring water to a boil.
2. Add oatmeal, reduce heat, and simmer, stirring occasionally, for 5–10 minutes or until water is absorbed and oats are tender.

Yields 2 cups

INGREDIENTS:

1 cup old-fashioned rolled oats

2 cups water

Kasha (Roasted Buckwheat)

*Kasha, most often found in Eastern European cooking,
is a nutty grain with a fluffy texture.*

1. In a medium saucepan, bring water and olive oil to a boil.
2. Add kasha, cover, and reduce heat. Simmer for 10 minutes. Fluff before serving.

Eastern European Comfort Food
Kasha, or roasted buckwheat, is a common breakfast food throughout Eastern Europe. Buckwheat, which is not related to wheat, is also commonly found a flour that is used in pancakes and other baked goods. Because it is a good source of protein, fiber, magnesium, and manganese, it is a good addition a well-stocked pantry.

Basic Grits

Grits are a good source of dietary fiber.

1. In a small saucepan, combine grits and water.
2. Bring to a boil, stirring constantly.
3. Reduce heat, cover, and simmer for 5 minutes.

Lentils

Lentils feature prominently in cuisines from around the world, including the Middle East and India. If your baby needs a smoother texture, purée lentils before serving.

1. Rinse lentils under running water, and pick over to remove any stones or debris.
2. Combine lentils and the 4 cups of water in medium saucepan and simmer gently with lid tilted for 30–45 minutes, or until lentils are tender.
3. Drain off excess water before serving.

Yields 2 cups

INGREDIENTS:
1 cup lentils
4 cups water

Split Peas

Split peas are a great source of protein, fiber and iron. If your baby needs a smoother texture, puree split peas before serving.

1. Rinse split peas under running water, and pick over to remove any stones or debris.
2. Combine split peas and the water in a small saucepan. Bring to a boil.
3. Reduce heat, cover, and simmer for 30–45 minutes.
4. Drain off extra water before serving.

Green or Yellow?
Split peas come in green and yellow. They can be used interchangeably, as they both cook up tender and are great sources of protein and iron.

Yields 2 cups

INGREDIENTS:
1 cup green split peas
2 cups water

Black Bean Mash

Yields 2 cups

INGREDIENTS:

1 cup dried black beans
(or 1 (15-ounce) can of
black beans)

3–4 cups water

1 tablespoon olive oil

*Dried beans are extremely affordable, where canned
beans are extremely convenient.*

1. Soak dried beans in water for 6–8 hours or overnight before cooking. Drain soaking water from beans and rinse.

2. In a medium saucepan combine beans with water, and bring to a simmer with the lid tilted. Cook 1–1½ hours or until tender. Drain and rinse cooked beans (or drain and rinse canned beans, if using).

3. In a medium saucepan or sauté pan, heat olive oil over medium heat. Add beans and heat through for 1–2 minutes, or until desired temperature is reached. Remove from heat and mash beans with a potato masher or fork.

Refried Pinto Beans

Yields 2 cups

INGREDIENTS:

1 cup dried pinto beans
(or 1 (15-ounce) can)

3–4 cups water

1 tablespoon olive oil

½ onion, finely chopped

1 clove garlic, minced

1 teaspoon cumin

This is a mild version of a classic Mexican dish.

1. Soak dried beans in water for 6–8 hours or overnight before cooking. Drain soaking water from beans, and rinse.

2. In a medium saucepan, combine beans with water, and bring to a simmer with lid tilted. Cook 1–1½ hours or until tender. Drain and rinse either cooked beans or canned beans, if using.

3. In a medium saucepan or sauté pan, heat olive oil over medium heat. Add onion and garlic. Cook until onion is tender, 3–5 minutes. Add beans and cumin, and heat through for 1–2 minutes, or until desired temperature is reached. Remove from heat, and mash with a potato masher or fork.

Apple & Pear Purée

For this recipe or other recipes that call for a sweeter pear, try a red Bartlett, comice, or forelle type.

Combine all ingredients.

Yields 4 tablespoons

INGREDIENTS:

2 tablespoons Apple Purée (page 35)

2 tablespoons Pear Purée (page 36)

Apricot, Pear, & Barley Cereal

This fiber-rich cereal is also a good source of vitamins A and C.

Combine all ingredients.

Yields 6 tablespoons

INGREDIENTS:

2 tablespoons iron-fortified barley cereal (prepared with breast milk or formula)

2 tablespoons Apricot Purée (page 38)

2 tablespoons Pear Purée (page 36)

Apple, Sweet Potato, & Cinnamon Purée

Yields 6 tablespoons

INGREDIENTS:

2 tablespoons Apple Purée (page 35)

4 tablespoons Sweet Potato Purée (page 34)

⅛ teaspoon cinnamon

As your baby gets older, you can begin to experiment with slightly thicker mashes and adding spices. If your baby has trouble with the thickness, add more apple purée to thin. Try the thicker mash again in a week or two.

Combine all ingredients.

Banana & Blueberry Purée

Yields 1½ cups

INGREDIENTS:

1 ripe banana

½ cup fresh or frozen blueberries

2 tablespoons water

Be sure that your baby is wearing a bib for this one—blueberries stain!

1. Purée all ingredients in blender or food processor.
2. Add water to reach desired consistency.

Butternut Squash & Corn Purée

Making a smooth purée is a safe way to serve the delicious taste of sweet corn to your baby.

1. In a medium saucepan, combine squash, water, and corn and bring to a boil.

2. Stir while cooking to ensure that squash cooks evenly.

3. Cook until tender, 8–10 minutes.

4. Transfer to a food processor or blender. Purée, using additional water as necessary to achieve age-appropriate consistency.

Yields 1½ cups

INGREDIENTS:

½ cup peeled butternut squash chunks

½ cup water

¼ cup frozen sweet corn

Fall Harvest Purée

This beta carotene–rich dish highlights some of autumn's best delights.

Combine all ingredients.

Yields 6 tablespoons

INGREDIENTS:

2 tablespoons Apple Purée (page 35)

2 tablespoons Pumpkin Purée (page 54)

2 tablespoons Sweet Potato Purée (page 34)

Homemade Applesauce

Make a stockpot full of this delicious sauce during the fall, and freeze in 1–cup containers. It will stay good for up to 6 months in your freezer.

Yields 2½ cups

INGREDIENTS:

3 sweet apples

⅛ teaspoon cinnamon

Enough water to cover apples

1. Peel apples and cut into chunks. In a large saucepan, combine apple chunks and cinnamon. Cover apples with water. Cook until apples are very tender and start to break apart.

2. Mash with a potato masher or the back of a spoon. Transfer to blender or food processor if a finer consistency is needed.

Applesauce for Baking

Many of the recipes for baked goods in this book use applesauce mixed with baking powder. Homemade applesauce is perfect for this. Mash the applesauce to a smooth consistency and then follow the baking recipe directions.

Apple & Carrot Mash

The natural sweetness of carrots is highlighted by the sweet taste of the applesauce in the sunny-colored dish.

Yields 1 cup

INGREDIENTS:

1 carrot

½ cup Homemade Applesauce (page 64)

1. Peel carrot and cut into small slices or chunks. Steam carrot using either a steamer basket or microwave.

2. Purée carrot using reserved steaming water to achieve age-appropriate consistency. Combine carrot and applesauce.

Not So Fast, Honey!

When it's time to start thinking about adding sweeteners to your baby's diet, whether it's for baking or cooking, one natural choice needs to wait. Babies should not have any honey until after one year. Their immature digestive systems cannot adequately process honey, and it can lead to a form of botulism, a serious food poisoning. If you need to turn to a sweetener before one year old, consider apple juice concentrate, maple syrup, or agave nectar.

Mango Banana Purée

One quarter of a banana should yield 2 tablespoons of mashed banana. Transfer the remainder of the banana to a freezer bag and freeze for use in a smoothie.

Combine all ingredients.

Yields 4 tablespoons

INGREDIENTS:

2 tablespoons Banana Mash (page 36)

2 tablespoons Mango Purée (page 39)

Two-Potato Mash

Because Yukon Gold potatoes are so flavorful, it is the perfect potato to use for this dish, which doesn't contain any added salt.

1. Wash and peel potato and cut into small chunks.
2. In a small saucepan, bring potato and water to a boil. Cook until tender.
3. Transfer potato to a food processor or blender with oil. Purée.
4. Combine both potato purées.

Yields 4 ounces

INGREDIENTS:

1 small Yukon Gold potato

⅛ cup water

½ teaspoon canola oil

4 tablespoons Sweet Potato Purée (page 34)

Papaya & Banana Mash

Yields 4 tablespoons

INGREDIENTS:

2 tablespoons Papaya
Purée (page 37)

2 tablespoons Banana
Mash (page 36)

*You can store a ripe banana in the refrigerator for a few days.
The peel will turn brown but the banana flesh will stay yellow.*

Combine all ingredients and mash with a fork until desired consistency.

Can You Freeze Banana Purée?

Bananas are best if mashed fresh. Bananas need lemon juice added to
them to prevent browning and young babies should not have citrus until
closer to one year of age. If you are making this for an older child, you
can add citrus and freeze, but otherwise, mash bananas fresh.

Peach Raspberry Purée

Yields ½ cup

INGREDIENTS:

¼ cup raspberries

4 tablespoons Peach
Purée (page 38)

*Raspberry bushes grow easily in backyards around the country.
Consider planting one for fresh-picked fruit during the summer.*

1. Wash raspberries and drain, but do not dry.

2. Transfer moist raspberries to a food processor or blender and purée.

3. Pass raspberry purée through a fine-meshed sieve or strainer to remove
   seeds.

4. Combine with Peach Purée.

Potato & Plum Purée

Different varieties of plums are ripe all throughout the summer, so take advantage of the luscious juiciness of this treat by mixing up some of this sweet and creamy dish.

1. Wash and peel potato and cut into small chunks.
2. In a small saucepan, bring potato and water to a boil. Cook until tender.
3. Peel plum, remove seed, and chop into chunks.
4. Combine fresh plum and cooked potato in food processor or blender. Purée until smooth.

Yields 6 tablespoons

INGREDIENTS:
1 small potato
⅛ cup water
1 small, ripe plum

Pumpkin & Parsnip Purée

What to do with parsnips that show up in your box of produce from the farm in early winter? Cook this sweet treat for your baby!

1. Peel parsnip and cut into small slices or chunks.
2. Steam parsnip using either a steamer basket or microwave.
3. Purée parsnip using reserved steaming water to achieve age-appropriate consistency.
4. Combine parsnip purée and Pumpkin Purée.

Yields 4 tablespoons

INGREDIENTS:
1 small parsnip
4 tablespoons Pumpkin Purée (page 54)

Rutabaga & Pear Purée

Yields 1 cup

INGREDIENTS:

1 rutabaga

⅛–¼ cup water

4 ounces Pear Purée
(page 36)

*Rutabagas are beta carotene–rich root vegetables that grow best
in cold climates, such as the northern United States and Canada.*

1. Peel rutabaga and cut off ends. Cut into chunks. In a small saucepan, combine rutabaga and water. Bring to a boil. Boil until soft, approximately 10 minutes.

2. Transfer rutabaga and reserved cooking water to a food processor or blender. Purée until smooth. Combine with Pear Purée.

Rutabaga, the Turnip's Cousin
Rutabaga, a sweet, delicious fall root vegetable, is actually a cross between a turnip and a cabbage. Because they're closely related to turnips, rutabagas and turnips can be used interchangeably in recipes.

Spinach & Potato Purée

Yields ½ cup

INGREDIENTS:

1 small potato

¼ cup chopped spinach

⅛–¼ cup water

*Fresh spinach holds a lot of dirt and sand. The best way to wash
it is to submerge it in a bowl of cold water, drain,
and repeat the process until the water remains clear.*

1. Wash, peel, and chop potato into small chunks.

2. In a small saucepan, combine potato, spinach, and water.

3. Bring to a boil, and cook until the potato is tender, approximately 5–10 minutes depending on the size of the chunks.

4. Transfer potato and spinach to a blender or food processor. Purée until smooth, adding as much reserved cooking water as necessary for age-appropriate consistency.

Sweet Potato & Carrot Purée

Vitamins A and C team up with a healthy dose of dietary fiber in this vibrant dish.

1. Peel carrot and cut into small slices or chunks.
2. Steam carrot using either a steamer basket or microwave.
3. Transfer carrot to a blender or food processor and purée using reserved steaming water to achieve age-appropriate consistency.
4. Combine carrot purée with Sweet Potato Purée.

Yields ½ cup

INGREDIENTS:

1 carrot

4 tablespoons Sweet Potato Purée (page 34)

Apricot & Banana Mash

Fresh apricots can be tart; sweet banana makes them easily acceptable to baby's tastes.

Combine all ingredients.

Yields 4 tablespoons

INGREDIENTS:

2 tablespoons Apricot Purée (page 38)

2 tablespoons Banana Mash (page 36)

Apricot & Apple Purée

*Freezing leftover purées allows you to make combinations
that take advantage of different growing seasons.*

Combine all ingredients.

Puréeing 101

When these recipes call for a purée, it means a solid food that has been turned into a smooth, almost liquid, consistency. Most soft fruits, plums, apricots, peaches, berries, and so on, can be washed, peeled (if they have a tougher skin, like peaches), and put in the food processor or blender. The juice in the fruit is probably adequate to achieve the right consistency without added water. Most vegetables will benefit from initial steaming before puréeing. Because vegetables are not as juicy as fruits, they might need some additional water or broth to achieve the right liquid texture.

Apple & Plum Compote

*Use a sweet variety of apple for this dish,
such as Golden Delicious, Fuji, or Pink Lady.*

1. Peel apple and plums and cut into chunks. In a large saucepan, combine apple and plum chunks with cinnamon. Cover fruit with water. Cook until apples are very tender and start to break apart, approximately 10 minutes depending on the size of the chunks.

2. Mash with a potato masher or the back of a spoon. Transfer to blender or food processor if a finer consistency is needed.

Can You Still Go Out to Eat?

For you, more and more restaurants are featuring organic ingredients. For your baby, you can easily pack up his food and bring it out with you. Since babies aren't picky about their dinner being served at any exact temperature, so long as you keep it safe by packing the food along with an ice pack, you should be good to go.

Butternut Squash with Apples & Pears

*Acorn squash or pumpkin can be substituted
for butternut squash in this recipe.*

1. In a medium saucepan, combine squash and water and bring to a boil. Stir while cooking to ensure that squash cooks evenly. Cook until tender, 8–10 minutes.

2. Transfer squash to a food processor or blender. Purée, using reserved cooking water as necessary to achieve age-appropriate consistency.

3. Combine squash with Apple Purée and Pear Purée.

Wash That Spoon!

To prevent contaminating a large batch of baby food, take out only what you think your baby will eat. Once the spoon has gone from your baby's mouth back into the bowl, leftovers must be discarded.

Yields 1½ cups

INGREDIENTS:

½ cup peeled butternut
squash chunks

¼ cup water

2 tablespoons Apple
Purée (page 35)

2 tablespoons Pear Purée
(page 36)

Butternut Squash with Carrots

*This is a great recipe to make your baby in the fall
when both of these foods are in season!*

1. Steam large butternut squash pieces for 25 minutes to soften and loosen the skin. Remove skin from squash and cut into 2" cubes.

2. In food processor or blender, add squash and process on and off until desired consistency reached. Combine 2 tablespoons of resulting butternut squash purée with carrot purée and serve. Freeze remaining butternut squash in an ice-cube tray.

How Do You Cook a Squash?

Butternut squash can be steamed, microwaved, or baked. To steam a squash: Cut in half and place in steamer for 20–30 minutes. To microwave a squash: Put a peeled squash in the microwave with 3 tablespoons of water for 8 minutes. To bake a squash: Cut squash and place in shallow pan with water and bake for 20 minutes in the oven.

Yields 4 tablespoons

INGREDIENTS:

½ cup peeled butternut
squash chunks

2 tablespoons store-
bought carrot purée

Mashed Turnip & Sweet Potato

*Although the outside of turnips can be white,
purple, or green, the inside is all white.*

Yields ½ cup

INGREDIENTS:

1 small turnip

⅛ cup water

*4 tablespoons Sweet
Potato Purée (page 34)*

1. Peel turnip and chop into small chunks. In a small saucepan, combine turnip and water. Bring to a boil and cook until the turnip is tender, approximately 10 minutes depending on the size of the chunks.

2. Transfer turnip to a blender or food processor. Purée. Combine turnip purée with Sweet Potato Purée.

Freezing Tips

Once you've frozen extra baby food in an ice cube tray, transfer the cubes to a freezer-safe bag or container. Be sure to put a label on the container describing the contents and adding the date. Fruits and vegetables can be frozen for up to six months, and meats can be frozen up to three months.

Peaches & Quinoa

*Quinoa is a great addition to soups for your baby. Add a small amount of quinoa
to your baby's favorite soup to give it a good texture.*

Yields 6 tablespoons

INGREDIENTS:

*2 ounces of Peach Purée
(page 38)*

*1 tablespoon cooked
Quinoa (page 57)*

1. Combine Peach Purée and cooked quinoa.

2. If necessary, use a food processor or blender until desired consistency reached.

Mother of all Grains

Quinoa has been grown in South America for more than 6,000 years. The Incas revered quinoa as the "mother of all grains" due to its unique nutritional properties. It has a good amount of balanced protein and is high in fiber, phosphorous, magnesium, and iron.

Avocado & Black Beans

In many Latin American countries, avocados and black beans are a first food!

Combine ingredients and mash together with a fork.

Yields 4 tablespoons

INGREDIENTS:

2 tablespoons Black Bean Mash (page 60)

2 tablespoons Avocado Mash (page 35)

Orzo & Sweet Pea Purée

Orzo means "barley" in Italian. This rice-shaped pasta is not made of rice or barley, but from a hard-wheat semolina.

1. Combine cooked orzo pasta and Sweet Pea Purée.

2. If necessary, use a food processor or blender until desired consistency is reached.

Making a Risotto?

Orzo pasta can be a great substitute for Arborio rice in many different recipes. Due to the size and shape of orzo pasta, many people think that it is a rice. It is not but has a similar consistency and properties and works just as well in Arborio rice in risotto recipes. Liven up your risottos with a little orzo pasta!

Yields 6 tablespoons

INGREDIENTS:

4 tablespoons of Sweet Pea Purée (page 32)

2 tablespoons cooked orzo pasta

Zucchini & Rice Cereal

Yields 4 tablespoons

INGREDIENTS:

1 medium zucchini

2 tablespoons prepared iron-fortified oatmeal cereal (with either breast milk or formula)

Zucchini squash comes in many colors: yellow, light green, and dark green! Use different types of zucchini together for a colorful dish.

1. Cut off ends of zucchini, do not peel.
2. Cut into slices and steam zucchini squash pieces for 4–6 minutes to soften.
3. In food processor or blender, process on and off until desired consistency is reached.
4. Combine 2 tablespoons of zucchini purée with 2 tablespoons of prepared iron-fortified cereal and serve. Freeze remaining zucchini purée in ice-cube trays.

Rice Cereal & Peach Purée

Yields 6 tablespoons

INGREDIENTS:

3 tablespoons prepared iron-fortified oatmeal cereal (with either breast milk or formula)

3 tablespoons Peach Purée (page 38)

Peaches are the second largest commercial fruit crop in the United States. The first major commercial fruit product is apples.

1. Combine prepared rice cereal and peach purée.
2. If necessary, use a food processor or blender until desired consistency is reached.

Peachy Facts

Peaches are revered in China as a symbol of long life. Many people in the United States grow peaches in their yards. Peach trees produce a pink beautiful flower. Interestingly, the peach is the state flower of Delaware and the state fruit of South Carolina and Georgia. The state of Georgia calls itself the "Peach State."

Apple & Banana Oatmeal Cereal

Most babies prefer the taste of sweet apples over tart, so it's best to stay away from Granny Smith apples when making apple purée for the earliest eaters.

Combine all ingredients.

Yields 6 tablespoons

INGREDIENTS:

2 tablespoons prepared iron-fortified oatmeal cereal (with either breast milk or formula)

2 tablespoons Apple Purée (page 35)

2 tablespoons Banana Mash (page 36)

Pinto Beans & Brown Rice

You can use canned pinto beans or you can cook pinto beans from dry beans. If choosing canned beans, choose organic beans and make sure they do not contain hot peppers!

1. Combine brown rice and pinto bean mash.

2. If necessary, use a food processor or blender until desired consistency reached.

Yields 4 tablespoons

INGREDIENTS:

2 tablespoons cooked brown rice

2 tablespoons Refried Pinto Beans (page 60)

Pinto Beans, Apples, & Barley

Apples add a little natural sweetness to this dish.

Combine all ingredients.

Yields 6 tablespoons

INGREDIENTS:

2 tablespoons prepared iron-fortified barley cereal (with either breast milk or formula)

2 tablespoons Refried Pinto Beans (page 60)

2 tablespoons Apple Purée (page 35)

Island Breakfast Cereal

Using frozen fruit in winter when local options are limited can bring a taste of the tropics to an otherwise gloomy day.

Combine all ingredients.

Yields 6 tablespoons

INGREDIENTS:

2 tablespoons prepared iron-fortified barley cereal (with either breast milk or formula)

2 tablespoons Papaya Purée (page 37)

2 tablespoons Mango Purée (page 39)

Thawing Frozen Purées

If you've frozen your purées in an ice cube tray, and then transferred them to a freezer-safe container, you have a collection of 2-tablespoon (1-ounce) servings of baby food. When it's time to thaw them, you can put the cubes you need in the refrigerator in the morning to thaw by evening, pack them with an ice pack in baby's diaper bag to be ready in a few hours, or microwave them, being sure to stir them well to eliminate hot spots. It's not safe to thaw the purée on the kitchen counter, as bacteria can start to grow in a partially defrosted cube.

Kasha with Peach & Pear Purée

Once your child has tried each of these components individually, have fun combining different combinations together to provide variety to your child's developing taste buds.

1. Combine above ingredients.
2. If necessary, use a food processor or blender until desired consistency is reached.

Want to Stop Your Grains from Sticking Together?

Before cooking buckwheat, rice, millet, barley, or kasha, wash the grains first in warm water and then follow with hot water. Warm water removes the starch from the surface of grains. The hot water then removes the fat that may rise to the surface of grains during their storage.

Yields 6 tablespoons

INGREDIENTS:

2 tablespoons Peach Purée (page 38)

2 tablespoons Pear Purée (page 36)

2 tablespoons cooked kasha cereal

Chicken with Cherries & Brown Rice

Cook a plain extra chicken breast when you cook dinner for your family to use in a purée for your infant.

1. In a large pot bring the 6 cups of water to a boil. Place chicken breast in pot and boil until done, approximately 10 minutes. Once done, cut into small pieces and allow to cool.
2. Combine chicken, cherries, and brown rice.
3. Use a food processor or blender until desired consistency reached. Use broth from cooking the chicken, breast milk, or iron-fortified formula to reach an age-appropriate consistency. If consistency is too chunky, drain through a sieve and purée remaining liquid.

Yields 2 cups

INGREDIENTS:

6 cups water

1 boneless, skinless chicken breast

½ cup pitted cherries

1 cup cooked brown rice

Chicken & Mango Purée

Yields 2 cups

INGREDIENTS:

6 cups water

1 boneless, skinless chicken breast

1 cup Mango Purée (page 39)

If fresh mangos are out of season, frozen mango can be substituted in this recipe.

1. In a large pot bring 6 cups of water to a boil.
2. Place chicken breast in pot and boil until done, approximately 10 minutes.
3. Once done, cut into small pieces and allow to cool.
4. Combine chicken and Mango Purée.
5. Use a food processor or blender until desired consistency reached. Use broth from cooking the chicken, breast milk, or iron-fortified formula to reach an age-appropriate consistency.
6. If consistency is too chunky, drain through a sieve and purée remaining liquid.

Chicken, Banana, & Coconut

Yields 2 cups

6 cups water

1 boneless, skinless chicken breast

1 small banana or ½ large banana

1 teaspoon coconut milk

This is a great dish for grownups, too! Cook the adult portion in a separate pot so that you can spice it up. Options to spice it up for adults include adding some red chili paste, diced onions, coconut milk, curry powder, and fresh cilantro. Serve over brown or Arborio rice.

1. In a large pot bring 6 cups of water to a boil. Place the chicken breast in the pot and boil until done, approximately 10 minutes. Once done, cut into small pieces and allow to cool.
2. Combine chicken, banana, and coconut milk. Use a food processor or blender until desired is consistency reached. Use broth from cooking the chicken, breast milk, or iron-fortified formula to reach an age-appropriate consistency. If consistency is too chunky, drain through a sieve and purée remaining liquid.

Chicken, Papaya, & Nutmeg Mash

This recipe works best with a very ripe papaya. If your papaya is underripe then it will be necessary to cut it into cubes and steam it for about 5 minutes.

1. In a pot bring 6 cups of water to a boil. Place chicken breast in pot and boil until done, approximately 10 minutes. Once done, cut into small pieces and allow to cool. Combine chicken, papaya, and nutmeg.

2. Use a food processor or blender until desired consistency reached. Use broth from cooking the chicken, breast milk, or iron-fortified formula to reach an age-appropriate consistency. If consistency is too chunky, drain through a sieve and purée remaining liquid.

What Is the Best Way to Ripen a Papaya?
Place it in a brown paper bag with an apple for the fastest ripening. Apples produce ethylene gas, which speeds up ripening.

Yields 2 cups

INGREDIENTS:

6 cups water

1 boneless, skinless chicken breast

½ cup ripe papaya

2 tablespoons of breast milk or formula

Dash of nutmeg

Chicken & Parsnip Purée

It is best to choose a small to medium-sized parsnip for this recipe. Large root vegetables have a tendency to be woody and bitter, which can turn some children off the taste of these vegetables.

1. Peel and dice parsnip. Bring 1 cup of water to a boil and cook parsnip until tender, about 15 minutes. Cut cooked chicken into small pieces. Combine chicken and parsnip.

2. Use a food processor or blender until desired consistency is reached. Use broth from cooking the chicken, breast milk, or iron-fortified formula to reach an age-appropriate consistency. If consistency is too chunky, drain through a sieve and purée remaining liquid.

Yields 2 cups

INGREDIENTS:

1 medium-sized parsnip

1 cup water

1 cooked boneless, skinless chicken breast

3 tablespoons breast milk, iron-fortified formula, or water

Chicken, Carrot, & Sweet Onion Mash

Yields 2 cups

INGREDIENTS:

6 cups water

1 boneless, skinless chicken breast

⅛ sweet onion

2 carrots, peeled

2 teaspoons olive oil

Sweet onions are a nice way to introduce your child to the flavor and health benefits of onions.

1. In a large pot bring 6 cups of water to a boil.

2. Preheat oven to 400°F.

3. Add chicken and onion to water and boil until done, approximately 10 minutes. Once done, drain chicken and onions and save. Cut chicken into small pieces and allow to cool. Cut carrots lengthwise and then into small pieces, coat with olive oil, and roast in oven for 15–20 minutes. Combine chicken, onions, and carrots.

4. Use a food processor or blender until desired consistency is reached. Use broth from cooking the chicken to reach an age-appropriate consistency. If consistency is too chunky, drain through a sieve and purée remaining liquid.

Beef Stew Mash

Yields 1 cup

INGREDIENTS:

2 ounces of beef

2 cups water

1 carrot, scrubbed and sliced

½ medium-sized russet potato, peeled and diced

Most of your family stew recipes can be transformed into baby foods. Just limit the amount of spices and make sure the ingredients are age appropriate. You can purée just about any food for your child!

1. In a medium-sized heavy saucepan, brown the beef.

2. In a small saucepan, bring 2 cups of water to a simmering boil. Add beef, cover, and cook 20 minutes. Add carrot and potato and cook another 15 minutes or until all ingredients are falling apart. Remove from heat and cool slightly.

3. Use a food processor or blender until desired consistency is reached. Use broth from cooking the beef to reach age-appropriate consistency.

4. If consistency is too chunky, drain through a sieve and purée remaining liquid.

Beef & Barley

For a shortcut, buy precooked beef from the store.

1. Cut beef into small pieces. Combine cooked beef, barley, and carrot purée together.

2. Use a food processor or blender until desired consistency is reached. Use beef or vegetable broth to reach an age-appropriate consistency. If consistency is too chunky, drain through a fine-mesh sieve.

Baby Food in a Slow Cooker?
Slow cookers are a great way to make baby foods. Place your meats, vegetables, spices, and water in a slow cooker. Turn it on and forget about it until later in the day. Meats and vegetables get cooked to a wonderful texture for puréeing. When done, purée the stew, serve, and then freeze the leftovers.

Yields 8 tablespoons

INGREDIENTS:

2 ounces of stew beef or other cut, cooked beef

3 tablespoons cooked pearl barley

2 tablespoons store-bought carrot purée

Minced Pork Chop with Applesauce

Make this as a family dinner for your whole family. Once the pork is cooked, purée the pork with apple purée for your infant. This allows you to not make extra meals for your infant but use what you are preparing for the rest of the family.

1. Cut pork chop into small pieces. Combine pork and Apple Purée together.

2. Use a food processor or blender until desired consistency is reached. Use chicken or vegetable broth to reach an age-appropriate consistency. If consistency is too chunky, drain through a sieve and purée remaining liquid.

Is There Iron in Pork?
Yes! There is 0.9 mg of iron in 1 ounce of pork. This iron is heme iron which is better absorbed by the body than plant sources of iron. Try to feed your baby two sources of iron-containing foods per day. For example, iron-fortified rice cereal in the morning and a meal containing meat later in the day.

Yields 2 cups

INGREDIENTS:

1 cooked pork chop

16 tablespoons Apple Purée (page 35)

Poached Fish & Carrots

Be sure to choose low-mercury and environmentally friendly fish.

Yields 2 cups

INGREDIENTS:

¼ pound Tilapia (U.S.-farmed)

16 tablespoons store-bought puréed carrots

1. Fill sauté pan with about 1"–2" water and bring to a boil. Add fish filet, cover, turn heat down to low, and allow to poach for 5"–10 minutes. Once done, drain fish, saving small amount of liquid, and chop. Ensure no bones remain in fish.

2. Combine fish and carrot purée. Use a food processor or blender until desired consistency is reached. Use broth from cooking the fish to reach an age-appropriate consistency. If consistency is too chunky, drain through a sieve and purée remaining liquid.

Healthy Fish

The Shedd Aquarium in Chicago produces a "Right Bite" guide, which shows you which fish are abundant, well cared for, and caught or farmed in environmentally friendly ways.

Lamb & Pumpkin Mash

Lamb is a good source of zinc. Zinc is important for a high-functioning immune system and it also is vital for your child's growth. Your child's body needs zinc to grow as tall as they genetically can!

Yields 2 cups

INGREDIENTS:

2 ounces ground lamb

½ cup canned pumpkin

1. In a medium saucepan with a teaspoon of olive oil, brown lamb meat until done. Browning the lamb should take about 5 minutes for this small amount.

2. Remove lamb from pan and combine with the pumpkin.

3. Use a food processor or blender until desired consistency is reached. Use vegetable or chicken broth to obtain an age-appropriate consistency.

4. If consistency is too chunky, drain through a fine-mesh sieve.

Chapter 5

Nine to Twelve Months

Lentil Soup **84**

Split Pea Soup **84**

Vegetable Rice Soup **85**

Tomato & Orzo Soup **85**

Split Pea Curry **86**

Alphabet Noodle Soup **86**

Chicken Noodle Soup **87**

Blueberry Mini Muffins **88**

Banana Bread **89**

Apple & Sweet Potato Mini Muffins **90**

Carrot & Zucchini Mini Muffins **91**

Oatmeal with Cinnamon Apples **91**

Yogurt Berry Parfait **92**

Strawberry Banana Yogurt **92**

Blueberry Syrup **93**

Oatmeal with Sautéed Plantains **94**

Mashed Potatoes & Parsnips **95**

Black Bean & Carrot Mash **96**

Mango & Brown Rice **97**

Tofu Bites **97**

Cauliflower & Potato Mash **98**

Roast Lamb, Rice, & Tomato Compote **99**

Coconut Pineapple Rice Pudding **99**

Barbecue Tofu & Quinoa **100**

Roasted Potato Rounds **100**

Organic Farmer's Pie **101**

Easy Gravy **102**

Vegetable Barley Casserole **103**

Lentils with Spinach & Quinoa **104**

Mashed Sweet Potatoes **105**

Whole Wheat Shells with Marinara Sauce **105**

Broccoli & Quinoa Casserole **106**

Chickpea, Carrot, & Cauliflower Mash **106**

Chicken, Sweet Pea, & Sweet
Potato Dinner **107**

Hummus **107**

Couscous with Grated Zucchini & Carrots **108**

Hawaiian Sweet Potatoes **109**

Tofu Avocado Spread **109**

Turkey Chili **110**

Whole-Wheat Rotini with Bolognese Sauce **111**

Apple-Roasted Carrots **112**

Orzo with Creamy Tomato Spinach Sauce **112**

Parsnip & Chicken Purée **113**

Strawberry Cantaloupe Sorbet **113**

Sweet Potato Spread **114**

Blackberry Frozen Yogurt **114**

Strawberry Applesauce **115**

Mango Honeydew Sorbet **115**

Happy Birthday Vanilla Cake **116**

Orange Coconut Sorbet **117**

Lentil Soup

Yields 6 cups

INGREDIENTS:

1 tablespoon olive oil

1 garlic clove

¾ cup diced onion

4 cups water

1 bouillon cube (vegan, chicken, or beef)

1 cup diced carrots

½ cup diced celery

½ cup lentils

2 cups diced tomatoes with liquid

Divide this soup and freeze in small portions to have meals ready for the future.

1. In a large stock pot, heat olive oil over medium–high heat.
2. Sauté garlic and onion for 5 minutes.
3. Add water, bouillon cube, carrots, and celery.
4. Rinse and pick over lentils, and add to pot.
5. Add tomatoes.
6. Cover and simmer for 45 minutes.

Split Pea Soup

Yields 6 cups

INGREDIENTS:

1 cup split peas

1 medium onion

1 medium carrot

1 medium baking potato

1 teaspoon olive oil

3 cups vegetable broth

¼ teaspoon dried summer savory

⅛ teaspoon cumin

1 bay leaf

This protein-rich soup is also a good source of vitamin A, vitamin C, potassium, and dietary fiber.

1. Pick over split peas and remove any debris. Rinse, drain, and set aside.
2. Finely chop onion, carrot, and potato.
3. In a stockpot, heat olive oil over medium–high heat. Add vegetables and sauté until soft, approximately 3 minutes. Add remaining ingredients. Stir. Simmer uncovered 40 minutes, or until split peas are very soft. Remove bay leaf. Add more vegetable broth for a thinner soup, if desired.

Different Tastes and Textures

The first year of eating is about getting used to new tastes and textures. Set the groundwork for good eating habits by exposing your baby to a variety of flavors, textures, and combinations. Throw away notions of what foods go together and be creative.

Vegetable Rice Soup

This soup cooks up thick so it's easy to keep on the spoon for feeding.
It also works well for an older baby who is learning self-feeding skills.

1. Finely chop all vegetables.

2. Combine all ingredients in a large stock pot. Bring to a boil. Reduce heat, cover, and simmer for 45 minutes or until rice is soft.

Flexible Grains
There is very little as frustrating as starting a recipe, confident that you have all of the ingredients on hand, and then discovering that you're missing a key component of your dish. Not to worry, because there is often a fine substitute right at hand. If you don't have brown rice, substitute white rice, orzo, barley, or quinoa.

Yields 10 cups

INGREDIENTS:

1 carrot

1 celery stalk

1 potato

½ small onion

1 small sweet potato

1 cup chopped spinach

1 cup brown rice

8 cups water

1 (15-ounce) can diced tomatoes

½ teaspoon dried oregano

½ teaspoon dried basil

½ teaspoon dried thyme

Tomato & Orzo Soup

This is an easy way to turn a can of soup into a family meal.

1. Put organic roasted red pepper and tomato soup in a medium saucepan. Add beans to the soup.

2. Combine soup and beans with pasta.

3. Top each serving with 1 tablespoon of the yogurt.

Will Your Baby Get Fat From Eating Fat?
No! Babies need adequate fat in their diets to grow properly and foster brain development. Do not be shy about adding fat to your baby's meals. In fact, infant food labels do not list calories from fat, saturated fat, or cholesterol content in order to prevent parents from limiting foods high in fat that babies need.

Yields 6 cups

INGREDIENTS:

4 cups roasted red pepper and tomato soup

1 cup of black beans, drained

2 cups cooked orzo pasta

6 tablespoons whole-milk plain yogurt

Split Pea Curry

*This dish is inspired by the flavorful curries that
make up the heart of Indian cooking.*

Yields 5 cups

INGREDIENTS:

1 cup split peas

½ cup carrots

1 cup cauliflower florets

2 baking potatoes

1 garlic clove

½ cup tomato sauce

*1½ teaspoons curry
powder*

1. Pick over split peas and remove any debris. Rinse, drain, and set aside. Dice carrots, cauliflower, and potatoes. Mince garlic.

2. Combine all ingredients in a large sauté pan or stock pot. Simmer for 45 minutes–1 hour, or until tender.

Making the Most of a Slow Cooker

Even parents with the best of intentions for providing home-cooked organic meals for their families can become overwhelmed by all of the demands that life with a baby brings. A slow cooker can be a great tool to help reduce some of that pressure. Soups, casseroles, and curries can be assembled during a nap or the night before and then cook unattended for six to eight hours.

Alphabet Noodle Soup

*As your children get older, use alphabet soup to help them learn
the alphabet. Who ever said that eating can't be educational?*

Yields 8 cups

INGREDIENTS:

*Approximately 10 cups
water (enough to cover
chicken)*

*1 large broiler-fryer
chicken*

*3–4 celery stalks,
chopped*

4–6 carrots, chopped

1 large onion

1–2 tomatoes

Salt and pepper

2 bay leaves

*2 teaspoons chicken
bouillon*

*1½ cups cooked alphabet
noodles*

1. Bring water to a boil. Add chicken and return to a boil.

2. Once boiling, reduce heat immediately. Skim any fat from the top of soup.

3. Add remaining ingredients and simmer for 1½ hours.

4. Remove chicken and set aside. Remove all vegetables and discard bay leaf.

5. Strain soup and allow to cool. Once cool, skim off hardened fat.

6. Reheat soup and add cooked alphabet noodles.

Chicken Noodle Soup

Chicken noodle soup is a great method to introduce chicken to your child. Cut pieces of chicken very tiny to avoid choking. Boiling the chicken in this soup gets the meat perfectly tender for your baby.

1. In a large saucepan, sauté the chicken, onion, celery, carrot, red pepper, and garlic in butter and oil for 5 minutes.
2. Stir in the flour, basil, oregano, and pepper until blended.
3. Slowly add organic chicken broth, tomatoes, and zucchini.
4. Bring to a boil. Reduce heat; cover and simmer for 1 hour.
5. Return to a boil; stir in the pasta and spinach.
6. Reduce heat; simmer, uncovered, for 12–15 minutes or until pasta is tender.

A Soup a Day

Soups are a fantastic base for infant meals. It is easy to incorporate many different vegetables in soups that your child may not adventure to taste on their own. The consistency of soup is ideal for making purées once soup is done, or puréeing to different thicker consistencies as your child grows and develops.

Yields 8 cups

INGREDIENTS:

1 pound boneless chicken breasts cut into ¼" pieces

½ red onion, diced

2 celery ribs, sliced

1 medium carrot, sliced

¼ red bell pepper, diced

3 garlic cloves, minced

2 tablespoons butter or stick trans fat–free margarine

2 tablespoons olive or canola oil

¼ cup all-purpose flour

1 teaspoon dried basil

½ teaspoon dried oregano

⅛ teaspoon pepper

3 (14½ ounce) cans chicken broth

1 (14½ ounce) can diced tomatoes, undrained

½ summer squash or zucchini, sliced

6 ounces uncooked whole wheat spiral pasta

5 ounces fresh spinach, chopped

Blueberry Mini Muffins

Yields 42 mini muffins

INGREDIENTS:

2 cups white whole-wheat flour

1½ teaspoons baking powder, divided

½ teaspoon salt

½ cup applesauce

½ cup flaxseed meal

¼ cup canola oil

½ teaspoon vanilla

¾ cup apple juice concentrate

¼ cup plain yogurt (dairy or soy)

¼ cup milk (dairy or soy)

1½ cups blueberries

Fresh or frozen blueberries work well in this recipe. If you are using frozen, the batter will take on a purple hue unless you thaw them first.

1. Preheat oven to 350°F.

2. In a medium bowl, combine flour, 1 teaspoon baking powder, and salt.

3. In a large bowl, combine applesauce with ½ teaspoon baking powder.

4. Add flaxseed meal, oil, vanilla, apple juice concentrate, yogurt, and milk. Combine well.

5. Slowly add dry ingredients to wet. Add blueberries.

6. Spoon batter into lightly oiled mini muffin pan.

7. Bake 25–30 minutes, or until a toothpick inserted into the center of a muffin comes out clean.

The Mighty Flaxseed

Flaxseeds are a great source of Omega-3 fatty acids and a good source of dietary fiber. Although flaxseeds are available whole or ground, it is believed that ground flaxseeds provide the better source of nutrition. In addition to incorporating this nutritional powerhouse into baked goods, ground flaxseed can also be sprinkled on cereal or yogurt.

Banana Bread

This banana bread has a great texture and a not-too-sweet banana flavor.

1. Preheat oven to 350°F.

2. In a medium bowl combine flour, 1 tablespoon baking powder, baking soda, and salt.

3. In a large bowl, combine applesauce with ½ teaspoon baking powder.

4. Thoroughly mix in butter or trans fat–free margarine, apple juice concentrate, agave nectar, and vanilla.

5. Mash bananas.

6. Mix bananas into wet ingredients.

7. Slowly mix dry ingredients into wet.

8. Pour batter into a lightly oiled standard loaf pan.

9. Bake 1 hour or until a toothpick inserted into the center of the loaf comes out clean.

10. Cool 10 minutes in pan, then cool completely on cooling rack.

Limiting Salt and Sugar

Habits, whether good or bad, can begin early. Since babies don't have preconceived notions about how specific foods are "supposed" to taste, let them taste the purity of the high-quality organic ingredients you are using. Babies don't expect foods to be salty or sweet, so if they aren't introduced to excessive salt and sugar, they can develop the good habit of liking food the way nature intended it to taste.

Yields 1 loaf

INGREDIENTS:

2 cups white whole wheat flour

1 tablespoon plus ½ teaspoon baking powder, divided

1 teaspoon baking soda

¾ teaspoon salt

½ cup applesauce

½ cup butter or trans fat–free margarine, softened

2 tablespoons apple juice concentrate

⅓ cup agave nectar

1 teaspoon vanilla

4 ripe bananas

Apple & Sweet Potato Mini Muffins

INGREDIENTS:

2 cups white whole-wheat flour

1½ teaspoons baking powder, divided

½ teaspoon salt

½ teaspoon cinnamon

½ cup applesauce

½ cup flaxseed meal

¼ cup canola oil

½ teaspoon vanilla

½ cup milk (dairy or soy)

1 cup frozen apple juice concentrate

1½ cups grated sweet potato

1 cup grated apple

Because these muffins aren't too sweet they're great as a take-along snack, warmed and topped with butter or Sweet Potato Spread (page 114).

1. Preheat oven to 350°F.

2. In a medium bowl, combine flour, 1 teaspoon baking powder, salt, and cinnamon.

3. In a large bowl, combine applesauce with ½ teaspoon baking powder.

4. Add flaxseed meal, oil, vanilla, milk, and apple juice concentrate. Stir to combine.

5. Slowly mix dry ingredients into wet.

6. Mix in sweet potato and apple.

7. Pour batter into a lightly oiled mini muffin pan.

8. Bake for 25–30 minutes or until a toothpick inserted in the middle of a muffin comes out dry.

Carrot & Zucchini Mini Muffins

What a fun way for baby to eat vegetables!
Mini muffins are just the right size for little fingers.

1. Preheat oven to 350°F.

2. In a medium mixing bowl, combine flour, 1 teaspoon baking powder, salt, and cinnamon.

3. In a large bowl, combine applesauce with ½ teaspoon baking powder. Add flaxseed meal, oil, vanilla, brown sugar, and syrup.

4. Slowly mix dry ingredients into wet. Mix in carrots and zucchini. Spoon into lightly oiled mini muffin pan.

5. Bake 15–20 minutes or until a toothpick inserted into the center of a muffin comes out clean.

Yields 42 mini muffins

INGREDIENTS:

2 cups white whole-wheat flour

1½ teaspoons baking powder, divided

½ teaspoon salt

1 teaspoon cinnamon

½ cup applesauce

½ cup flaxseed meal

¼ cup canola oil

½ teaspoon vanilla

¼ cup packed brown sugar

½ cup maple syrup

1 cup grated carrots

1 cup grated zucchini

Oatmeal with Cinnamon Apples

This hearty dish is great in the fall when apples are abundant.
Pick apples at your local apple farm and use them for breakfast!

1. In a small saucepan, combine water, apple juice, and apple. Bring to a boil.

2. Once boiling, stir in rolled oats and cinnamon. Return to a boil.

3. Reduce heat down to low and simmer to desired thickness, about 3–5 minutes.

4. Add agave nectar to reach desired sweetness.

5. Pour milk over servings and serve.

Yields 2 cups

INGREDIENTS:

½ cup water

½ cup apple juice

1 golden delicious apple, peeled, cored and chopped

⅔ cup rolled oats

1 teaspoon ground cinnamon

1–2 tablespoons light agave nectar

1 cup milk

Yogurt Berry Parfait

Wheat germ contains a small amount of fat, which makes it spoil quickly.
Store your wheat germ in the fridge to extend its life.

1. Pour the wheat germ into the yogurt and mix well.

2. In a clear glass sundae jar, alternate layers of the yogurt and berries.

Is Wheat Germ a Germ?

No! Wheat germ is the "embryo" part of the wheat kernel. Wheat germ will become the sprout to grow into wheat grass. It is a very nutritious part of the wheat kernel and contains the following nutrients: vitamin E, folic acid, magnesium, phosphorus, thiamine, zinc. It also contains essential fatty acids and is a good source of fiber.

Yields 2 cups

INGREDIENTS:

1¼ teaspoons wheat germ

8 ounces vanilla yogurt

1 cup seasonal berries

Strawberry Banana Yogurt

This recipe makes a great side dish to go with Moist Yogurt Pancakes,
which can be found on page 204.

Combine all ingredients.

Yields 2 cups

INGREDIENTS:

1 cup vanilla yogurt

½ cup strawberries

½ banana

½ teaspoon cinnamon

Blueberry Syrup

Serve this delicious syrup over whole-grain waffles. Your toddler will love it!

1. In a small saucepan, combine blueberries and apple juice concentrate.
2. Simmer 10 minutes.
3. While the fruit is simmering, combine cornstarch and water in a small bowl.
4. Add cornstarch and water mixture to blueberries.
5. Simmer and stir continuously, until thickened.

Blueberries on Ice
Freezing blueberries at home is a great way to make the taste of summer last all year. Wash the blueberries, dry them, and pick out any damaged berries. Then, spread the berries out on a cookie sheet and freeze. Once frozen solid, transfer the berries to a freezer-safe container, where they can be enjoyed for up to six months.

Yields 2 cups

INGREDIENTS:

2 cups blueberries

⅓ cup apple juice concentrate

1 tablespoon cornstarch

2 tablespoons cold water

Oatmeal with Sautéed Plantains

Yields 2 cup

INGREDIENTS:

1 yellow plantain (very ripe)

1 tablespoon brown sugar

1 teaspoon butter

½ cup water

½ cup apple juice

⅔ cup rolled oats

1 teaspoon ground cinnamon

*Plantains are a Central American staple;
they can be cooked in sweet or savory dishes.*

1. Peel and cut plantain into ½" pieces.

2. Put brown sugar in plastic bag and place plantain pieces in bag, shaking the bag to coat them.

3. Heat butter in small pan over medium heat, place plantains in pan and cook until the sugar begins to caramelize, about 2 minutes each side; remove from heat.

4. In a small saucepan, combine water, and apple juice. Bring to a boil.

5. Once boiling, stir in rolled oats and cinnamon. Return to a boil.

6. Reduce heat to low and simmer to desired thickness, 3–5 minutes.

7. Top oat mixture with sautéed plantains and serve.

Plantains Versus Bananas

Plantains are firmer and have a lower sugar content than bananas. Plantains need to be cooked but bananas are mostly eaten raw. In tropical areas of the world, plantains are often a first food for babies. Plantains are a staple item in these areas and are consumed on a daily basis.

Mashed Potatoes & Parsnips

Yukon Gold potatoes have a rich flavor, creamy texture, and beautiful color.

1. Peel potatoes and parsnips.

2. Roughly chop vegetables and place in a medium saucepan.

3. Cover with water.

4. Bring mixture to a boil, reduce heat to a simmer.

5. Cook until vegetables are tender, approximately 10–15 minutes depending on size of chopped pieces.

6. Drain, reserving cooking liquid.

7. Return vegetables to pot, mash with a potato masher or fork, stir in olive oil, and salt if using.

8. Add reserved cooking water, 1 tablespoon at a time, until mash is the desired consistency.

Parsnips, a Late-Fall Treat

Parsnips look very similar to white carrots. Because they are at their sweetest after having been exposed to cold temperatures, they are best in the late fall or early winter. Cook them in the same way as carrots for great-tasting results.

Yields 3 cups

INGREDIENTS:

4 Yukon Gold potatoes
2 parsnips
Water to cover
1 tablespoon olive oil
¼ teaspoon salt, optional

Black Bean & Carrot Mash

Yields 2½ cups

INGREDIENTS:

1 (14-ounce) can black beans

4 ounces store-bought puréed carrots

The addition of carrots to the black beans is a great way to boost the vitamin A content of the black beans.

1. In a medium saucepan, combine black beans and carrot purée over medium heat.

2. Allow black beans to soften, about 5–10 minutes.

3. Mash mixture with a potato masher while cooking on stove.

4. Remove from heat and serve.

Black Beans as a SuperFood?
Black beans contain the same amount of antioxidants as grapes and cranberries. The darker the beans, the more antioxidants they contain. Also, looking for an iron-rich food for your baby? Look no further than black beans. They contain almost 4 grams of iron per cup of black beans.

Mango & Brown Rice

For a twist to this recipe, cook the brown rice in coconut milk to give this dish more of an Asian influence and introduce your child to the flavor of coconut!

1. Combine cooked brown rice and chopped mangos.

2. Squeeze lime juice on top for flavor.

Healthiest Oil on Earth?
Coconut oil has a high amount of medium chain triglycerides (MCT). These oils are hard to find in our diet. MCT oil is processed differently than the long-chain fats that are in animal products. These MCT oils may have a positive effect on cholesterol and heart disease. Small amounts of coconut oil can be part of a healthy diet.

Yields 5 cups

INGREDIENTS:
2 cups cooked brown rice
2 mangos, chopped
1 tablespoon lime juice

Tofu Bites

Who needs highly processed chicken nuggets, when these tasty, high-protein treats are so easy to make?

1. Preheat oven to 425°F.

2. Drain tofu and cut into 24 rectangle-shaped bites.

3. Combine flour and garlic pepper in a shallow bowl.

4. Dredge each tofu through the flour mixture.

5. Spread olive oil on a cookie sheet.

6. Place coated triangles on oiled cookie sheet.

7. Bake 10 minutes or until golden brown.

Yields 24 bites

INGREDIENTS:
1 pound tofu (firm or extra-firm)
¼ cup whole wheat flour
1 teaspoon garlic pepper
2 teaspoons olive oil

Cauliflower & Potato Mash

Yields 5 cups

INGREDIENTS:

2 large potatoes, chopped

1 head of cauliflower, cut into florets

1 cup whole milk (dairy or soy)

1 tablespoon butter or trans fat–free margarine

Here is a twist on mashed potatoes! Add other items to these "mashed potatoes" based on your child's taste. Try adding peas to this mash for a little more texture.

1. Place potatoes in a medium-sized pot and cover with water. Boil the potatoes for 10 minutes until soft; drain, and return to pot.

2. Steam the cauliflower until tender; drain, and add to pot with potatoes.

3. Add milk and butter to potatoes and cauliflower.

4. Mash with a potato masher or use a beater to get a thinner purée.

The Different Colors of Cauliflower

There are many colors of cauliflower. Purple cauliflower contains the antioxidant anthocyanin, which is also in red wine and cabbage. Green cauliflower is called broccoflower. And orange cauliflower contains twenty-five times the amount of vitamin A that is in white cauliflower . . . it competes well with carrots.

Roast Lamb, Rice, & Tomato Compote

*This recipe helps you use the lamb that you're serving the
whole family in an appropriate way for your baby.*

Purée all ingredients in a blender or food processor.

Avoiding Hot Spots

Some babies prefer their food to be slightly warmed. The microwave
can be a convenient tool for heating up your baby's food. Be careful,
though, to stir the food thoroughly, because the microwave can cause
some spots in the food to be much hotter than other spots. Test the
food it once it's stirred to be sure that it's not too hot for baby's sensitive
mouth.

Yields 1 cup

INGREDIENTS:

*2 ounces roasted lamb
meat*

¼ cup cooked brown rice

*4 tablespoons Sweet
Potato Purée (page 34)*

¼ cup diced tomatoes

Coconut Pineapple Rice Pudding

*With these three ingredients in the pantry,
making this tasty, wholesome dessert is a snap.*

1. Preheat oven to 325°F.

2. Rinse rice.

3. In a small saucepan, bring coconut milk and crushed pineapple with
   juice to a boil.

4. Combine rice with liquid in a covered casserole dish.

5. Bake for 1 hour.

Yields 4 cups

INGREDIENTS:

1 cup Arborio rice

*1 (15-ounce) can coconut
milk*

*1 (15-ounce) can crushed
pineapple in juice*

Barbecue Tofu & Quinoa

Quinoa and tofu combine for a protein-rich meal with a lot of flavor.

Yields 5 cups

INGREDIENTS:

1 pound firm or extra-firm tofu

1 cup mushroom caps (button or cremini)

¼ small onion

1 large red bell pepper

1 tablespoon olive oil

½ cup barbecue sauce

2 cups prepared quinoa

1. Cut tofu into 1" cubes.

2. Dice mushrooms, onion, and red pepper.

3. Heat olive oil over high heat, then add tofu. Cook 3 minutes, turning tofu as it cooks. Add vegetables and cook 5 minutes more. Add sauce and cook 5 more minutes. Serve over prepared quinoa.

Simple Barbecue Sauce
To make a tasty, basic barbecue sauce, combine ¼ cup soy sauce, 2 tablespoons blackstrap molasses, 3 tablespoons honey or agave nectar, and ¼ cup ketchup.

Roasted Potato Rounds

Baking potatoes or Yukon Gold potatoes can be substituted for red potatoes.

Yields 24 rounds

INGREDIENTS:

3 large red potatoes

2 tablespoons olive oil

Sprinkling of sea salt

1. Preheat oven to 475°F.

2. Wash and thinly slice potatoes.

3. Spread 1 tablespoon olive oil on baking sheet.

4. Spread potato slices on top of oil.

5. Top with remaining oil and salt.

6. Bake 13–15 minutes, until soft and golden.

Organic Farmer's Pie

*Serve this tender casserole with Easy Gravy (page 102) and
Homemade Applesauce (page 64) for an autumnal feast.*

1. Preheat oven to 350°F.
2. Peel and dice sweet potatoes.
3. In a large saucepan, cover sweet potatoes with water.
4. Bring to a boil; boil uncovered until tender, approximately 10 minutes.
5. While potatoes are cooking, heat olive oil in a medium skillet.
6. Add garlic and vegetables. Sauté until soft, approximately 5 minutes.
7. Add veggie burger crumbles and heat through.
8. When sweet potatoes are tender, drain and return them to the pot.
9. Mash the sweet potatoes with yogurt and salt using a potato masher or fork.
10. Scrape the burger mixture into a 3-quart casserole dish.
11. Spread the sweet potatoes on top.
12. Bake uncovered for 40 minutes.

Yields a 3-quart casserole dish

INGREDIENTS:

2 large sweet potatoes

Water to cover

1 tablespoon olive oil

2 cloves garlic, minced

¼ cup grated onion

¼ cup grated zucchini

¼ cup grated carrot

3 cups veggie burger crumbles

½ cup plain yogurt (dairy or soy)

½ teaspoon salt

Easy Gravy

Yields 1 cup

INGREDIENTS:

1 bouillon cube (vegan, chicken, or beef)

1 cup plus 2 tablespoons water

2 teaspoons soy sauce

¼ teaspoon poultry seasoning

1 tablespoon corn starch

For many young eaters, sauces and dips make every dish more exciting. This easy gravy can dress up many different entrées, from Organic Farmer's Pie (page 101) to broiled chicken.

1. Dissolve bouillon cube in 1 cup boiling water.

2. Add soy sauce and poultry seasoning to bouillon.

3. In a separate small bowl, thoroughly combine corn starch with 2 tablespoons water.

4. Add diluted corn starch to bouillon mixture, stirring until combined and thickened.

Sauces Can Make Dinnertime Easier

Around 18 months, even the easiest eater can start to be picky. Diets that used to be rich with fruits, vegetables, grains, and proteins can whittle down to just a few items in what seems like the blink of an eye. Offering a favorite sauce, whether it's ketchup, gravy, or dip can keep little ones eating a greater variety. While ketchup-dipped cantaloupe probably sounds unappealing to an adult, it might just be a culinary delight to a child.

Vegetable Barley Casserole

For a variation, stir in one cup shredded,
boiled chicken after the casserole is finished.

1. Preheat oven to 350°F.

2. Peel and thinly slice carrots.

3. Thoroughly wash and dry kale. Trim and remove stems.

4. In a food processor, finely chop kale.

5. Add water to chopped kale 2 tablespoons at a time to make a paste.

6. Bring 3 cups water to a boil.

7. Dilute bouillon cube in water.

8. Combine all ingredients in a 3-quart casserole dish.

9. Cover and bake 1½ hours.

Yields 4½ cups

INGREDIENTS:

3 carrots

1 bunch kale

3¼ cups water, divided

1 bouillon cube (vegan, chicken, or beef)

1 cup pearled barley

½ small diced onion

Lentils with Spinach & Quinoa

INGREDIENTS:

1 cup of lentils

½ cup quinoa

1 cup water

½ teaspoon garlic

1 teaspoon oil

3 cups fresh spinach

You do not want to mix old lentils with new lentils. The older lentils are, the longer they take to cook. Lentils will cook unevenly if you mix old and new lentils.

1. Pick over lentils and remove any debris. Set aside.

2. Add quinoa and water in a microwaveable glass bowl. Cover and heat on high for 4 minutes. Remove from microwave and stir. Heat again for 2 minutes, stir, and let stand for 1 minute.

3. In a medium pan, sauté garlic and oil until clear over low heat.

4. Add lentils to pan, cover with vegetable broth, increase heat to medium–high and bring to a boil for 2–3 minutes. Reduce heat to medium and cook until the lentils are tender.

5. When lentils are tender, add spinach to broth. Allow spinach to soften to desired consistency.

6. Drain lentils and spinach. Combine quinoa with the lentil and spinach mixture. Serve.

Lentil Cooking Tips

Wait! Do not add salt to the water in cooking your lentils as these might toughen the beans. Want another tip? Wait to add any acidic items to lentils until late in the cooking process as acidic foods make lentils take longer to cook.

Mashed Sweet Potatoes

If part of your sweet potato is bad, you cannot just remove the bad part and use the rest of the potato. If part of it is bad, you have to get rid of the whole potato!

1. Peel sweet potatoes and cube them.
2. Bring a pot of water to a boil. Place potatoes in boiling water and boil for about 20 minutes.
3. Drain potatoes and place in mixing bowl.
4. Add butter and mash.

Whole-Wheat Shells with Marinara Sauce

You can also use this sauce in the Italian Eggplant recipe (page 148).

1. In a medium saucepan, heat olive oil over medium heat.
2. Add garlic and sauté for 2 minutes until fragrant.
3. Add tomatoes, paste, agave nectar, basil, and oregano; stir thoroughly.
4. Simmer uncovered for approximately 1 hour or until desired texture.
5. Serve sauce over whole-wheat pasta.

Broccoli & Quinoa Casserole

Yields 6 cups

INGREDIENTS:

1 cup creamy corn soup

½ cup shredded Cheddar cheese (dairy or soy)

1 large bunch of broccoli

3 cups cooked quinoa

This dish is genuine comfort food that has a great consistency for a younger child, but will please the rest of the family as well. By combining the cooked ingredients without an added baking step, the dish remains very tender and easy for little ones to manage.

1. In a small saucepan, heat soup over medium–high heat. Add cheese and stir until melted. Set aside.

2. Cut broccoli into small florets and steam until tender. Combine quinoa, cheese sauce, and broccoli in a serving bowl or casserole dish.

Is Quinoa a Grain?

Although quinoa looks like a grain and cooks like a grain, it is not a true cereal grain. It is actually the seeds of the chenopodium or goosefoot plant. Its relatives include beets, spinach, and Swiss chard.

Chickpea, Carrot, & Cauliflower Mash

Yields 4 cups

INGREDIENTS:

2 carrots

1 cup cauliflower florets

2 cups cooked chickpeas (or 1 (15-ounce) can)

¼ cup vegetable broth or water

Cauliflower contains many cancer-fighting nutrients, so start your baby off on the right foot with this tasty recipe.

1. Peel and slice carrots.

2. Steam carrots and cauliflower until very tender.

3. Drain and rinse chickpeas.

4. Combine all ingredients and mash with a potato masher or fork.

5. Add broth or water as necessary to reach an age-appropriate consistency.

Chicken, Sweet Pea, & Sweet Potato Dinner

If you're making a soup with chicken, take some of the chicken meat out, purée it, and freeze it for dishes like this. You'll still have plenty of chicken in the original soup, and you'll buy yourself a quick and easy dinner option down the line.

1. Purée chicken in a food processor or blender. Add water or broth as needed to achieve a smooth purée.
2. Combine this new chicken purée with the vegetable purées.

Cool Meats, Dude

Having a hard time blending your meats into purées? Meats tend to blend better if you wait until they cool to purée them. This is especially true with meats that have been baked instead of boiled. Boiled meats shred nicely, which can make puréeing them a little easier.

Yields ¾ cup

INGREDIENTS:

2 ounces boiled, shredded chicken

4 tablespoons Sweet Pea Purée (page 32)

4 tablespoons Sweet Potato Purée (page 34)

Hummus

This creamy, mild hummus is just right for younger taste buds.

1. If using canned garbanzo beans, drain and rinse beans.
2. Combine all ingredients in a food processor or blender.
3. Process until smooth.

Yields 2 cups

INGREDIENTS:

2 cups cooked garbanzo beans (homemade or canned)

2 teaspoons lemon juice

3 tablespoons olive oil

1 clove garlic

¼ teaspoon cumin

⅛ teaspoon salt

Couscous with Grated Zucchini & Carrots

Yields 2 cups

INGREDIENTS:

1 cup whole-wheat couscous

1 cup water

2 tablespoons butter or canola oil

1 teaspoon ground flaxseeds

½ cup zucchini, grated

½ cup carrot rounds

½ teaspoon garlic

1 teaspoon oil

1 cup canned white beans

Butter or oil added to this dish prevents the couscous from forming clumps or curds. Remember that your baby needs fat for healthy brain and eye development.

1. Add couscous, water, and butter or canola oil in a microwaveable glass bowl. Cover and heat on high for 2–3 minutes. Remove from microwave and fluff with fork. Sprinkle ground flaxseeds on couscous and blend with fork.

2. Place carrot rounds and zucchini in a microwaveable bowl and steam until tender.

3. In a medium saucepan, sauté garlic in oil over medium heat until clear.

4. Add beans to cooked zucchini and carrots and heat through.

5. Combine couscous, beans, zucchini, and carrots.

How Do You Use Flaxseeds?

One way to use flaxseeds is to purchase fresh flaxseeds. Store them in the refrigerator and grind them right before use. Get an inexpensive coffee grinder that you use specifically for this purpose. Grind in small batches and store in an airtight container in the fridge. Use these quickly once they have been ground.

Hawaiian Sweet Potatoes

*Roasting the sweet potatoes with the pineapple gives
this dish a festive air without any added sugar.*

1. Preheat oven to 375°F.
2. Wash sweet potato and cut into wedges lengthwise. Arrange sweet potato wedges in a small baking dish. Cover sweet potatoes with pineapple pieces and juice. Bake 45–55 minutes, or until sweet potatoes are tender.

The World-Traveling Pineapple
Although pineapples are native to Paraguay and Brazil, they made their way around the world on sailing vessels. Sailors ate them to prevent scurvy. The same vitamin C that kept sailors healthy also helps keep today's little ones healthy.

Yields 2 cups

INGREDIENTS:
1 large sweet potato
1 cup chopped pineapple

Tofu Avocado Spread

*This creamy spread is rich in protein and potassium and
pairs nicely with a piece of whole-grain toast.*

1. Mash tofu and avocado.
2. Add soy sauce; combine well.

Is Your Avocado Ripe?
Hold the avocado in your hand give it a soft squeeze. A nearly ripe avocado will yield slightly under the pressure. Avoid those that feel loose in their skin as these are overripe. If it feels like a stone, it isn't ripe yet.

Yields ½ cup

INGREDIENTS:
¼ cup firm tofu
½ ripe avocado
¼ teaspoon soy sauce

Turkey Chili

*If this chili is not spicy enough for the adults, add extra chili powder,
green chilies, or serrano peppers to the adult portion and heat through.*

1. In a large pot, heat the canola oil over medium heat. Add onion and garlic; cook and stir for 3 minutes until clear.

2. Add ground turkey. Stir until crumbly and no longer pink.

3. Add the butternut squash, broth, tomatoes, black beans, hominy, and tomato sauce; season with chili powder, cumin, and cinnamon.

4. Bring to a simmer, then reduce heat to medium-low, cover, and simmer until the squash is tender, about 20 minutes.

5. Top each bowl with 1–2 tablespoons of yogurt to serve.

Yields 12 cups

INGREDIENTS:

2 tablespoons canola oil

1 red onion, chopped

1 cloves garlic, minced

1 pound ground turkey breast

1 pound butternut squash, peeled, seeded, and cut into 1" cubes

½ cup vegetable broth

2 (14½-ounce) cans petite diced tomatoes

1 (15-ounce) can black beans with liquid

1 (15½-ounce) can white hominy, drained

1 (8-ounce) can tomato sauce

2 teaspoons chili powder

1 tablespoon ground cumin

⅛ teaspoon cinnamon

8-ounce container of plain yogurt

Whole-Wheat Rotini with Bolognese Sauce

In Italy, bowls of pasta are layered differently. The sauce is the most important part of the meal so the pasta is added to the sauce, instead of the sauce being added on top of the pasta.

1. In a large pot, heat olive oil and butter over medium heat.

2. Add onion, celery, and carrot and sauté until onion is clear.

3. Add ground beef and cook thoroughly.

4. Add tomato sauce and paste and heat through.

5. Mix whole-wheat rotini and sauce, top with Parmesan cheese, and serve.

Want to Have Lunch in Rome?

In Italy, lunch is the largest meal of the day. Breakfast is typically small, lunch often has many courses, and then dinner tends to be smaller portions of leftovers from lunch. Italian diets are rich in whole grains, vegetables, fish, and olive oil. This pattern of eating is often associated with low rates of heart disease.

Yields 2 cups of sauce

INGREDIENTS:

2 tablespoons olive oil

2 tablespoons butter or trans fat–free margarine

½ Vidalia onion, diced

½ celery stalk, diced

½ carrot diced

1 pound ground beef

15 ounces tomato sauce

2 tablespoons tomato paste

Whole-wheat rotini, cooked

Parmesan cheese, grated

Apple-Roasted Carrots

*Cooked carrot slices make a great food for self-feeding.
The rounds are just the right size for little fingers.*

Yields ½ cup

INGREDIENTS:

4 carrots

¼ cup apple juice concentrate

1 tablespoon olive oil

1. Preheat oven to 450°F.

2. Peel and thinly slice carrots.

3. Toss carrots with apple juice concentrate in a medium bowl.

4. Spread carrot slices on a baking sheet that has been lightly coated in olive oil.

5. Bake 10–12 minutes, or until carrots are tender.

Orzo with Creamy Tomato Spinach Sauce

If using frozen spinach, thaw before using in this recipe.

Yields 2½ cups

INGREDIENTS:

¾ cup orzo (or other very small pasta)

½ cup pasta sauce

¼ cup silken tofu

¼ cup chopped spinach

1. Cook orzo according to pasta directions. Drain and set aside.

2. In a food processor, combine pasta sauce, tofu, and spinach. Process until smooth.

3. Transfer sauce to a small saucepan. Heat through.

4. Stir orzo into sauce.

Tofu, an Early Finger Food

When adults eat tofu, it is usually cooked; but cold tofu is a great early finger food for children. Cut firm or extra-firm tofu into small blocks for self-feeding.

Parsnip & Chicken Purée

*Broth adds extra flavor to this dish, while providing the
liquid necessary to attain the proper consistency.*

1. Peel parsnips and cut into small slices or chunks.

2. Steam parsnip using either a steamer basket or microwave.

3. Purée parsnip and chicken with broth.

Yields ½ cup

INGREDIENTS:

2 small parsnips

*2 ounces boiled,
shredded chicken*

*¼ cup vegetable or
chicken broth*

Strawberry Cantaloupe Sorbet

*Since this frozen treat has no added sugar, it can be served
as a healthy snack on a hot day, as well as a dessert.*

1. In a food processor or blender, purée all ingredients together. Pour into
   a freezer-safe container.

2. After 1½–2 hours, fluff sorbet with a fork, then return to freezer. After
   2 more hours, fluff sorbet with a fork and return to freezer. Continue
   this process until ready to serve.

Pyrex Casserole Dishes Are Not Just for Baking
A covered Pyrex casserole with a shallow rectangle shape makes it
easy to store sorbet in a crowded freezer and the easy-to-remove lids
keep freezer odors out, while keeping liquid in. If Pyrex isn't available, a
stainless steel mixing bowl covered with aluminum foil works well, too.

Yields 4 cups

INGREDIENTS:

½ medium cantaloupe

1½ cups strawberries

½ cup apple juice

Sweet Potato Spread

INGREDIENTS:

1 cup grated raw sweet potato

¾ cup water

1 teaspoon maple syrup

¼ teaspoon cinnamon

⅛ teaspoon nutmeg

2 tablespoons cream cheese (dairy or soy)

Serve this sweet spread to add vitamins to graham crackers or whole grain toast.

1. Bring sweet potato and water to a boil, keep boiling for 5 minutes.
2. Reduce heat to low and stir in remaining ingredients.
3. Keep stirring until cream cheese is melted and all ingredients are combined.

Blackberry Frozen Yogurt

Yields 1½ cups

INGREDIENTS:

½ cup frozen blackberries

1 tablespoon apple juice concentrate

8 ounces of vanilla yogurt (dairy or soy)

Blueberries, raspberries, or strawberries can be substituted for blackberries in this recipe.

1. Blend all ingredients in a food processor or blender.
2. Transfer to a freezer-safe container.
3. Freeze for 1 hour. Remove from freezer and fluff with a fork.
4. Return to freezer, repeating process until ready to serve.

Strawberry Applesauce

This recipe uses the Homemade Applesauce recipe on page 64 as a base. Make your applesauce from that recipe and then add the strawberries.

1. Peel and dice apples.

2. Wash and cut strawberries.

3. In a medium saucepan, add all ingredients. Cover and simmer for about 10–15 minutes, until fruit is tender. Mash with potato masher or purée in blender to desired consistency.

Apples and Carrots
Many fruits combined with apples will create wonderful "sauces." Try unique combinations of fruits and vegetables. For example, create a mixed-berry applesauce using blackberries and blueberries. Whip up an orange applesauce, or even try a carrot applesauce!

Yields 2 cups

INGREDIENTS:
1 cup apples
1 cup strawberries
¼ cup apple juice.

Mango Honeydew Sorbet

Sweet honeydew and flavorful mango combine for an interesting frozen combination.

1. In a food processor or blender, purée all ingredients together.

2. Pour into a freezer-safe container.

3. After 1½–2 hours, fluff sorbet with a fork, then return to freezer.

4. After 2 hours, fluff sorbet with a fork.

5. Continue this process until ready to serve.

Yields 4 cups

INGREDIENTS:
½ medium honeydew
1½ cups mango chunks
½ cup apple juice

Happy Birthday Vanilla Cake

INGREDIENTS:

1 cup white, all-purpose flour

½ cup oat flour

2¼ teaspoons baking powder, divided

¼ teaspoon salt

¼ cup applesauce

½ cup apple juice concentrate

½ cup milk (dairy or soy)

¼ cup canola oil

¼ cup maple syrup

1½ teaspoons vanilla

This birthday cake gets its sweetness from apple juice and maple syrup instead of from refined sugar.

1. Preheat oven to 375°F.

2. Lightly oil an 8"–9" square or round cake pan.

3. In a medium mixing bowl, combine flours, 2 teaspoons baking powder, and salt.

4. In a large mixing bowl, combine applesauce with ¼ teaspoon baking powder.

5. Add apple juice concentrate, milk, oil, syrup, and vanilla to the applesauce.

6. Mix dry ingredients into wet, one half at a time.

7. Scrape batter into pan.

8. Bake 25 minutes, or until a toothpick inserted into the middle comes out clean.

Make Your Own Oat Flour

Making your own oat flour is easy. Just take old-fashioned rolled oats and blend them in the blender or food processor. Keep blending until you have a fine, powdery flour. Replacing a portion of white flour with oat flour will provide some whole-grain goodness to your dessert recipes.

Orange Coconut Sorbet

Sweet and creamy, this dessert adds important fat and vitamin C.

1. Combine juice and milk.

2. Pour into a covered freezer-safe container.

3. After 1½–2 hours, fluff with a fork, and return to freezer.

4. Continue freezing and fluffing until ready to serve.

Softening Sorbet

Sorbet can harden if left in the freezer overnight. Take sorbet out of the freezer and let sit on the counter for 5 minutes to allow it to soften before serving.

INGREDIENTS:

2 cup orange juice

1 cup coconut milk

2 tablespoons agave nectar

Chapter 6

Twelve to Eighteen Months

Broccoli Cheese Soup   120

Cream of Potato Soup   121

Citrusy Rice Salad   121

Creamy Cauliflower Soup   122

Chicken Salad   123

Creamy Pasta Salad   123

Quinoa Bean Salad   124

Lemony Rice & Asparagus Salad   125

Zucchini Corn Muffins   126

Spicy Pumpkin Muffins   127

Corn Muffins   128

Blueberry Pancakes   129

Strawberry, Blueberry, & Banana Smoothie   130

French Toast   130

Peach Raspberry Compote   131

Cantaloupe Papaya Smoothie   131

Maple Barley Breakfast   132

Spinach Tomato Scramble   132

Banana Yogurt Milkshake   133

Orange Pineapple Smoothie   133

Mushroom Barley Casserole   134

Baked Honey Pescado   134

Broccoli with Meat & Rigatoni   135

Honeyed Carrots   135

Chicken Pot Pie Muffins   136

Arrounce Verde con Frijoles Negro   137

Macaroni & Cheese   138

Cheesy Grits   138

Vegetable Tofu Pot Pie   139

Easy Baked Chicken   140

Homestyle Stuffing   141

Maple Acorn Squash   142

Lentils & Brown Rice   142

Turkey Divan Muffins   143

Spaghetti Squash with Italian Herbs   143

Roasted Potato Salad   144

Vegetable Baked Risotto   144

Creamed Spinach   145

Italian Beans & Barley   145

Caribbean Baked Risotto   146

Creamy Salsa Dip   146

Red Beans & Rice   147

Italian Eggplant   148

Mangosteen Cereal Mix   149

Take-Along Cereal Snack   149

Fruit Kabobs   150

Vanilla Raspberry Sorbet   150

Tropical Pudding Pie Dip   151

Sweet Sunflower Seed Butter Dip   151

Cinnamon Yogurt Fruit Dip   152

Pink Milk   152

Broccoli Cheese Soup

Yields 8 to 9 cups

INGREDIENTS:

½ cup butter

7 tablespoons all-purpose flour

5 cups 2-percent milk, divided

2 vegan vegetable bouillon cubes with sea salt

2½ cups grated Cheddar cheese, divided

1½ heads of broccoli florets, finely chopped

This is a great soup on a cold winter day! Use frozen broccoli for convenience and if needed, this soup can be puréed to achieve the appropriate consistency for your toddler.

1. In a large saucepan, melt ½ cup butter. Add flour to butter to create a thick paste. Add 2 cups milk and bouillon cubes. On a low heat, cook until sauce begins to thicken.

2. Add 3 cups milk. Then slowly add the ½ cup of Cheddar cheese, stirring to allow the cheese to melt as added, continue adding the cheese in ½ cup measurements until a total of 2½ cups has been added.

3. Add broccoli florets and allow to cook until tender.

Get Creative

The base of this soup can be used for many other soups. Get creative and add different combinations to the soup. Make a baked potato soup, a fish and potato soup, or a corn chowder soup. Soup bases come in handy in all types of cooking. The first step of this recipe can be used to replace a can of condensed soup.

Cream of Potato Soup

Slow cookers can be an easy way to prepare meals for your infant or toddler. Assemble the ingredients in the morning and then forget about it until it's time for dinner!

1. Put all ingredients except evaporated milk into a slow cooker.
2. Cover and cook on low for 10–12 hours or on high for 3–4 hours.
3. Stir in evaporated milk during the last hour.
4. Control consistency in the soup by adding instant mashed potatoes, if needed.

Yields 6 servings

INGREDIENTS:

6 potatoes, peeled and cubed

2 onions, chopped

1 carrot, sliced

1 stalk celery, sliced

4 chicken bouillon cubes

1 tablespoon parsley flakes

5 cups water

⅓ cup butter

13 ounces evaporated milk

Citrusy Rice Salad

Keep the extra dressing in a separate container to redress any leftover salad.

1. Steam green beans until tender. Plunge into cold water to stop cooking process.
2. Cut fruit and beans into bite-sized pieces.
3. Thinly slice white portion of scallion.
4. Combine rice, fruit, and vegetables.
5. In a jar with a tight-fitting lid, combine orange juice, agave nectar, and olive oil. Shake to combine.
6. Toss salad with dressing to taste.

Yields 3 cups

INGREDIENTS:

¼ cup green beans

¼ cup chopped orange pieces

¼ cup pineapple chunks

2 scallions

2 cups cooked short-grain brown rice

¼ cup orange juice

1 teaspoon agave nectar

¼ cup olive oil

Creamy Cauliflower Soup

INGREDIENTS:

½ onion, chopped

1 tablespoon olive oil

3 medium potatoes, peeled and diced

1 medium head cauliflower, chopped

4 cups vegetable broth

2 tablespoons nutritional yeast

½ teaspoon white pepper

½ teaspoon sea salt

1 bay leaf

1 cup plain yogurt (soy or dairy)

For added texture, remove ⅓ of the soup before puréeing.
After soup is puréed, return to pot and combine with reserved soup.

1. In a large stock pot, sauté onion in olive oil.

2. Add remaining ingredients, bring to a boil.

3. Reduce heat to a simmer. Simmer approximately 30 minutes until potatoes and cauliflower are tender.

4. Remove bay leaf.

5. Purée soup in blender.

The White "Green" Vegetable

The saying "eat your green vegetables" should have the amendment—"and cauliflower." This late-season nutritional powerhouse is a cruciferous vegetable; it's in the same family as broccoli, cabbage, and kale. It has high levels of vitamin C and significant amounts of vitamin B_6, folate, and dietary fiber.

Chicken Salad

The consistency of this chicken salad will be better for your child closer to 18 months. Serve this on whole-wheat crackers or whole-wheat pita. Use this to stuff pea pods or celery as a fun snack for your children.

Combine all ingredients.

Yields 10 ounces

INGREDIENTS:

10 ounces canned white meat chicken, drained

2 tablespoons dried blueberries

¼ cup vegenaise

Creamy Pasta Salad

This dressing works with many vegetables. Use your family's different combinations of favorite vegetables for this salad to mix up the variety in the diet. Try artichoke hearts, olives, broccoli, cauliflower, or summer squashes!

1. Combine pasta, cucumber, carrot coins, tomatoes, and chicken.
2. Combine all ingredients for the dressing, toss with salad.

Yields 4½ cups

INGREDIENTS:

Pasta Salad

3 cups whole-wheat rotini, cooked

½ cucumber, diced

½ cup cooked carrot coins

½ cup cherry tomatoes, sliced

4 ounces cooked chicken, chopped

Dressing

½ cup light mayonnaise or vegenaise

¼ cup ranch dressing

3 tablespoons milk

2 tablespoons red wine vinegar

¼ teaspoon mustard

Quinoa Bean Salad

Yields 6 cups

INGREDIENTS:

1 cup quinoa

2 cups water

1 (12-ounce) can of kidney beans

1 cup of frozen corn

1 red pepper, finely chopped

Juice of 1 lemon

⅓ cup cilantro, finely chopped

3 tablespoons of balsamic vinegar

½ cup of olive oil

2 tablespoons of cumin

Salt to taste

The key to successful quinoa is to thoroughly rinse your quinoa before you cook it. This rinsing helps the quinoa from becoming bitter tasting.

1. Rinse the quinoa under cold running water until the water runs clear.

2. In a medium saucepan, place quinoa and water. Turn on medium heat and cook for 10–15 minutes or until all the water is absorbed. Fluff with fork.

3. Combine quinoa with remaining ingredients. Mix thoroughly, chill, and serve.

Quinoa Is a Complete Protein

Protein is made up of tiny particles called amino acids. There are nine essential amino acids that our bodies need to obtain from food since our bodies do not make them. Quinoa contains all nine of these essential amino acids. As long as your family eats a variety of food, you should be getting enough protein without worrying about combining foods to make complete proteins.

Lemony Rice & Asparagus Salad

Save extra dressing for leftover rice salad. Overnight, the rice will absorb the dressing and will benefit from the extra flavor.

1. In a medium saucepan, bring rice and water to a boil.
2. Reduce heat, cover, and simmer 20 minutes, or until liquid is absorbed.
3. Let rice sit covered 5 minutes before fluffing with a fork.
4. While rice cooks, clean asparagus and remove tough ends.
5. Chop asparagus into 1" pieces.
6. Steam asparagus until bright and tender.
7. Mince dill.
8. Combine olive oil and lemon juice in a lidded jar. Shake to combine.
9. Combine rice, asparagus, dill, and ½ cup of the dressing.
10. Chill before serving.

The Plant that Keeps on Giving

Asparagus, a perennial plant, is a member of the lily family. Asparagus spears are the shoots that grow from a crown that is planted approximately three feet underground. Although the shoots or spears are not picked for the first three years, the same plant can produce spears for fifteen to twenty years.

Yields 4 cups

INGREDIENTS:

2 cups enriched white rice

4 cups water

1 bunch asparagus

2 tablespoons fresh dill

¼ cup olive oil

½ cup lemon juice

Zucchini Corn Muffins

Corn muffins get a boost of vitamins A and C from fresh zucchini in this tasty quick bread recipe.

Yields 12 muffins

INGREDIENTS:

1 cup cornmeal

1 cup white whole wheat flour

2¼ teaspoons baking powder, divided

1 teaspoon baking soda

½ teaspoon salt

¼ cup applesauce

½ cup apple juice concentrate

¾ cup milk (dairy or soy)

3 tablespoons melted butter or trans fat–free margarine

1 cup grated zucchini

1. Preheat oven to 400°F.

2. In a medium bowl, combine cornmeal, flour, 2 teaspoons baking powder, baking soda, and salt.

3. In a large bowl, combine applesauce with ¼ teaspoon baking powder.

4. Add apple juice concentrate, milk, and melted butter or trans fat–free margarine to the applesauce.

5. Slowly mix dry ingredients into wet.

6. Mix in zucchini.

7. Spoon into oiled muffin pan.

8. Bake 18–22 minutes, or until a toothpick inserted into the center of a muffin comes out clean.

Spicy Pumpkin Muffins

*These muffins are extremely moist and packed with
vitamin A, potassium, calcium, and fiber.*

1. Preheat oven to 350°F.

2. In a medium bowl, combine flour, 1½ teaspoons baking powder, salt, cinnamon, and nutmeg.

3. In a large bowl, combine applesauce with ¾ teaspoon baking powder.

4. Add oil, molasses, agave nectar, vanilla, and pumpkin to applesauce mixture. Stir to combine.

5. Slowly add dry ingredients to wet.

6. Spoon into oiled muffin pan.

7. Bake 25–30 minutes, or until a toothpick inserted into the center of a muffin comes out clean.

Blackstrap Molasses

Blackstrap molasses is a byproduct of the process that converts sugar cane into table sugar. It is the byproduct of the third boiling. Molasses from other stages of the sugar-production process are available as well—however, they don't have the same nutritional makeup as blackstrap molasses. Blackstrap molasses is a good source of calcium, copper, potassium, and manganese. It is also a rich sweetener that adds depth to baked beans, barbecue sauce, and gingerbread.

Yields 12 muffins

INGREDIENTS:

2½ cups white whole-wheat flour

2¼ teaspoons baking powder, divided

¾ teaspoon salt

1½ teaspoons cinnamon

½ teaspoon nutmeg

¾ cup applesauce

¼ cup canola oil

¼ cup blackstrap molasses

½ cup agave nectar

1 teaspoon vanilla

2 cups cooked pumpkin (or 15-ounce can)

Corn Muffins

Yields 12 muffins

INGREDIENTS:

1 cup cornmeal

1 cup white whole-wheat flour

2¼ teaspoons baking powder, divided

1 teaspoon baking soda

½ cup agave nectar

¼ cup applesauce

1 cup milk (dairy or soy)

3 tablespoons canola oil

Serve these corn muffins with White Chili (page 218) or Lentil Soup (page 84).

1. Preheat oven to 400°F.

2. In a medium bowl, combine cornmeal, flour, 2 teaspoons of baking powder, and baking soda.

3. In a large bowl, combine applesauce and ¼ teaspoon baking powder.

4. Add agave nectar, milk, and oil to applesauce mixture.

5. Slowly mix dry ingredients into wet, being careful not to overstir.

6. Divide batter into lightly oiled muffin pan.

7. Bake 25–30 minutes, or until a toothpick inserted into the center comes out clean.

As American as Cornbread?

Cornbread's history is tied to the history of the United States. Long before Europeans settled in the colonies of the New World, Native Americans were grinding corn into cornmeal. Upon arriving in their new home, the European settlers learned to make what is now known as cornbread.

Blueberry Pancakes

What weekend morning is complete without pancakes? These pancakes are a nice break from pre-mixed pancake mixes. They are healthful and taste great. Try them with strawberries, bananas, or chocolate chips!

1. Lightly oil a griddle and preheat to low-medium heat.

2. In large bowl, mix pastry flour, brown sugar, baking powder, salt, and flaxseed meal.

3. In separate bowl, mix old fashioned oats, and buttermilk. Then add beaten eggs and canola oil with a whisk until smooth and well blended.

4. Mix wet and dry ingredients together. Fold in blueberries.

5. Pour ¼ cup batter at a time onto the hot griddle. Cook until bubbles are seen and then flip.

Fun Pancake Facts

Do you know how many times did the person holding the world record for pancake flipping flip? The answer is: 416 times in 2 minutes! Do you celebrate pancake day? The official Pancake Day is the same day as Mardi Gras, or Fat Tuesday. It is the feast day before the start of the Lenten season of fasting.

Yields 15 pancakes (¼ cup batter each)

INGREDIENTS:

1 cup whole-wheat pastry flour

2 tablespoons brown sugar

2 tablespoons baking powder

¼ teaspoon salt

1 tablespoon flaxseed meal

1½ cups old fashioned oats

2 cups buttermilk

3 eggs, beaten

¼ cup canola oil

1 pint fresh blueberries

Strawberry, Blueberry, & Banana Smoothie

This smoothie has a delightful purple hue.

Combine all ingredients in a blender. Blend all ingredients until smooth.

Yields 2¼ cups

INGREDIENTS:

½ cup frozen strawberries

½ cup frozen blueberries

½ frozen banana

½ cup apple juice

1 cup milk (dairy or soy)

French Toast

Make a large batch of these on the weekend and freeze. These are great frozen and then reheated in a toaster oven for a easy weekday breakfast. Serve with Blueberry Syrup on page 93.

1. Lightly oil a griddle and preheat to medium heat.
2. In a medium bowl, combine eggs, milk, cinnamon, and vanilla.
3. Dip each slice of bread in egg mixture and place on griddle.
4. Cook until golden brown on each side.

Yields 8 slices

INGREDIENTS:

4 eggs

2 tablespoons whole milk

¼ teaspoon cinnamon

½ teaspoon vanilla extract

8 slices whole-wheat bread

Peach Raspberry Compote

*Serve this compote with French Toast (page 130)
or Moist Yogurt Pancakes (page 204).*

Simmer all ingredients until fruit starts to soften and
break down, approximately 10 minutes.

What a Peach

The peach, a sweet, vitamin-rich summer fruit, is so delightful that Americans use its name to conjure up all kinds of positive images. From the complimentary, "She's a peach," to the upbeat, "I'm feeling peachy," the peach has become a synonym for sweetness. Although the nectarine is a smooth-skinned variety of peach, you just don't hear anyone saying, "You're such a nectarine!"

Yields 2 cups

INGREDIENTS:
1 cup chopped peaches
1 cup raspberries
2 tablespoons apple juice concentrate

Cantaloupe Papaya Smoothie

*This smoothie is a vibrant orange color.
It pleases the eyes as well as the taste buds.*

Combine all ingredients in a blender. Blend all ingredients until smooth.

Yields 2¼ cups

INGREDIENTS:
1 cup frozen cantaloupe chunks
½ cup frozen papaya chunks
½ cup orange juice
1 cup milk (dairy or soy)

Maple Barley Breakfast

Yields 1 cup

INGREDIENTS:

½ cup milk (dairy or soy)

⅔ cup cooked barley

1 tablespoon maple syrup

Cook a batch of barley and put it use in several recipes, like this comforting breakfast or Italian Beans & Barley (page 145).

1. In a small saucepan, warm milk.
2. Top barley with warm milk and maple syrup.

Barley—A Fiber-Rich Grain

Although pearled barley is not a whole grain (the hull has been removed), it is still high in fiber. This is because dietary fiber is found throughout the barley grain. Barley can be a helpful digestive aid in children with constipation due to its high-fiber content.

Spinach Tomato Scramble

Yields 6 servings

INGREDIENTS:

3 whole omega-3 fortified eggs

6 omega-3 fortified egg whites

¼ cup whole milk (dairy or soy)

1 teaspoon olive oil

½ cup spinach, chopped in food processor very fine

½ cup tomatoes chopped or mild salsa

½ cup shredded Swiss cheese (optional)

You can try to substitute chopped collard greens, kale, or other greens in this recipe to give your child's diet a greater variety of green vegetables.

1. Blend eggs, egg whites, and milk using a whisk.
2. Add 1 teaspoon olive oil to a medium skillet and heat on medium.
3. Once heated, pour egg mixture into pan and stir with spatula.
4. Mix in spinach and tomatoes or salsa.
5. Sprinkle with cheese, if desired.
6. Continue to stir and scramble until done.
7. Remove from heat and serve.

Banana Yogurt Milkshake

Agave nectar or honey can be used to sweeten this to your taste. Use different flavored yogurts to make different flavored milkshakes. Blending crushed ice in the milkshake creates a thicker shake.

Combine all ingredients in a blender.

Milkshake Day
Want to celebrate your favorite milkshake? Who doesn't? You can start in June and finish in September. June 20 is National Milkshake Day. Go out and celebrate milkshake day as a family! Due to the popularity of chocolate milkshakes, they get their own separate holiday. September 12 is designated as National Chocolate Milkshake Day!

Yields 2 cups

INGREDIENTS:
1 banana
1 tablespoon lemon juice
8 ounces vanilla yogurt (dairy or soy)
1 cup milk (dairy or soy)
1 tablespoon ground flaxseeds

Orange Pineapple Smoothie

The combination of orange and pineapple is sure to bring a little sun (not to mention lots of vitamin C) into even the gloomiest day.

Blend all ingredients.

Folic Acid for Your Next Baby
Women of childbearing age are strongly encouraged to consume 400 micrograms of folate or folic acid every day (this is the RDA for folate, a B vitamin). Folate is the form of the vitamin found naturally occurring in food, and folic acid is the form used to enrich foods like bread or breakfast cereal. Taking the RDA of folate/folic acid by pregnant women has been found to significantly reduce the incidence of neural tube birth defects. Since these defects usually occur before a woman even knows she is pregnant, it is important for any woman who could become pregnant to ensure that she is consuming the RDA for this important vitamin. Both oranges and orange juice are good sources of folate.

Yields 2¼ cups

INGREDIENTS:
1 cup frozen pineapple chunks
½ frozen banana
¾ cup orange juice
¾ cup milk (dairy or soy)

Mushroom Barley Casserole

Experiment with this dish by adding a green vegetable (e.g., broccoli, asparagus, or zucchini) before cooking.

1 Preheat oven to 325°F.

2. Combine all ingredients in a covered 3-quart casserole dish.

3. Bake for 1½ hours.

Baked Honey Pescado

This makes a very sweet fish. Adults may like it with the following modifications: no agave nectar and 2½ tablespoons of Dijon mustard. It is also great with a crusty loaf of bread topped with Herbed Butter, which is found on page 216.

1. Preheat oven to 400°F.

2. In a small bowl, combine honey, agave nectar, Dijon mustard, vegenaise, lemon juice, and sea salt.

3. Place fish in a lightly oiled shallow baking dish. Spread mixture of top of fish. Bake for 15 minutes or until fish flakes lightly with a fork.

Looking for White Sea Bass?

It often goes by a few different names such as kingcroaker, weakfish, or seatrout. It is a firm, whitish fish that has a mild flavor. This is a best choice for seafood as it is not overfished and is not at risk for mercury contamination.

Broccoli with Meat & Rigatoni

*The meat in this dish can easily be omitted for a vegetarian dish.
Another option would be to try this with protein crumbles as a meat substitute.*

1. Cook rigatoni pasta according to directions, drain, and set aside.

2. In medium pan, brown ground beef. Drain and set aside.

3. In a large skillet, heat 3 tablespoons olive oil and butter. Sauté garlic until browned over medium heat. Add broccoli and stir gently until coated. Add chicken broth and simmer until broccoli is al dente. (Al dente means that it is still slightly firm. This amount of broccoli should take about 8 minutes to become al dente.)

4. Add half the basil, drained rigatoni, and ground beef to skillet and mix thoroughly. Transfer to serving bowl, top with remaining basil, parsley, and Parmesan cheese.

Yields 8 cups

INGREDIENTS:

1 pound whole-wheat rigatoni pasta

½ pound ground beef

3 tablespoons olive oil

1 tablespoons butter

4 garlic cloves, minced

1 bunch broccoli departed into florets

1 cup free range chicken or beef broth

1 cup fresh basil, coarsely chopped, divided

Fresh parsley, chopped

Parmesan cheese

Honeyed Carrots

*Carrots are loaded with vitamin A and E
and are great for babies and toddlers.*

1. Steam carrot coins in the microwave until tender.

2. In medium saucepan, melt butter over medium heat.

3. In small bowl, combine honey, agave nectar, and lemon or lime juice.

4. Add carrots and honey mixture to saucepan with butter.

5. Heat through and mix until carrots are coated with honey mixture.

6. Remove with slotted spoon and serve. Sprinkle with salt to taste.

Yields 1 pound of carrots

INGREDIENTS:

1 pound carrot coins, steamed

1 tablespoons butter or trans fat–free margarine

2 tablespoons wildflower honey

1 tablespoon agave nectar

1 tablespoon lemon or lime juice

Salt to taste

Chicken Pot Pie Muffins

Yields 12 muffins

INGREDIENTS:

1¾ cup chicken broth

¼ cup butter

4 cups whole-wheat croutons with garlic

1 packet dry ranch seasoning dip

1½ cups shredded chicken, cooked

1 cup frozen mixed vegetables (peas, carrots, green beans)

1 (8-ounce) can of white corn, drained

1 tablespoon wheat germ

1 tablespoon ground flaxseed meal

3 tablespoons water

3 eggs

1½ cup shredded Cheddar cheese

Timesaver tip: Purchase a rotisserie chicken at your grocery store to use for the shredded chicken. This makes assembling this dish a snap.

1. Preheat oven to 375°F.

2. In a small saucepan, combine broth and butter and heat over medium heat until butter is melted.

3. In large mixing bowl, combine croutons and dry ranch packet. Then add chicken, mixed vegetables, corn, and wheat germ to bowl and mix well.

4. In a small bowl, mix flaxseed meal and water and allow to sit for 2–3 minutes. Add 3 eggs and whisk with fork. Pour this mixture into large mixing bowl.

5. Pour egg and flax mixture into mixing bowl and mix.

6. Pour butter and broth mixture into the large mixing bowl and mix all ingredients together well.

7. Scoop mixture out into muffin tins. Top each muffin with Cheddar cheese.

8. Bake for 18–20 minutes until done.

Finger Food Anyone?

The croutons in this dish make an easy way to have the crust of the chicken pot pie. The end product with the croutons, chicken, and vegetables is an easy finger food for your toddler. They will enjoy becoming independent at this age with feeding. Let them make a mess with this chicken pot pie.

Arroz Verde con Frijoles Negro

*For a fun twist, serve this dish with warmed
whole-grain tortillas instead of forks.*

1. In a large saucepan, bring 4½ cups vegetable broth, bay leaf, and rice to a boil.
2. Reduce heat, cover, and simmer 40 minutes.
3. While rice is cooking, thoroughly wash spinach and remove stems.
4. Combine spinach, lemon juice, and garlic in food processor.
5. Process into a paste adding extra vegetable broth when necessary.
6. Remove bay leaf from rice, fluff with a fork, stir in drained and rinsed beans and spinach mixture.
7. Add pepper to taste.

International Year of Rice
Did you know that 2004 was the International Year of Rice? This special year was marked with events in Asia, Europe, Latin America, Africa, and North America.

Yields 6 cups

INGREDIENTS:

5 cups vegetable broth, divided

1 bay leaf

2 cups short-grain brown rice

1 bunch spinach

2 tablespoons lemon juice

2 garlic cloves

2 cups cooked black beans

Pepper to taste

Macaroni & Cheese

Pasta comes in so many styles so it's perfectly acceptable to veer from the traditional elbow macaroni. Experiment with other fun shapes your child may like.

Yields 10 cups

INGREDIENTS:

10 cups water

½ pound whole-wheat elbow macaroni

6 tablespoons butter

6 tablespoons all-purpose flour

3 cups 2-percent milk

1½ cup grated mild Cheddar cheese

½ cup grated sharp Cheddar cheese

½ teaspoon salt

¼ teaspoon pepper

⅛ teaspoon dry mustard

1. In a large pot, boil the 10 cups water. Add whole-wheat elbow macaroni and cook until tender. Drain and rinse well under cold running water.

2. In a large saucepan over medium–heat, melt butter. Add flour and continue stirring until the mixture thickens. Add milk and continue to stir until this thickens up.

3. Remove from heat and add Cheddar cheese, salt, pepper, and dry mustard. If needed, return to low heat and stir to melt cheese. Add cooked elbow macaroni and mix well. Serve.

Cheesy Grits

Cheese grits are a traditional breakfast food and side dish of the American South.

Yields 2¼ cups

INGREDIENTS:

½ cup grits

2 cups water

1 teaspoon butter or trans fat–free margarine

¼ cup Cheddar cheese (dairy or soy)

1. In a small saucepan, combine grits, water, and butter or trans fat–free margarine.

2. Bring to a boil, stirring constantly.

3. Reduce heat, cover, and simmer for 5 minutes.

4. Add grated cheese. Stir until cheese is melted.

Honored Grits

Grits, a dish made from ground, dried corn, was named the "Official Prepared Food" of Georgia in 2002. This honor marks the important place that this porridge has held in Southern cooking throughout American history.

Vegetable Tofu Pot Pie

*Serve this warm, comforting dish with
Strawberry Applesauce (page 115) for dessert.*

1. Preheat oven to 350°F.

2. Peel potatoes and carrots.

3. Chop all vegetables into bite-sized pieces.

4. Heat olive oil over medium–high heat. Add potatoes, carrots, onion, and broccoli. Sauté for 3–5 minutes, until slightly soft. Add mushrooms, sauté 1 more minute.

5. In a medium bowl, mix together broth, nutritional yeast, and spices.

6. Dilute corn starch with cold water. Add to broth mixture.

7. Cut tofu into 1" cubes.

8. Toss vegetables and tofu with sauce.

9. Pour into a 2-–3-quart, round casserole dish. Add pie crust to top of casserole, pinch edges around top of dish. Prick pie crust with a fork.

10. Bake 45–55 minutes, or until crust is golden and sauce is bubbling through holes in the crust.

Nutritional Yeast

Nutritional yeast is an inactive yeast that is grown on molasses. It is used as a flavoring agent and as a nutritional supplement, as it provides protein and B vitamins. Some nutritional yeast is enriched with vitamin B_{12}, a vitamin often lacking in the diets of vegetarians and vegans. Do not confuse inactive nutritional yeast with active yeast, such as baker's yeast. If consumed raw, active yeasts can continue to grow in the intestinal tract, robbing the body of essential nutrients.

Yields 6 cups

INGREDIENTS:

2–3 potatoes

2 carrots

1 small onion

1 cup broccoli florets

4 large mushrooms

2 tablespoons olive oil

1½ cups vegetable broth

1 tablespoon nutritional yeast

1 tablespoon garlic pepper

1 tablespoon poultry seasoning

1 teaspoon dried dill

1 tablespoon corn starch

2 tablespoons cold water

½ pound extra-firm tofu

1 frozen pie crust

Easy Baked Chicken

Yields 4 chicken breasts

INGREDIENTS:

*1 pound boneless,
skinless chicken breasts*

*1 (12-ounce) container of
full-fat Greek plain yogurt*

*This is a simple but delicious recipe. The yogurt protects the
chicken from becoming dry and gives it a nice flavor. This chicken
is also a good base to add your family's favorite seasoning to it.
Mix the yogurt with barbecue sauce for a fun twist.*

1. Preheat oven to 350°F.

2. Coat chicken with yogurt and place in baking dish.

3. Bake covered in aluminum foil for 10 minutes.

4. Remove foil and allow chicken to complete cooking uncovered about
   10 more minutes.

Greek Yogurt versus Regular Yogurt

Greek yogurt is known for its unique creamy texture. Greek yogurt is
strained while still warm, which allows most of the whey to be removed.
The end result is a thick and creamy yogurt that is high in protein, low
in lactose, and tolerates heat well. Even the low-fat versions of Greek
yogurt have the thick and creamy texture.

Homestyle Stuffing

This stuffing is a breeze to make. Pair this with the Easy Baked Chicken on page 140 and the Cucumber Tomato Salad on page 155.

1. Preheat oven to 375°F.

2. In a small saucepan, combine broth and butter and heat over medium heat until butter melted.

3. In large mixing bowl, combine croutons and stuffing seasoning packet. Then add cooked nitrate-free sausage, steamed carrots, steamed celery, and wheat germ to bowl and mix well.

4. In a small bowl, mix flaxseed meal and water and allow to sit for 2–3 minutes. Add 3 eggs and whisk with a fork. Pour this mixture into large mixing bowl.

5. Pour egg and flax mixture into mixing bowl and mix.

6. Pour butter and broth mixture into large mixing bowl and mix all ingredients together well.

7. Scoop mixture out into muffin tins. Top each muffin with Cheddar cheese.

8. Bake for 18–20 minutes until done.

Want to Make Your Own Stuffing Packet?

You do not need to buy premade seasoning packets. Instead, you can use the spices in your cabinet to save money. Mix the following together: 1 teaspoon ground sage, 1 teaspoon chicken bouillon granules, 1 tablespoon dried celery flakes, 2 teaspoons dried onion, 2 teaspoons dried parsley, and ⅛ teaspoon ground pepper.

Yields 12 muffins

INGREDIENTS:

1¾ cup beef broth

¼ cup butter or trans fat–free margarine

4 cups whole wheat croutons with garlic

1 packet dry stuffing seasoning mix

1 pound nitrate-free sausage, cooked and crumbled

1 cup carrots, steamed and diced

1 cup celery, steamed and diced

1 tablespoon wheat germ

1 tablespoon ground flaxseed meal

3 tablespoons water

3 eggs

1½ cup shredded Cheddar cheese

Maple Acorn Squash

Yields 2 halves

INGREDIENTS:

1 acorn squash

2 tablespoons maple syrup

Cooking acorn squash in a water bath results in an extremely tender side dish.

1. Preheat oven to 375°F.
2. Cut squash in half. Scoop out seeds and discard. Place squash, cut-side down, in a square baking pan. Fill with water until it is 1"–2" deep.
3. Bake 45 minutes or until flesh is very tender. Pour out water, turn squash cut-side up and pour 1 tablespoon maple syrup into each half.
4. Turn oven to broiler setting. Broil for 2 minutes.

Lentils & Brown Rice

Yields 3 cups

INGREDIENTS:

1 cup short-grain brown rice

2¼ cups water

2 medium carrots, peeled and thinly sliced

½ cup dried lentils

¼ teaspoon cumin

1 bouillon cube (vegan, chicken, or beef)

1 tablespoon olive oil

Frozen carrot slices work well in this dish if fresh aren't available.

1. Combine all ingredients in a medium saucepan.
2. Bring to a boil.
3. Reduce heat, cover pan, and simmer on low heat for 40 minutes.
4. Turn off heat, let sit 5 minutes covered, then fluff and serve.

Turkey Divan Muffins

This is a great recipe for leftovers from Thanksgiving. It is an enjoyable way to use up your Thanksgiving turkey when people are tired of leftover sandwiches.

1. Preheat oven to 400°F. Lightly oil muffin tin pan.

2. Put ¼ cup cooked brown rice in the bottom of each muffin tin. Add ¼ teaspoon wheat germ to each muffin, on top of rice. Then add small amounts of turkey, water chestnuts, white corn, and frozen broccoli to each muffin.

3. Combine soup, water, and dry mustard with a whisk. Pour into each muffin. Top each muffin with 1 tablespoon Cheddar cheese and bake for 15–20 minutes.

Yields 12 muffins

INGREDIENTS:

3 cups cooked brown rice

3 tablespoons wheat germ

2½ cups cooked turkey, shredded

¼ cup water chestnuts, diced

¼ cup white corn

2½ cups frozen broccoli

10 ounces cream of chicken soup

1¼ cup water

¼ teaspoon dry mustard

¾ cup shredded Cheddar cheese

Spaghetti Squash with Italian Herbs

Spaghetti squash is also delicious when it is served with a tomato sauce, like Marinara Sauce (page 105).

1. Preheat oven to 350°F.

2. Pierce squash with a fork in several places.

3. Bake 1½ hours (1 hour for a small squash).

4. Cut in half and remove seeds. Scrape flesh with the tines of a fork to form spaghetti-like threads.

5. Heat olive oil over medium heat. Add minced garlic and herbs. Cook 2 minutes or until garlic is golden, but not brown.

6. Toss "spaghetti" with oil and herbs. Top with Parmesan cheese if using.

Yields 4–6 cups

INGREDIENTS:

1 spaghetti squash

2 tablespoons olive oil

1 garlic clove

1 teaspoon dried basil

1 teaspoon dried oregano

¼ cup Parmesan cheese (optional)

Roasted Potato Salad

Yields 4 cups

INGREDIENTS:

2 pounds new potatoes

4 tablespoons Herbs de Provence vinaigrette

½ red onion, chopped

¼ cup Parmesan cheese, grated

½ teaspoon sea salt

¼ teaspoon pepper

Roasting potatoes adds some variety to the traditional boiled potatoes that are usually used in potato salads. Roasting is an easy process that adds a nice, surprising flavor to your potato salad.

1. Cut raw potatoes into small bite-sized pieces and toss with vinaigrette.

2. Arrange on a baking sheet and put into cold oven.

3. Heat up oven to 450°F and roast potatoes for about 20–30 minutes. Turn potatoes about half way through the roasting process to allow even roasting.

4. Remove from oven and toss with remaining ingredients.

5. Serve.

Vegetable Baked Risotto

Yields 4½ cups

INGREDIENTS:

1 cup Arborio rice

½ cup green beans

3 cups vegetable broth

1 cup broccoli florets

1 small zucchini, coarsely chopped

1 garlic clove, minced

1 cup cooked great northern beans

1 teaspoon dried basil

1 teaspoon dried oregano

This delicious dish delivers protein, iron, fiber, and a variety of vitamins.

1. Preheat oven to 325°F.

2. Rinse rice.

3. Trim ends from green beans, cut into 1" pieces.

4. Combine all ingredients in a covered casserole dish.

5. Bake 1 hour.

Creamed Spinach

Serve creamed spinach on a baked potato for a more filling dish.

1. Roughly chop spinach. Wilt spinach in a dry skillet over medium heat.

2. Combine wilted spinach with roll in a food processor. Process until finely chopped.

3. In a medium skillet, heat olive oil over medium heat. Sauté minced garlic in oil until fragrant. Add flour, then salt and pepper. Add 2 tablespoons milk. Add spinach mixture. Add more milk until desired consistency.

4. Heat through.

Yields 1½ cups

INGREDIENTS:

1 bunch spinach, washed and with stems removed

½ dinner roll or biscuit

2 tablespoons olive oil

1 clove garlic, minced

2 tablespoons white whole-wheat flour

½ teaspoon salt

¼ teaspoon pepper

2–4 tablespoons milk (dairy or soy)

Italian Beans & Barley

For convenience, canned garbanzo beans and canned tomatoes work well in this recipe. Drain and rinse beans if using canned, but do not drain tomatoes.

1. In a large skillet, heat olive oil over medium heat.

2. Add minced garlic to olive oil. Cook for 2–3 minutes, until garlic is golden and fragrant.

3. Add green beans, and cook for another 5 minutes.

4. Add remaining ingredients, combine, and heat through.

Yields 5 cups

INGREDIENTS:

2 tablespoons olive oil

1 clove garlic, minced

2 cups chopped green beans

2 cups cooked garbanzo beans

1 cup diced tomatoes

3 cups cooked barley

Caribbean Baked Risotto

Yields 4½ cups

INGREDIENTS:

1 cup Arborio rice

1 cup coconut milk

3 cups vegetable broth

½ cup cooked pumpkin

1 cup pineapple pieces

½ cup cooked black beans

1 garlic clove, minced

1 cup chopped spinach

This dish is a complete meal incorporating fruit, vegetable, protein, and grain.

1. Preheat oven to 325°F.
2. Rinse rice. Combine all ingredients in a covered casserole dish. Bake 1 hour.

Risotto

Risotto is a traditional Italian creamy rice dish. It is typically made by stirring a small amount of hot liquid, usually broth or stock, into Arborio rice until the liquid is absorbed. This process continues until all of the liquid has been absorbed and the rice is fully cooked with a creamy, starchy sauce. Baking Arborio rice brings about a similar result without standing in front of a stove for close to an hour, a luxury not many new parents can afford!

Creamy Salsa Dip

Yields 2 tablespoons

INGREDIENTS:

1 tablespoon cream cheese (dairy or soy)

1 tablespoon mild salsa

½ teaspoon agave nectar

This dip makes snack time, fiesta time. Serve with Baked Tortilla Chips (page 230), Baked Pita Chips (page 186) or steamed veggies.

Combine all ingredients and stir thoroughly.

Red Beans & Rice

Rice and beans are a staple food in many parts of the world. They go together because beans provide a protein that is lacking in amino acids, but is rounded out by serving it alongside nuts or grains, like rice, to make a complete protein.

1. In medium saucepan, heat olive oil.

2. Once hot, add beans, marinara sauce, carrot purée, wheat germ, oregano, basil, thyme, and water to saucepan and simmer on low heat until heated through.

3. Remove from heat. Mix with 4 cups brown rice and serve.

When Do People Eat Red Beans and Rice?

Red beans and rice is a typical Louisiana Creole dish. This dish is traditionally served on Mondays. Why? It started as a way to use leftovers from Sunday night dinners. This version is not the traditional Creole red beans and rice which might to too spicy for young toddlers. Feel free to spice it for adult member of the family with some added cayenne pepper or hot sauce.

Yields 6 cups

INGREDIENTS:

2 teaspoons olive oil

1 (15-ounce) can of kidney beans

1 cup marinara sauce

½ cup carrot purée

1 tablespoon wheat germ

½ teaspoon dried oregano

½ teaspoon dried basil

⅛ teaspoon dried thyme

¼ cup water

4 cups cooked brown rice

Italian Eggplant

Yields 9" × 13" pan

INGREDIENTS:

1 large eggplant

1 tablespoon salt

1 cup Italian-seasoned breadcrumbs

2 tablespoons olive oil

3 cups pasta sauce (either homemade or jarred)

4 ounces mozzarella cheese (dairy or soy)

Whole-wheat pasta tossed with olive oil makes a great complement to this entrée.

1. Thinly slice eggplant. (The slicing attachment on a food processor works well for this.)

2. Sprinkle eggplant slices with salt, set aside for 20 minutes, then rinse.

3. Preheat oven to 350°F.

4. Combine breadcrumbs and olive oil.

5. Toss eggplant in breadcrumb mixture.

6. In a lasagna pan, alternate layers of sauce and eggplant, beginning and ending with sauce.

7. Top with chopped mozzarella cheese.

8. Bake for 50–60 minutes, until cheese is melted and eggplant is tender when pierced with a fork.

To Peel or Not to Peel?

It is best to keep the skin on eggplant when cooking, as that is the part of the eggplant with the greatest amount of dietary fiber. To ensure that the skin will be tender upon cooking, use young, smaller eggplants rather than older eggplants, which might have tougher skin.

Mangosteen Cereal Mix

Mix it up! Use different types of cereals that are on hand. Different flavored fruit leathers and dried blueberries make a nice addition. Dried blueberries are small and are not a choking hazard like raisins or cranberries.

1. Cut fruit leathers into tiny bite-sized pieces.
2. Combine all ingredients in a glass container.

What Are Mangosteens?

They are a tropical fruit and grow mostly in Southeast Asia. The rind of this fruit is purple and the inside fruit is white. This fruit is new to the arena of antioxidants but shows promise as being a good source of antioxidants. You can only find whole fresh mangosteens in Canada and Hawaii. Due to government regulations, only the juice can be imported to the United States, not the whole fruit.

Yields 8 cups

INGREDIENTS:

6 mangosteen fruit leathers

2 cups cinnamon whole-wheat cereal

2 cups corn cereal shaped in tiny balls

2 cups dried blueberries

1.7 ounces freeze-dried mango pieces

Take-Along Cereal Snack

Since raisins can be a choking hazard for children under three, dehydrated fruits step in to create a tasty nutritious snack.

1. Combine all ingredients.
2. Store in an air-tight container or bag.

Yields 4½ cups

INGREDIENTS:

3 cups O-type cereal

1 cup dried, diced apples

½ cup dried strawberry pieces

Fruit Kabobs

Yields 4 kabobs

INGREDIENTS:

¼ cup cantaloupe cubes

¼ cup honeydew cubes

¼ cup pineapple cubes

¼ cup peach cubes

Small plastic straws (or drink stirrers)

*Using plastic straws instead of sharp toothpicks or skewers
makes this a safer treat for little fingers to manage.*

1. Cut each fruit into 1" cubes.

2. Thread the fruit on the straws, alternating fruit pieces.

Have Fun with Food

Creating playful presentations can be fun for parents and children alike.
Making smiley-face pancakes using artfully arranged blueberries or
creating a flower out of fruit salad can make meal time a happy time for
everyone.

Vanilla Raspberry Sorbet

Yields 2¼ cups

INGREDIENTS:

2 cups raspberries

1½ teaspoons vanilla

3 tablespoons apple juice concentrate

*For a seedless sorbet, press mixture through
a fine-mesh sieve before freezing.*

1. In a blender, combine all ingredients. Blend all ingredients until smooth.

2. Pour into a freezer-safe container.

3. Freeze for 2 hours, then fluff with a fork.

4. Return to freezer.

5. Continue fluffing and freezing every 1½–2 hours until serving.

A Black-Belt in Good Health

Both raspberries and blackberries are rich with antioxidants. Antioxidants are believed to protect your body's cells from damage caused by
tobacco, radiation, and even the unhealthy byproducts of food you eat.

Tropical Pudding Pie Dip

This tropical dip is a hit with kids! Serve this dip with an arrangement of in-season fruit to help your children try new fruits.

1. Combine vanilla pudding and milk with a beater.
2. Once blended well, add remaining ingredients and blend until smooth.
3. Chill and serve.

Yields 3 cups

INGREDIENTS:

1 small package all natural instant vanilla pudding

1½ cups whole milk

1 cup light sour cream

⅓ cup orange-pineapple juice

½ teaspoon orange or lemon zest

Sweet Sunflower Seed Butter Dip

Serve this sweet dipping sauce with cold steamed broccoli florets and carrots.

Combine all ingredients in a small bowl and stir well.

Yields 2 tablespoons

INGREDIENTS:

1 tablespoon vanilla yogurt (dairy or soy)

1 tablespoon sunflower seed butter

1 teaspoon agave nectar

Cinnamon Yogurt Fruit Dip

Yields 1 cup

INGREDIENTS:

1 (8-ounce) container of vanilla yogurt (dairy or soy)

2 teaspoon wildflower honey or agave nectar

½ teaspoon cinnamon

Children love to dip and this is a quick and easy yogurt dip that can be used with fruit or with vegetables. Using dips is a great way to increase your children's intake of healthy fruits and vegetables.

1. Combine and stir all ingredients until smooth.
2. Drizzle over fruit or use as a dip.

Cinnamon Is More than a Tasty Spice!
Researchers have shown that ½ teaspoon of cinnamon per day may help to lower blood glucose in people with type-2 diabetes and may also help to control cholesterol and help improve brain function. Use cinnamon daily in your family meals or steep a cinnamon stick in teas or juice.

Pink Milk

Yields 2 cups

INGREDIENTS:

2 cups milk (dairy or soy)

¼ cup strawberries

Why use mixes that are loaded with sugar and artificial colors and flavors to give milk a fun boost, when the natural alternative is so easy?

Combine all ingredients in a blender. Blend ingredients until smooth.

Chapter 7

Eighteen to Twenty-Four Months

Summer Barley Salad **154**

Tofu Salad **155**

Cucumber Tomato Salad **155**

Mango Cole Slaw **156**

Tabouli Salad **157**

Sweet Potato Biscuits **157**

Traditional Potato Salad **158**

Thumbprint Cookies **159**

Raspberry Strawberry Muffins **160**

Breakfast Burrito **161**

Barley with Bananas & Blueberries **161**

Egg & Cheese Strata **162**

Sunflower Seed Butter & Banana Smoothie **163**

Blueberry & Banana Yogurt **163**

Mixed Fruit Yogurt Smoothie **164**

Cherry Apple Coconut Rice Pudding **164**

Roasted Winter Vegetables **165**

Barbecue Chicken Pizza **165**

Chicken & Broccoli Stir Fry **166**

Mixed-Vegetable Stir Fry **167**

Chicken & Udon Noodles **168**

Frosted Cauliflower **169**

Roasted Carrots **170**

Pumpkin Risotto **171**

Quinoa Primavera **172**

Hummus & Mango Sandwich **173**

Pinto Bean Roll-Ups **173**

Grilled Cheese with Squash & Corn Purée **174**

Pork & Beans **175**

Bean & Avocado Quesadilla **176**

Black Bean Roll-Ups **177**

Cheesy Polenta with Roasted Vegetables **178**

Black Bean Cakes **179**

Pineapple Salsa **179**

Orange Beets **180**

Broiled Pineapple with Frozen Yogurt **181**

Potato Smash Up **181**

Barbecue Meatloaf Muffins **182**

Creamy Spinach Pita Pizza **183**

Chicken Enchiladas **184**

Taco Dinner **185**

Baked Pita Chips **186**

Green Boats **187**

Eggy Boats **187**

Caribbean Dream Boats **188**

Zucchini Yachts **189**

Limeade Sorbet **190**

Hummus Yogurt Dipping Sauce **191**

Yogurt Applesauce Dip **191**

Happy Second Birthday Carrot Cake **192**

Cream Cheese Frosting **193**

Chocolate Pomegranate Dip **194**

Fresh Fruit Slush **194**

Summer Barley Salad

Yields 3 cups

INGREDIENTS:

½ cup green beans

2 scallions

½ cup strawberries, sliced

2 cups Basic Barley
(page 56)

½ cup red wine
vinaigrette

*The combination of steamed vegetable and sweet fruit
brings a nice balance to this salad. You can substitute whatever is fresh at the farmers' market for this recipe.*

1. Trim ends off green beans. Chop into 1" pieces and steam until tender.

2. Finely chop white portion of scallions.

3. Toss all ingredients with the vinaigrette.

4. Chill before serving.

Red Wine Vinaigrette

Here is a simple recipe to make your own red wine vinaigrette. Combine
the following ingredients in a tightly lidded jar: ¼ cup olive oil, ⅛ cup red
wine vinegar, ⅛ cup lemon juice, and 1 tablespoon agave nectar. Shake
before using.

Tofu Salad

*Use this cool, summery salad as a filling for a
pita pocket or tucked into a small melon half.*

1. Mash tofu until crumbly with a fork.
2. Add remaining ingredients, stir to combine.

Tofu Storage
Store any leftover tofu in a sealed container. Fresh water should cover
the tofu. Change the water every day, and the tofu should remain fresh
for up to one week.

Yields 3 cups

INGREDIENTS:

*1 pound firm or extra-firm
tofu*

*½ cup mayonnaise
(regular or vegan)*

*2 tablespoons prepared
yellow mustard*

½ teaspoon dried dill

*¼ minced sweet onion,
like Vidalia*

½ cup shredded carrot

Cucumber Tomato Salad

*Serve this dish as a topping to crusty fresh bread, or as a
topping for fish or chicken. Consider giving your toddler
a small bowl and some chips and allow them to "dip."*

1. Dice tomatoes, cucumber, and onion.
2. In large mixing bowl, combine all ingredients.
3. Salt and pepper to taste.

Picking an Olive Oil Can Be Confusing
There are four descriptors that shows the degree of processing in the
olive oil. Extra virgin olive oil means that this is the oil from the first
pressing of the olives. Virgin olive oil is from the second pressing. Pure
olive oil is then refined and filtered slightly. Extra light oil has been highly
refined and retains only a mild olive flavor.

Yields 4 cups

INGREDIENTS:

4 tomatoes

1 cucumber

½ red onion

*1 tablespoon minced
garlic*

*2 tablespoons extra virgin
olive oil*

*3 tablespoons red wine
vinegar*

Salt and pepper to taste

Mango Cole Slaw

Yields 8 cups

INGREDIENTS:

3 stalks of collard greens

5 cups shredded cabbage or bagged cole slaw mix

3 ripe mangos or 3 cups frozen mango

¼ cup red onion, chopped

2 tablespoons olive oil

1 tablespoon balsamic vinegar

1 tablespoon light agave nectar

The collard greens and cole slaw can be cooked for this recipe if your child is not ready to handle the crunchy texture of the raw vegetables.

1. Chop collard greens into tiny pieces.

2. In large mixing bowl, combine cole slaw mixture, collard greens, mango, and onion.

3. In small mixing bowl, combine olive oil, vinegar, and agave nectar and mix well to create dressing.

4. Pour dressing over contents in large mixing bowl.

5. Toss and serve.

Why Are Collard Greens Good for You?

Collard greens are excellent sources of vitamins K, A, and C. Furthermore, they are a good source of the nutrient manganese. What is manganese? It helps your body use the vitamin C in your diet. Manganese is also vital to the chemical properties that help create natural antioxidants in your body.

Tabouli Salad

The perfect summer salad. Make this salad at the peak of tomato season to use some of the best tomatoes produced all year.

1. Combine all ingredients.
2. Chill for 2–3 hours and then serve.

Yields 8 cups

INGREDIENTS:

3 cups quinoa, cooked

1 cup cannellini beans

1½ cups parsley, finely chopped

3 large tomatoes

3 green onions, sliced

1 tablespoon mint, finely chopped

¼ cup extra virgin olive oil

¼ cup lemon juice

Sweet Potato Biscuits

These easy-to-make little breads get a vitamin boost (and a nice golden color) from sweet potatoes.

1. Preheat oven to 425°F.
2. In a large bowl, combine applesauce with ½ teaspoon baking powder.
3. Add sweet potato, olive oil, and milk.
4. In a medium bowl, combine flour, 2 teaspoons baking powder, baking soda, and salt.
5. Slowly mix dry ingredients into wet.
6. Drop batter onto greased cookie sheet.
7. Bake 10 minutes.

Yields 16 biscuits

INGREDIENTS:

½ cup applesauce

2½ teaspoons baking powder, divided

1 cup Sweet Potato Purée (page 34)

2 tablespoons olive oil

⅜ cup milk (dairy or soy)

3 cups white whole-wheat flour

1 teaspoon baking soda

½ teaspoon salt

Traditional Potato Salad

*Combining sweet potatoes and russet potatoes
is a nice twist to a familiar dish.*

Yields 6 cups

INGREDIENTS:

4 russet potatoes

2 sweet potatoes

3 omega-3 fortified eggs

½ cup of sweet green peas

2 scallions, chopped

½ cup light mayonnaise or vegenaise

1 tablespoon yellow mustard

Sea salt and pepper to taste

1. In a large saucepan, boil potatoes until soft. Once soft, remove from heat and cut potatoes into bite-sized pieces.

2. In small pot, cover eggs with cold water and bring to boil. Cover and remove from heat for approximately 10 minutes. Remove from water, cool, and chop.

3. Place eggs and potatoes in a large mixing bowl.

4. Add peas, scallions, mayonnaise, and mustard and mix thoroughly.

5. Salt and pepper to taste.

6. Refrigerate until ready to serve.

Are Sweet Potatoes Really Potatoes?

No! There are more than 100 varieties of edible potatoes but the sweet potato is not one of them. These two root vegetables are completely different. The potato's scientific name is Solanum tuberosum and its relatives are tomatoes, eggplants, and peppers. The sweet potato's scientific name is *Ipomoea batatas*, which is in the bindweed, or morning glory, family. Sweet potatoes are more closely related to flowers that they are to a regular potato.

Thumbprint Cookies

These cookies get all of their sweetness from fruit. Experiment with different flavors of fruit spread (e.g., strawberry, apricot, blueberry or plum).

1. Preheat oven to 350°F.
2. In a medium bowl, combine flour and salt.
3. In a large bowl, combine applesauce with baking powder.
4. Add apple juice concentrate, milk, butter or trans fat–free margarine, and vanilla to the applesauce mixture. Mix well.
5. Slowly add dry ingredients to wet. Stir to combine.
6. Form batter into 1" balls. Make a depression in the middle of each ball with thumb or back of a spoon.
7. Fill depressions with fruit spread.
8. Bake for 10–12 minutes.

What Is White Whole-Wheat Flour?

White whole-wheat flour is a whole-grain flour made from an albino variety of wheat. Just like the browner whole-wheat flour, white whole-wheat flour is made from all parts of the grain, so it has the nutritional benefits of a whole grain. It has a sweeter taste than whole-wheat flour made from the red variety of wheat, and it is usually processed into a finer flour than traditional whole-wheat flour.

Yields 30 cookies

INGREDIENTS:

2 cups white whole-wheat flour

¼ teaspoon salt

¼ cup applesauce

¼ teaspoon baking powder

⅓ cup apple juice concentrate

2 tablespoons milk (dairy or soy)

⅔ cup butter or trans fat–free margarine, softened

1 teaspoon vanilla

½ cup all-fruit spread

Raspberry Strawberry Muffins

Yields 12 muffins

INGREDIENTS:

2 cups white whole-wheat flour

1½ teaspoons baking powder, divided

½ teaspoon salt

½ cup applesauce

½ cup flaxseed meal

¼ cup canola oil

½ teaspoon vanilla

¾ cup maple syrup

¼ cup plain yogurt (dairy or soy)

¼ cup milk (dairy or soy)

¾ cup raspberries

¾ cup chopped strawberries

Freeze any leftover muffins and reheat when needed.

1. Preheat oven to 350°F.

2. In a medium bowl, combine flour, 1 teaspoon baking powder, and salt.

3. In a large bowl, combine applesauce with ½ teaspoon baking powder.

4. Add flaxseed meal, oil, vanilla, syrup, yogurt, and milk to the applesauce mixture. Combine well.

5. Slowly add dry ingredients to wet. Add raspberries and strawberries.

6. Spoon batter into lightly oiled muffin pan.

7. Bake 25–30 minutes, or until a toothpick inserted into the center of a muffin comes out clean.

Taking It on the Road

Cereal mixes, muffins, fruit-sweetened cookies, and dehydrated fruit are all great snacks to throw in baby's diaper bag for a nutritious snack. Children need to eat throughout the day and having a wholesome option on hand can contribute to a fun outing.

Breakfast Burrito

Purées and mashes are not just for babies. Use purées to boost the nutritional value of your family's meals. Adding a purée is an excellent method to increase the nutrient density of your meals and snacks without the battles.

1. In medium saucepan, heat Black Bean & Carrot Mash until hot.
2. In a small bowl, combine eggs and milk and whisk with fork.
3. In a skillet, add egg mixture and cheese and cook over medium heat until done.
4. Spread tortilla with a thin layer of Black Bean and Carrot Mash, top with scrambled eggs and cheese mixture.
5. Roll up tortilla and top with salsa. Serve.

Yields 1 burrito

INGREDIENTS:

¼ cup Black Bean and Carrot Mash (page 96)

2 omega-3 fortified free-range eggs

1 tablespoon milk

¼ cup shredded cheese

1 whole wheat tortilla

Salsa (for garnish)

Barley with Bananas & Blueberries

Try barley for a breakfast cereal with different fruit combinations (e.g., strawberries, peaches, apricots).

Top barley with fruit and milk.

Local Color

Fresh blueberries are a delight that can be found around the country at local farmers' markets from May to October. They grow in many regions of the United States and Canada, including the Northeast, the Eastern Seaboard, the Midwest, and the Pacific Northwest. Whether eating them freshly washed straight from the colander, mixing them into cereal or yogurt, or cooking them into a favorite recipe, these little blue darlings are sure to delight.

Yields 1¼ cup

INGREDIENTS:

⅔ cup cooked barley

2 tablespoons blueberries

2 tablespoons banana slices

⅓ cup milk (dairy or soy)

Egg & Cheese Strata

INGREDIENTS:

6 slices whole-wheat
bread

¼ cup butter

1 cup shredded cheese

6 omega-3 fortified free
range eggs

1 cup whole milk

½ cup butternut squash
purée

¼ teaspoon Dijon mustard

This is great to whip together the night before a family brunch or to have the morning after a sleepover party. Add some vegetables like roasted tomatoes, mushrooms, or spinach to boost the nutrition content of this dish.

1. Butter slices of whole-wheat bread, cut into 1" cubes.

2. In medium bowl, combine bread and cheese and put into lightly greased pie pan.

3. Whisk together eggs, whole milk, butternut squash purée, and mustard. Pour egg mixture over bread and cheese. Cover and refrigerate overnight.

4. Bake at 375°F for 20–30 minutes or until top is brown and bubbly.

The Protein in Eggs Is Highly Bioavailable

What does that mean? The protein in eggs is easily and readily used by the human body for growth and development. It is the standard to which all other proteins are compared. In fact, 93.7 percent of the egg protein is used by the body, which is the highest of all protein sources. Eggs also contain all the essential amino acids, so they are a complete protein.

Sunflower Seed Butter & Banana Smoothie

For children who are going through a "picky" phase, this smoothie provides protein, calcium, and potassium in the guise of a treat.

1. Combine all ingredients.
2. Blend until smooth.

Sunflower Seeds—Not Just for the Birds
Sunflower seeds, the mainstay of many wild birdfeeders and baseball pitchers, are a great source of nutrition for your family. They are great sources of vitamin E and folate, plus a host of minerals. They are also a good source of protein and good fats. Grind some up into sunflower seed butter and add them to your recipes for a creamy, health-improving boost.

Yields 5 cups

INGREDIENTS:

1½ frozen bananas

⅓ cup sunflower seed butter

⅓ cup apple juice

2 cups milk (dairy or soy)

2 teaspoons agave nectar

Blueberry & Banana Yogurt

Yogurt gets a nutrition and texture boost with the addition of fresh banana and crispy rice.

1. Mash banana.
2. Combine with blueberry yogurt.
3. Stir in crispy rice cereal.

Yields 2 cups

INGREDIENTS:

½ ripe banana

8 ounces blueberry yogurt

¼ cup crispy rice cereal

Mixed Fruit Yogurt Smoothie

Yields 5 cups

INGREDIENTS:

1 cup frozen cantaloupe chunks

1 cup frozen pineapple pieces

1 cup frozen blueberries

1 cup vanilla yogurt (dairy or soy)

1 cup milk (dairy or soy)

1 cup apple juice

Feel free to substitute other fruits, such as honeydew, strawberries, or bananas.

1. Combine all ingredients.
2. Blend well.

Nondairy Milk Alternatives

Not all young children are able to tolerate organic cow's milk. Fortunately, there are a number of nondairy milk alternatives available at well-stocked grocery stores. These are not meant to replace formula, but to be used in place of whole milk when an alternative is recommended. Look for vitamin-enriched milk alternatives. High-quality options include soy, rice, oat, or even hemp milk.

Cherry Apple Coconut Rice Pudding

Yields 4 cups

INGREDIENTS:

1 cup Arborio rice

1 (15-ounce) can coconut milk

1 cup frozen cherries, thawed

1 cup chunky applesauce

Since frozen cherries already have the pits removed, using them dramatically limits the prep time in this dish.

1. Preheat oven to 325°F.
2. Rinse rice.
3. Combine all ingredients in a covered 2–3-quart casserole dish.
4. Bake for 1 hour.

Roasted Winter Vegetables

*This method works well for any root vegetable,
including turnips, rutabagas, and beets.*

1. Preheat oven to 425°F.
2. Peel all vegetables and cut into chunks. (Remove seeds from squash before cutting.)
3. Toss in olive oil and salt and pepper, if using.
4. Spread in a single layer on a cookie sheet.
5. Bake until tender and sweet, approximately 20 minutes.

Yields 6 cups

INGREDIENTS:

1 large sweet potato

1 small butternut squash

2 medium parsnips

2 tablespoons olive oil

Salt and pepper to taste

Barbecue Chicken Pizza

*Prebaking the pizza crust helps this pizza not become soggy.
If you make your own pizza crust from scratch or use a
prepared dough, bake the crust first and then follow this recipe.*

1. Preheat oven to 425°F.
2. In small bowl, combine BBQ sauce and marinara sauce. Spread on prebaked pizza crust.
3. Top pizza with chicken, cheeses, and red onions. Bake about 15 minutes.
4. Remove from oven, sprinkle with cilantro. Serve.

Yields 1 large pizza

INGREDIENTS:

3 tablespoons BBQ sauce

½ cup marinara sauce

1 prebaked whole-wheat pizza crust

8 ounces shredded chicken

¾ cup mozzarella cheese

¾ cup cheddar cheese

⅓ cup red onion, sliced thin

2 tablespoons chopped cilantro (optional)

Chicken & Broccoli Stir-Fry

Yields 8 cups

INGREDIENTS:

1 pound boneless, skinless chicken breasts

2 garlic cloves, minced

3 tablespoons honey

1 tablespoon light agave nectar

2 tablespoons low-sodium soy sauce

2 tablespoons orange juice

½ teaspoon fresh ginger, grated

⅛ teaspoon sea salt

⅛ teaspoon black pepper

1 package frozen broccoli stir-fry mix (broccoli, water chestnuts, peppers, corn)

2 teaspoons corn starch

2 teaspoons cold water

4 cups cooked brown rice

If broccoli is in season, use fresh organic vegetables. Combine broccoli, water chestnuts, baby corn, and red peppers and make your own stir-fry mix.

1. Cut chicken into small strips.

2. Combine garlic, honey, agave nectar, soy sauce, orange juice, ginger, salt, and pepper in a medium bowl and marinate the chicken in this mixture for 1 hour.

3. In a large, lightly oiled skillet, stir-fry chicken and marinade until chicken turns light brown. Remove from skillet but keep warm.

4. In same skillet, stir-fry the vegetables until heated through. Return chicken and marinade to pan.

5. In small bowl, combine cornstarch and cold water and mix until no lumps.

6. Place corn starch in skillet with chicken and vegetables. Allow this to come to a boil and cook for 1–2 minutes or until thickened.

7. Serve over brown rice.

The Origin of Stir-Frying

In China, the origin of stir-frying had nothing to do with healthful cooking. It developed during a period of time in China where cooking materials and food were in short supply. Items had to be cooked fast without wasting any food and with minimum fuel. Now, we know it is a healthful way to cook vegetables and preserve their nutrients.

Mixed-Vegetable Stir-Fry

*For a heartier dish, add 1 cup of the protein of your choice
(chicken strips, beef strips, or tofu) and serve over brown rice.*

1. In a small bowl, combine broth, vinegar, and soy sauce.

2. Dilute corn starch in cold water and add to broth mixture.

3. In a wok or large frying pan, heat oil over high heat.

4. Add garlic and ginger, cook for 30 seconds.

5. Add carrots, onion, and broccoli. Cook for 2 minutes.

6. Add bok choy and cabbage. Cook for 1 minute.

7. Add assembled sauce and cook for two minutes. Cook until vegetables are tender, but not mushy.

Yields 5 cups

INGREDIENTS:

1 cup broth (vegetable, chicken, or beef)

1 tablespoon rice vinegar

1½ teaspoons soy sauce

1 tablespoon corn starch

2 tablespoons cold water

1–2 tablespoons canola oil

2 cloves of garlic, minced

1¼" piece of ginger, minced

2 carrots, chopped

½ onion, chopped

2 cups broccoli florets

1 cup bok choy, chopped

1 cup cabbage, chopped

Chicken & Udon Noodles

Yields 6 cups

INGREDIENTS:

1 pound boneless, skinless chicken breasts

1 cup teriyaki sauce

1 (12-ounce) can crushed pineapple in natural juices

8 cups of water

9-ounce package of udon noodles

¾ cup sunflower nut butter

½ cup light coconut milk

½ cup vegetable or chicken broth

2¼ tablespoons of Carrot Purée (page 69)

2 teaspoons garlic, minced

½ teaspoon ground ginger

2 tablespoons fresh lime juice

⅛ teaspoon red pepper flakes (optional)

The spices in this dish can vary. Add more red pepper flakes for adult dishes and keep the spice to a minimum if your children are not used to spicy food. In many areas of the world, baby food is spicy and children accept and tolerate spicy foods as young toddlers.

1. Preheat oven to 350°F.

2. Arrange chicken in 9" × 13" baking dish and pour in teriyaki sauce and juice from crushed pineapple. Bake until chicken's internal temperature reaches 170°F.

3. In large pot, boil the 8 cups of water. Once boiling, place udon noodles in water and boil until tender, approximately 8–10 minutes. Drain noodles and rinse with cold water.

4. Blend sunflower nut butter, coconut milk, broth, Carrot Purée, garlic, ginger, and lime juice in blender until smooth. Use extra broth to thin to desired consistency.

5. Return noodles to cooking pot and pour content of blender onto noodles and stir to combine.

6. Cut or shred chicken into age-appropriate pieces for your child, and top with crushed pineapple and red pepper flakes if using. Serve with a side of the udon noodles and sauce.

Frosted Cauliflower

*For a more striking presentation, this can be made with the whole
head intact and then divided into florets when serving.*

1. Preheat oven to 350°F.

2. Bring a large pot of water to a boil.

3. Cut cauliflower into florets.

4. Drop florets into boiling water, cook for 1–2 minutes. Drain and rinse
   under cold water.

5. In a small bowl, mix together yogurt, mustard, and agave nectar.

6. Toss cauliflower in sauce.

7. Transfer to 1½-quart casserole dish, cover with cheese.

8. Bake, uncovered, for 20–25 minutes, or until cheese is melted.

Using Convenience Foods

With the increased interest in organic foods, a number of organic convenience foods have become available at well-stocked grocery stores.
Make these foods even more nutritious by adding a personal touch. For
example, you could add steamed cauliflower or broccoli florets to macaroni and cheese, add colorful bell pepper rings to a frozen cheese pizza,
or top frozen waffles with fresh fruit and vanilla yogurt.

Yields 3 cups

INGREDIENTS:

1 head cauliflower

*¼ cup plain yogurt (dairy
or soy)*

*2 tablespoons prepared
yellow mustard*

1 teaspoon agave nectar

*½ cup shredded Cheddar
cheese (dairy or soy)*

Roasted Carrots

Yields 1½ pounds

INGREDIENTS:

8 ounces baby carrots, cut into thirds

1 tablespoon butter or trans fat–free margarine, melted

⅛ teaspoon cinnamon

1 tablespoon agave nectar

1 pound red seedless grapes, cut in quarters

1 pear, sliced

Careful preparation is needed in this dish to ensure that your children are not at risk for choking. Cut each grape into quarters. Roast the carrots so that they are soft and easily chewed by your toddler. Cut them into pieces that are smaller than the windpipe.

1. Preheat oven to 450°F.

2. In the microwave, steam carrots until slightly tender.

3. In a separate bowl, melt butter and combine with cinnamon and agave nectar.

4. In a medium bowl combine all ingredients together.

5. Spread mixture out on a baking sheet and roast in oven for 10–15 minutes or until tender.

Roasting Fruit in the Oven?

Roasting fruit is a wonderful way to bring its sweetness. Winter fruits tend to roast better than summer fruits. Pears, apples, and oranges all roast wonderfully. Lightly toss them with olive oil and a little sea salt and roast them in a 450–500°F oven for about 15 minutes to bring out their roasted taste.

Pumpkin Risotto

This colorful dish makes a lovely meal when paired with a green salad or green vegetable.

1. Preheat oven to 350°F.
2. In a small skillet, heat olive oil and butter or trans fat–free margarine over medium–high heat.
3. When oil mixture is sizzling, add sage and minced garlic. Sauté for 1 minute.
4. Transfer herb mixture to a 3-quart casserole dish.
5. Add remaining ingredients and cover.
6. Bake 1 hour. Stir before serving.

Pumpkins

There are many different varieties of pumpkins—and the ones you carve on Halloween won't taste particularly good! Look for the ones called "cooking pumpkins," "pie pumpkins," or some other designation that indicates they are meant to be eaten, not carved.

Yields 5 cups

INGREDIENTS:

1 tablespoon olive oil

1 tablespoon butter or trans fat–free margarine

1 tablespoon fresh sage

1 garlic clove, minced

¼ cup chopped onion

1 cup Arborio rice

1 cup canned pumpkin

3 cups vegetable broth

Quinoa Primavera

Yields 8 cups

INGREDIENTS:

1½ cup rinsed quinoa

3 cups water

1 cup of frozen corn, thawed

1 red pepper, finely chopped

1 green pepper, finely chopped

1 cucumber, finely chopped

Juice of 1 lemon

3 tablespoons of flax oil

3 tablespoons olive oil

3 tablespoons rice wine vinegar

Salt to taste

This dish is easy to vary according to your family's tastes. You can make this dish with many different vegetables. Vary the produce options depending on the season for freshest flavor.

1. Place quinoa and water in a medium saucepan. Turn on medium heat and cook for 10–15 minutes or until all the water is absorbed. Fluff with fork.

2. Combine quinoa with remaining ingredients. Mix thoroughly, chill, and serve.

What Is Rice Wine Vinegar?

Rice wine vinegar is popular light vinegar that is widely used in Asian cuisine. It is a vinegar made from rice wine and has a mellow and slightly sweet flavor. It is a nice addition to any marinade or vinaigrette dressing, or you can drizzle it over fish before cooking to give a light flavor.

Hummus & Mango Sandwich

This creamy, sweet sandwich provides protein, fiber, iron, and vitamins A and C.

1. Spread hummus over the surface of the bread, and cut bread in half.

2. Top one half with mango slices.

3. Cover with other half.

4. Cut sandwich in 2 pieces.

How to Choose a Mango

When selecting a mango, two senses come into play to determine which fruit is best. First, smell the mango at the stem end. It should have a nice fruity aroma. Second, touch the mango. It should feel firm, yet yield to gentle pressure in the same way as a peach.

Yields 2 mini sandwiches

INGREDIENTS:

1 piece of whole-grain bread

1 tablespoon Hummus (page 107)

⅛ cup mango slices

Pinto Bean Roll-Ups

Serve these sandwiches with Creamy Salsa Dip (page 146).

1. Spread pinto bean purée over the surface of the tortilla.

2. Sprinkle on carrots and cabbage.

3. Tightly roll tortilla into a tube.

4. Cut tortilla tube into 3 pieces.

Yields 3 (2") roll-ups

INGREDIENTS:

2 tablespoons Refried Pinto Beans (page 60)

1 whole-wheat tortilla

2 tablespoons shredded carrots

2 tablespoons shredded cabbage

Grilled Cheese with Squash & Corn Purée

Yields 1 sandwich

INGREDIENTS:

2 slices whole-grain bread

1 tablespoon olive oil, butter, or trans fat–free margarine

¼ cup Butternut Squash and Corn Purée (page 63)

¼ cup shredded Mexican-flavored cheese

1 slice provolone cheese

This recipe is a creative way to sneak vegetables into a child who might be picky about eating certain vegetables. Offer some corn or squash on the side of this so they are still exposed to a variety of fruits and vegetables.

1. Spread the outside of both pieces of bread with olive oil, butter, or trans fat–free spread.

2. Heat a medium skillet over medium heat.

3. Spread ⅛ cup of Butternut Squash and Corn Purée on the inside of one slice of bread and put in skillet.

4. Top with ¼ cup shredded Mexican-flavored cheese.

5. Add slice of provolone cheese.

6. Top sandwich with remaining piece of bread, coated with ⅛ cup Butternut Squash and Corn Purée on the inside.

7. Turn sandwich once. Heat in skillet until cheese is melted.

8. Remove from heat and serve.

One Squash, Two Squash, Three Squash, Four
Summer squashes are thinner squashes that bruise more easily. Winter squashes are more hearty and thick skinned. Both of these are excellent sources of nutrients. Squash is also a good source of calcium!

Pork & Beans

This can also be used as a side dish. Serve this recipe with fresh Fruit Salad (page 199), or the Mango Cole Slaw found on page 156.

1. In slow cooker, place pork ribs and beef broth. Cook on high for about 4 hours.

2. Once done, remove pork from cooker and shred it.

3. In small saucepan, heat black beans until heated through.

4. Mix pork with 6 ounces barbecue sauce and black beans.

5. Serve on whole-wheat rolls and top with desired amount of barbecue sauce.

There's More to Pork and Beans

Pork and beans does not have to be chopped hot dogs and pinto beans. Adding spices and vegetables such as roasted red peppers, tomatoes, green peppers, and onions can also give your pulled pork a little kick. This pulled pork–and-bean mixture can also be wrapped in corn tortillas and topped with shredded cabbage to make a nice pork taco.

Yields 6 cups

INGREDIENTS:

2 pounds boneless pork ribs

14 ounces beef broth

1 (12-ounce) can black beans, drained

12 ounces mild barbecue sauce, divided

Whole-wheat rolls

Bean & Avocado Quesadilla

Yields 1 quesadilla

INGREDIENTS:

2 whole-wheat tortillas

½ cup Black Bean &
Carrot Mash (page 96)

1 ripe avocado

¼ cup shredded cheese

1 teaspoon canola oil

Salsa (for garnish)

Many of the infant purées can be added to quesadillas. Try a butternut squash and pinto bean quesadillas or a pumpkin black bean quesadilla . . . be creative!

1. Spread 1 tortilla with a thin layer of Black Bean & Carrot Mash.

2. Cut avocado and scrape out the insides. Mash avocado with a fork.

3. Add avocado mash on top of black bean layer on the tortilla.

4. Sprinkle cheese on top of this layer and top with second tortilla.

5. In medium saucepan, heat canola oil. Place quesadilla in skillet. Heat until cheese begins to melt. Flip and cook to golden brown. Remove from heat and cut into 8 triangles.

6. Top with desired amount of salsa. Serve.

Black Bean Roll-Ups

This is a great meal for fast weeknight dinners. The combination of beans, carrots, whole grains, and healthy fats provides a quick and balanced meal. Serve with some fresh fruit on the side.

1. Heat olive oil in skillet over medium–high heat.

2. Add onion and garlic to skillet and sauté until clear.

3. Add black beans, Carrot Purée, and cumin to the skillet.

4. Mash with potato masher until reach desired consistency.

5. Cook until heated, about 10 minutes, and remove from heat.

6. Heat tortillas in the microwave for 30 seconds on high to warm.

7. Top one tortilla with a thin layer of bean spread and then Avocado Mash. Repeat with second tortilla.

8. Roll each tortilla.

9. Cut each tortilla into 4 pieces.

Birthday or Sleepover Party Food

Spirals or roll-ups are typically a hit with children. You can make several different types of roll-up and cut them into bite-sized pieces. Arrange them on a plate and let your child and their friends dig in. Children may be more willing to try new foods when they see other children try them. Peer pressure in reverse!

Yields 16 spirals

INGREDIENTS:

1 teaspoon olive oil

¼ cup onion, minced

1 teaspoon garlic, minced

1 (15-ounce) can of black beans, drained and rinsed

8 tablespoons of Carrot Purée (page 69)

1 teaspoon cumin

4 whole-wheat tortillas

4 tablespoons Avocado Mash (page 35)

Cheesy Polenta with Roasted Vegetables

Yields 5 cups

INGREDIENTS:

2 carrots

4 asparagus spears

6 mushrooms (button or cremini)

2 tablespoons olive oil

⅛ teaspoon salt

3 cups water

1 cup polenta

½ cup Cheddar cheese (dairy or soy)

Combining the creamy polenta with the tender roasted vegetables yields a comforting stew.

1. Preheat oven to 425°F.

2. Peel carrots and cut into ¼" wide matchsticks.

3. Break off tough ends of asparagus, and cut into 1"-long pieces.

4. Cut mushrooms in half.

5. Toss vegetables in olive oil and salt. Spread on baking sheet and cook until tender, approximately 10–15 minutes.

6. While vegetables are cooking, bring water to a boil in a medium saucepan. Slowly whisk in polenta and keep whisking until polenta thickens and pull away from the sides of the pan.

7. Sprinkle on cheese, and stir to melt.

8. In a large bowl, stir to combine polenta and vegetables.

Polenta, the Pasta of Northern Italy

Although Italy is known as the home of pasta and pizza, corn polenta has been a basic food item there since the late fifteenth century. Because corn, introduced to Italy from the New World, grows most easily in Northern Italy, polenta quickly became a culinary mainstay. It continues to be a very important component of Northern Italian cooking.

Black Bean Cakes

*Serve these black bean cakes with Spinach Tomato Scramble (page 132)
or Tofu Scramble (page 206).*

1. Drain and rinse black beans.

2. Mash beans with a potato masher or fork.

3. Combine mashed beans with salsa and breadcrumbs. Form mixture into small cakes.

4. In a medium skillet, heat oil over medium–high heat.

5. Cook cakes on each side, approximately 2–3 minutes per side.

Yields 6 cakes

INGREDIENTS:

2 cups cooked black beans (or 1 (15-ounce) can)

3 tablespoons mild salsa

2 tablespoons breadcrumbs

1 tablespoon canola oil

Pineapple Salsa

*Grilled pineapple can make a nice addition to this salsa. Cut a fresh
pineapple in to ½" thick slices. Place on medium–hot grill and grill for
5–7 minutes per side. Allow to cool before using in cold salsa dish.*

1. In a large bowl, combine pineapple, red and yellow peppers, black beans, red onion, and cilantro and mix well.

2. In a small bowl, combine orange-pineapple juice and lime juice. Pour into large bowl.

3. Mix all ingredients together, season with salt and pepper to taste.

Yields 4 cups

INGREDIENTS:

1 cup diced fresh pineapple

½ cup red bell pepper, diced

½ cup yellow bell pepper, diced

½ cup black beans, drained and rinsed

¼ cup red onion, diced

¼ cup cilantro, finely chopped

¼ cup orange-pineapple juice

2 tablespoons lime juice

Salt and pepper to taste

Orange Beets

Yields 4 cups

INGREDIENTS:

1 package of peeled and
steamed ready-to-eat
baby beets

1 can mandarin oranges

1 fresh apple, cut into
slices

¼ cup canola oil

3 tablespoons orange
juice

1 tablespoon lemon juice

1 teaspoon orange peel
zest

*How to boil your own beets: First, cut away the tops and 1" of the stem.
Wash the beets but do not peel them. Place in a pot with boiling water
cook for 1½ to 2 hours. The skins slip off easily when done.*

1. Cut beets into small slices.

2. In a large mixing bowl, combine beets with mandarin oranges and apple slices.

3. In a small bowl, combine oil, orange juice, lemon juice, and orange zest.

4. Toss dressing over fruit and chill. Serve.

Beets Not Your Child's Favorite Food?

It can take a while for your child to develop a taste for beets. Beets have one of the highest natural sugar content of any vegetable so they are great for roasting. Try roasting beets to bring out a sweeter flavor that might tempt your child. You can also try canned beets.

Broiled Pineapple with Frozen Yogurt

This "dessert" provides protein, calcium, and vitamin C.

1. Transfer yogurt to a freezer-safe container.

2. Freeze for one hour, stir, and return to freezer.

3. Preheat oven to broiler setting.

4. Broil pineapple until slightly browned, approximately 10 minutes.

5. Serve broiled pineapple topped with vanilla frozen yogurt.

Yields 2 cups

INGREDIENTS:

8 ounces of vanilla yogurt (dairy or soy)

1 cup pineapple chunks

Potato Smash Up

You can also leave the skin on the russet potatoes for a different texture in this dish. Both russet and new potatoes taste nice with the skin on. Sweet potato skin, however, does not usually taste good in recipes.

1. Peel potatoes and squash and cube them into pieces of about the same size. Usually 1–2" cubes work the best.

2. Bring a pot of water to a boil. Place potatoes and squash in boiling water and boil for about 20 minutes.

3. Drain potatoes and squash and place in mixing bowl.

4. Add butter and smash with a potato masher or hand mixer.

5. Add milk to reach desired texture.

Yields 6 cups

INGREDIENTS:

2 sweet potatoes

2 russet potatoes

1½ cups butternut squash

¼ cup butter or trans fat–free margarine

½ to 1 cup whole milk (dairy or soy)

Barbecue Meatloaf Muffins

Yields 12 muffins

INGREDIENTS:

1 tablespoon flaxseed meal

3 tablespoons water

1½ pounds 95-percent lean ground beef

1 cup tomato juice

¾ cup rolled oats

¼ cup chopped onion

2 garlic cloves, minced

2 tablespoons oregano

1½ cups barbecue sauce

Meatloaf without an egg? That's right, the flaxseed meal and water will thicken after 2–3 minutes and act as an egg replacer in this recipe.

1. Mix flaxseed meal and water. Stir and allow to sit for 2–3 minutes.

2. Preheat oven to 350°F.

3. Combine beef, tomato juice, rolled oats, onion, garlic, and oregano. Add flaxseed mixture to the beef mixture and knead until well mixed.

4. Portion out mixture into a regular-sized muffin tin. Top each muffin with 2 tablespoons barbecue sauce.

5. Bake until muffins reach an internal temperature of 160°F.

Flaxseed Meal Can Replace Eggs

Flaxseed meal can be used to replace the egg that is traditionally used in meatloaf. Flaxseed meal is a source of Omega-3 fatty acids, which are often lacking in the American diet. There is evidence to show that flaxseed is good for improving overall general health and preventing diseases.

Creamy Spinach Pita Pizza

Creamed spinach takes the place of traditional pizza sauce in this alternative Italian-style pie.

1. Spread spinach on surface of pita.

2. Top with tomato.

3. Sprinkle on Parmesan, if using.

4. Broil for 2 minutes; watch to prevent burning.

Pizza Crust Ideas

When it comes to pizza crust, don't feel like you have to stick to the traditional method of preparing your own dough. Consider these alternative ideas to form the base of a pizza: pita bread, English muffin, prepared pizza crust, tortilla, or a whole-grain waffle. With a little imagination, a pizza party is always possible.

Yields 1 pizza

INGREDIENTS:

¼ cup Creamed Spinach (page 145)

1 whole-grain pita bread

2 slices of tomato

1 tablespoon Parmesan cheese (optional)

Chicken Enchiladas

Yields 6 enchiladas

INGREDIENTS:

1 tablespoon butter

¼ cup chopped scallions

1 teaspoon garlic, minced

1 can cream of chicken soup

1 cup light sour cream

2 cups chicken, cooked and shredded

1 cup black beans, drained

1 cup mozzarella cheese

2 ripe tomatoes, chopped

6 whole-wheat flour tortillas

¼ cup milk

1 cup shredded Cheddar cheese

*Using cream of chicken soup in place of enchilada sauce
is a simple way to keep the heat down.*

1. Preheat oven to 350°F. Lightly grease a 9" × 13" baking dish.

2. In a medium saucepan, melt butter and sauté scallions and garlic until tender.

3. Add cream of chicken soup and sour cream. Heat all and mix together well.

4. Remove ¾ of sauce from pan and set aside. To the remaining ¼ in the pan, add chicken, black beans, mozzarella cheese, and tomatoes. Stir to combine.

5. Fill each whole-wheat tortilla with the chicken mixture and roll up. Place seam-side down in the prepared baking dish.

6. In a small bowl, combine the reserved ¾ of the sauce with the milk. Spoon this mixture over the rolled tortillas and top with Cheddar cheese.

7. Bake for 30–40 minutes until cheese is bubbly.

Taco Dinner

*This recipe has very little spice to it since it is geared toward toddlers.
To make this recipe acceptable for the whole family, pull your toddler's
portion of meat and corn out of the skillet, then add your taco
seasoning or green onions to the remaining meat.*

1. In a medium skillet, brown ground beef and drain.

2. Return beef to skillet and add corn.

3. Heat corn taco shells according to package directions in the oven.

4. Once shells are crisp, top each one with beef and corn mixture, shredded cabbage, Cheddar cheese, and tomatoes.

Forget Taco Seasoning Packets

Make your own! Mix the following: 1 tablespoon chili powder; ¼ teaspoon each of garlic powder, onion powder, crushed red pepper flakes, and dried oregano; ½ teaspoon each of cumin and paprika; and 1 teaspoon each of sea salt and black pepper.

Yields 12 tacos

INGREDIENTS:

1 pound ground beef

1 cup frozen corn, thawed

12 corn taco shells

2 cups shredded green cabbage

1 cup Cheddar cheese

1 cup diced tomatoes

Baked Pita Chips

Yields 48 chips

INGREDIENTS:

6 whole-wheat pita
pockets

½ cup olive oil

½ teaspoon garlic salt

*These make great chips for hummus. Serve these with the Hummus on page 107
or with the Hummus Yogurt Dipping Sauce on page 191.*

1. Preheat oven to 400°F.

2. Lay out 6 whole wheat pitas and brush both sides with olive oil.

3. Cut each whole-wheat pita pocket into 8 chips.

4. Sprinkle with garlic salt. Spread pita chips out on a baking sheet.

5. Bake for about 7 minutes or until pita turns brown and crispy.

Pita, Pita, Pita

Whole-wheat pita bread is a great base for many toddler meals. First, it is wonderful to use for dips. Second, it also makes a great pizza crust for making individual pizzas. Additionally, pitas can be made into pockets and can be used to stuff with sandwich fixings for a quick and healthy meal. When heating pita, sprinkle both sides with water to prevent splitting.

Green Boats

Green boats are a fun way to introduce celery. Get creative and let your children "race" these boats around their plate and across the finish line into their mouths!

1. Cut celery stalks into 4" pieces.

2. Spoon 2 tablespoons of cream cheese into celery and level with a knife.

3. Sprinkle lightly with paprika.

4. Top each with a cheddar cheese "sail."

5. Cover, chill, and serve.

Yields 8–12 boats

INGREDIENTS:

4 washed celery stalks

1 (8-ounce) package vegetable cream cheese

Paprika seasoning

Cheddar cheese slices, cut into triangles

Eggy Boats

Egg yolks naturally contain vitamin D.

1. Wash pea pods and dry thoroughly.

2. Slice the top of the pea pod (the straight side) open to make "pea pod boats."

3. Mash hard boiled eggs with a fork and mix with veganaise (or mayonnaise) and butternut squash.

4. Add salt and pepper to taste.

5. Spoon 1 tablespoon into each pea pod and top with olive slices as "lifesavers."

6. Cover, chill, and serve.

Yields 25 boats

INGREDIENTS:

25 pea pods

6 hard-boiled free range eggs

¼ cup vegenaise or light mayonnaise

2 tablespoons butternut squash purée

½ cup black or green olive slices

Salt and pepper to taste

Caribbean Dream Boats

Yields 8–12 boats

INGREDIENTS:

4 washed celery stalks

1 (8-ounce) package light cream cheese (dairy or soy)

1 (8-ounce) can crushed pineapple, drained

¼ cup shredded coconut

Tropical drink umbrellas

These are a great playgroup snack! Celery is 95 percent water but also provides fiber, folate, and potassium in one little powerhouse vegetable. It is a great vehicle for your older toddler's spreads and dips.

1. Cut celery stalks into 4" pieces.

2. Combine cream cheese and pineapple in a bowl.

3. Spoon 2 tablespoons of the cream cheese mixture into celery and level with a knife.

4. Sprinkle lightly with coconut.

5. Top each with a tropical drink umbrella.

6. Cover, chill, and serve.

Mix It Up!

Creativity goes a long way with children. Have fun making different arrangements with their food to tempt them to try new things. Make faces on pizzas or tortillas with vegetables or make a "scene" with their whole plate. Let your children create art with their food, and then watch them eat it!

Zucchini Yachts

This recipe makes a great dish for a group. Serve this with Green Boats on page 187, Eggy Boats on page 187, and Caribbean Dream Boats on page 188 and have a boat parade for your children!

1. Slice zucchini lengthwise to form 2 long boats.
2. Scrape out shallow middle of the zucchini to form the hull of the boat.
3. Combine yellow squash, onion, mango, and cilantro with red wine vinegar and olive oil until coated thoroughly.
4. Fill the zucchini boats with this mixture.
5. Serve on a slice of romaine lettuce for the "water."

Zucchini Vessels

Hollowed out zucchinis make great vessels to hold different foods. Fill the zucchini with egg salad, chicken salad, or a fruit salad. Nutritionally, your children will get small amount of folate, potassium, vitamin A, and manganese when eating zucchini.

Yields 2 yachts

INGREDIENTS:

1 zucchini

1 summer yellow squash, chopped

¼ red onion, chopped

1 ripe mango

½ cup finely chopped cilantro

2 tablespoons red wine vinegar

1 tablespoon olive oil

Limeade Sorbet

Yields 2¼ cups

INGREDIENTS:

1½ cups prepared limeade from frozen concentrate

¾ cup frozen white grapes

Although grapes are a choking hazard for children under 3, blending them into the limeade makes their sweetness safe and accessible.

1. Combine limeade and frozen grapes in a blender. Blend all ingredients until smooth.

2. Pour into a freezer-safe container.

3. Freeze for 2 hours, then fluff with a fork.

4. Return to freezer.

5. Continue fluffing every 1½–2 hours until serving.

Make Your Own Limeade or Lemonade

Limeade, and its more popular sister, lemonade, are made from mixing the juice of either limes or lemons with white grape juice and agave nectar. Different proportions yield sweeter or tarter results, but try this recipe for a starting place: ¼ cup lime or lemon juice, 2 cups white grape juice, and 1 teaspoon agave nectar. Combine all ingredients and stir. Serve over ice.

Hummus Yogurt Dipping Sauce

This yogurt hummus tastes great when served with homemade Baked Pita Chips (page 186). You can also serve with fresh vegetables for dipping.

1. Drain can of beans and save liquid.
2. In a food processor, combine all ingredients and blend well.
3. Use reserved liquid from garbanzo beans to thin to desired consistency.

Yields 2½ cups

INGREDIENTS:

1 (14.5-ounce) can garbanzo beans

1–2 cloves garlic, crushed

1 tablespoon lemon juice

½ cup plus 1 tablespoon plain Greek yogurt

1 teaspoon sea salt

½ teaspoon cumin

Yogurt Applesauce Dip

This dip works well for all kinds of fruit or animal crackers.

Combine all ingredients and stir well.

Yields 2 tablespoons

INGREDIENTS:

1 tablespoon applesauce

1 tablespoon vanilla yogurt

¼ teaspoon cinnamon

Happy Second Birthday Carrot Cake

Yields 8" cake

INGREDIENTS:

1½ cups white whole-wheat flour

½ cup oat flour

2 teaspoons baking powder, divided

1 teaspoon baking soda

¼ teaspoon salt

1 cup canned crushed pineapple

¼ cup softened butter or trans-fat free margarine

½ cup maple syrup

1 teaspoon vanilla

2 medium carrots, peeled and grated

This extra-moist cake gets all of its sweetness from pineapple and maple syrup, rather than refined sugar.

1. Preheat oven to 350°F.

2. In a medium bowl, combine flours, 1½ teaspoons baking powder, baking soda, and salt.

3. In a large bowl, combine pineapple purée with ½ teaspoon baking powder.

4. Add butter or margarine, maple syrup, and vanilla. Mix well with a wooden spoon.

5. Slowly mix dry ingredients into wet.

6. Mix in grated carrots.

7. Scrape batter into a lightly oiled 8" baking pan.

8. Bake 45–50 minutes, or until a toothpick inserted into the middle of the cake comes out clean.

Make Your Own Pineapple Purée

If you would prefer to use fresh pineapple instead of canned, crushed pineapple in this recipe, you can make your own puree. First, cut the ends off a fresh pineapple. Then, cut the pineapple in quarters. Cut off the tough outer skin, and cut out the fibrous core. Then, cut the pineapple in chunks, toss in the food processor, and purée.

Cream Cheese Frosting

This no-sugar-added frosting pairs very nicely with
Happy Second Birthday Carrot Cake (page 192).

Using a blender or electric mixer, combine all ingredients.

Yields 1⅓ cups

INGREDIENTS:

1 cup cream cheese
(dairy or soy)

⅓ cup pineapple purée
or canned crushed
pineapple

2 tablespoons apple juice
concentrate

Chocolate Pomegranate Dip

Yields 3 cups

INGREDIENTS:

1 small package all-natural instant chocolate pudding

1½ cups whole milk

1 cup light sour cream

⅓ cup pomegranate juice

½ teaspoon orange zest

Pomegranates are also a delicious source of potassium, vitamin C, and fiber. Many children who do not eat five servings of fruit or vegetables per day do not get enough potassium.

1. Combine chocolate pudding and milk with a beater. Once blended well, then add remaining ingredients and blend until smooth.

2. Chill and serve.

Pomegranate—an Antioxidant Powerhouse

Research shows that commercial pomegranate juice has 3 times the antioxidant activity as red wine and green tea. Antioxidants have been shown to help in the prevention of cancer and heart disease. Try to incorporate pomegranate juice into your children's diets. Once they are older than four years old and less likely to choke, you can serve them pomegranate fruit.

Fresh Fruit Slush

Yields 3 cups

INGREDIENTS:

1 (10-ounce) package frozen unsweetened peach slices, thawed

1 (10-ounce) package frozen unsweetened sliced strawberries, thawed

2 tablespoons light agave nectar

1 tablespoon lemon juice

1 teaspoon lime juice

¼ teaspoon vanilla extract

This tangy mixture can be used as a light dip for fruit or can be used a dressing to drizzle over fresh fruit. Frozen mangos and strawberries can also be used together as an alternative to peaches.

1. Combine the all the ingredients in a food processor.

2. Process until smooth.

Chapter 8
Twenty-Four to Thirty-Six Months

Minestrone Soup **196**

Avocado Summer Salad **197**

Citrus Fruit Salad **197**

Green Salad with Mock Caesar Dressing **198**

Carrot Pineapple Salad **199**

Fruit Salad **199**

Sunflower Seed Butter Cookies **200**

Coconut Chocolate Chip Muffins **201**

Oatmeal Cookies **202**

Apple Pear Crisp **203**

Strawberry Topping **203**

Moist Yogurt Pancakes **204**

Vanilla Maple Rice Pudding **205**

Tofu Scramble **206**

Tropical Fruit Smoothie **206**

English Muffins with Cinnamon Butter **207**

Breakfast Pizza **208**

Quesadilla with Tomato & Avocado **209**

Burritos **210**

Easy Spanish Rice **210**

Tofu Lasagna **211**

Mixed Vegetable Kabobs **212**

English Muffin Pizzas **213**

Beef Brochettes **214**

Spinach Lasagna **215**

Corn on the Cob with Herbed Butter **216**

Turkey Cheese Roll-Ups **216**

Shepherd's Pie **217**

Veggie Roll-Ups **218**

White Chili **218**

Sweet Potato Fries **219**

Pinto Bean Burgers **220**

Secret Beef Burgers **221**

Grilled Summer Vegetables **222**

Asparagus & Swiss Cheese Quiche **222**

Lentil-Stuffed Green Peppers **223**

Baja-Style Fish Tacos **224**

Tofu-Stuffed Shells **225**

Herbed Broccoli **226**

Guacamole **226**

Corn Cakes with Black Bean Salsa **227**

Spinach & Ricotta-Stuffed Shells **228**

Vegetable Lasagna **229**

Baked Tortilla Chips **230**

Roasted Red Pepper Hummus **231**

Blueberry Sorbet **232**

Lemon Raspberry Ice Pops **232**

Avocado Yogurt Dip **233**

Hot Chocolate **233**

Minestrone Soup

Yields 12 cups

INGREDIENTS:

3 cloves garlic, minced

1 red onion, chopped

1 tablespoon olive oil

6 cups vegetable stock

2 (14½-ounce) cans stewed tomatoes with Italian seasoning

1 large potato, cubed

2 stalks celery, chopped

2 carrots, chopped

¼ large head cabbage, finely chopped

½ tablespoon thyme

½ tablespoon oregano

2 tablespoon chopped fresh basil

1 (15-ounce) can cannellini beans

2 cups fresh corn kernels

1 large zucchini, sliced

¼ cup parsley, chopped

1 cup orzo pasta, uncooked

Salt and pepper to taste

Parmesan cheese (optional)

This hearty, healthy, and delicious soup is great for a crowd. Use this for winter gatherings or potluck dinners. Serve this soup with a hot loaf of whole-wheat bread for a crowd-pleasing dish.

1. In a large soup pot, sauté garlic and onion in olive oil until clear.
2. Add in the vegetable stock, the undrained tomatoes, potato, celery, carrots, cabbage, thyme, oregano, and basil.
3. Bring to a boil and then reduce heat. Simmer for about 15 minutes.
4. Stir in the beans, corn, zucchini, parsley, and pasta.
5. Simmer for 10–15 more minutes until the vegetables are tender.
6. Season with salt and pepper. Sprinkle with Parmesan cheese to serve.

Beaneaters!

Cannellini beans are so popular in the Tuscany region in Italy that the Tuscan people have been nicknamed *mangiafagiole* which means beaneaters. These beans can be used in place of Great Northern Beans or Navy Beans in most recipes. They are high in fiber, folate, iron, and magnesium.

Avocado Summer Salad

*This recipe works nicely with many different summer fruits.
Experiment with a variety of berries to provide different
sources of vitamins, minerals, and antioxidants.*

1. Remove the pit from the avocados and slice into long strips. Arrange slices on a plate. Squeeze lime juice over the avocados to help maintain freshness.
2. Pit and dice the nectarines.
3. Mix together the nectarines, strawberries, and onion in a bowl.
4. Top avocados with the mixture of nectarines, strawberries, and onions.
5. Season with salt and pepper.

Yields 5 cups

INGREDIENTS:

2 ripe avocados

3 tablespoons fresh squeezed lime juice

2 fresh nectarines

¾ cup strawberries, diced

¼ cup sweet onion, diced

Salt and ground black pepper to taste

Citrus Fruit Salad

*Pair this recipe with the Cinnamon Yogurt Fruit Dip on page 152.
These two dishes together provide great sources of vitamin C and calcium.
Jicama also provides a source of folic acid in this dish.*

1. Combine oranges, pineapple, blueberries, and jicama together.
2. Top with shredded coconut to taste.

Yields 5 cups

INGREDIENTS:

2 oranges, peeled and sliced

1 cup pineapple, sliced

1 cup blueberries

½ cup jicama, cut into matchsticks

Shredded coconut

Green Salad with Mock Caesar Dressing

Silken tofu can make a great addition to creamy dishes.
Tofu absorbs the flavor of almost any food that you place it with.
In a dressing, your children will never know that they are eating tofu!

Yields 8 cups

INGREDIENTS:

1 head of romaine lettuce, washed and torn

2 tomatoes, cut into wedges

2 cups whole-wheat croutons

2 garlic cloves

2 tablespoons Dijon mustard

12 ounces silken tofu

½ cup lemon juice

1 tablespoon Worcestershire sauce

1 teaspoon ground black pepper

Grated Parmesan cheese for garnish

1. Combine lettuce, tomatoes, and croutons in large mixing bowl.

2. In a blender, combine garlic, mustard, tofu, lemon juice, Worcestershire sauce, and pepper and blend until smooth to create a dressing.

3. Toss salad with desired amount of dressing and sprinkle with Parmesan cheese.

Which Tofu to Pick?

There are different types of tofu: silken or soft, firm, and extra-firm. When following a tofu recipe, pay attention to the type of tofu it calls for. Silken tofu is best for puddings and dips while stir-fries mostly use firm tofu.

Carrot Pineapple Salad

This side dish makes a great compliment to the Beef Brochettes on page 214. Leftovers of this salad are great for your toddler. This dish continues to soften and get sweeter over time, so make an extra batch to keep in the fridge.

1. In small mixing bowl, combine all ingredients.
2. Stir well and serve.

Blueberries Are Tops

According to research at Tufts University, blueberries are the stars of antioxidants. They contain the highest level of antioxidants in any food. Here's an interesting fact: As blueberries ripen, the amount of antioxidants in them may increase. Picking ripe blueberries to use in your dishes can boost the antioxidant capacity.

Yields 2½ cups

INGREDIENTS:

1 cup carrots, shredded

1 cup crushed pineapple, drained

½ cup dried blueberries

2 tablespoons of vanilla yogurt

½ teaspoon cinnamon

Fruit Salad

Added sweetener or dressing isn't necessary when you mix colorful, flavorful fruit.

Combine all ingredients.

An Old-Fashioned Watermelon Basket

To make a fun presentation for fruit salad, cut a watermelon in half and scoop out the pink flesh, leaving behind the green and white shell. Cut up the watermelon and other fruits, combine and use the watermelon shell as your serving bowl.

Yields 3 cups

INGREDIENTS:

½ cup honeydew cubes

½ cup cantaloupe cubes

½ cup seedless watermelon cubes

½ cup blueberries

½ cup pineapple cubes

½ cup strawberry slices

Sunflower Seed Butter Cookies

Yields 48 cookies

INGREDIENTS:

1⅔ cups white whole-wheat flour

1 teaspoon baking powder, divided

½ teaspoon baking soda

¼ teaspoon salt

½ cup applesauce

1 cup sunflower seed butter

¼ cup canola oil

⅔ cup packed brown sugar

½ cup maple syrup

Little ones will love the sweetness of these cookies, and you will love knowing that they're packed with high-protein sunflower seed butter.

1. Preheat oven to 350°F.
2. In a medium bowl, combine flour, ½ teaspoon baking powder, baking soda, and salt.
3. In a larger bowl, combine applesauce with baking powder.
4. Add sunflower seed butter, oil, brown sugar, and maple syrup to applesauce mixture.
5. Slowly mix dry ingredients into wet.
6. Drop batter by the heaping teaspoon onto ungreased cookie sheets.
7. Bake 10–12 minutes.

Coconut Chocolate Chip Muffins

With brown sugar and chocolate chips, these muffins are really a dessert. Unlike many desserts, however, they come with the benefit of whole-grain goodness.

1. Preheat oven to 350°F.
2. In a medium mixing bowl combine flour, 1 teaspoon baking powder, and salt.
3. In a large mixing bowl combine applesauce with ½ teaspoon baking powder.
4. Add flaxseed meal, canola oil, brown sugar, and coconut milk to the applesauce mixture.
5. Slowly add dry ingredients to wet. Stir to combine.
6. Stir in chocolate chips and coconut flakes.
7. Bake 25 minutes, or until a toothpick inserted in the center of a muffin comes out clean.

Monkey Face

The name "coconut" comes from the Spanish word *coco*, meaning monkey's face. Early Spanish explorers thought the three indentations (or eyes) on the coconut resembled the face of a monkey.

Yields 12 muffins

INGREDIENTS:

2 cups white whole-wheat flour

1½ teaspoons baking powder, divided

½ teaspoon salt

½ cup applesauce

½ cup flaxseed meal

¼ cup canola oil

¾ cup packed light brown sugar

¼ cup coconut milk

1 cup chocolate chips

¾ cup coconut flakes

Oatmeal Cookies

Yields 48 cookies

INGREDIENTS:

1½ cups white whole-wheat flour

1½ cups rolled oats

½ teaspoon cinnamon

½ teaspoon baking soda

½ teaspoon salt

½ teaspoon baking powder

½ cup applesauce

½ cup apple juice concentrate

½ cup maple syrup

½ cup canola oil

Change the flavor of these cookies by adding either 1 cup of chopped apples or 1 cup of chocolate chips to the batter before baking.

1. Preheat oven to 350°F.

2. In a medium bowl, combine flour, oats, cinnamon, baking soda, and salt.

3. In a large bowl, combine applesauce and baking powder.

4. Add apple juice concentrate, maple syrup, and canola oil to the applesauce mixture.

5. Slowly add dry ingredients to wet; stirring to combine.

6. Drop batter by heaping teaspoonfuls onto ungreased cookie sheets.

7. Bake 10–12 minutes, until golden brown.

Apple Pear Crisp

This fruity dessert is great served with some vanilla frozen yogurt.

1. Preheat oven to 400°F.
2. Peel, core, and thinly slice pears and apples.
3. In a small bowl combine brown sugar, vanilla, flour, oats, and butter.
4. Spray a 2-quart casserole dish with canola oil.
5. Spread fruit in bottom of casserole dish.
6. Top with sugar mixture.
7. Bake for 40 minutes.

Yields 4 cups

INGREDIENTS:

3 medium pears

3 large apples

¾ cup packed light brown sugar

1 teaspoon vanilla

½ cup white whole-wheat flour

¼ cup old-fashioned rolled oats

¼ cup butter or trans fat–free margarine, melted

Canola oil spray

Strawberry Topping

This very simple sauce is a tasty topping for ice cream, Moist Yogurt Pancakes (page 204), or Oatmeal (page 57).

1. In a small saucepan, combine strawberries and water.
2. Cook over medium heat, breaking up strawberries with the back of a spoon as they cook.
3. Serve warm or at room temperature.

Yields 1 cup

INGREDIENTS:

1 cup strawberries

¼ cup water

Moist Yogurt Pancakes

Yields 20 small pan-cakes

INGREDIENTS:

1½ cups unbleached all-purpose flour

½ cup oat flour

2½ teaspoons baking powder, divided

2 teaspoons baking soda

¼ teaspoon salt

½ cup applesauce

½ cup apple juice concentrate

2 cups plain yogurt (dairy or soy)

1 teaspoon vanilla

2 tablespoons butter or trans fat–free margarine, melted

Canola oil for pan

Pair these pancakes with either Blueberry Syrup (page 93) or Strawberry Topping (page 203) for a breakfast sensation.

1. In a medium bowl, combine flours, 2 teaspoons baking powder, baking soda, and salt.

2. In a large bowl, combine applesauce with ½ teaspoon baking powder.

3. Add apple juice concentrate, yogurt, vanilla, and melted butter or trans fat–free margarine to the applesauce mixture.

4. Slowly stir dry ingredients into wet, stirring just to combine.

5. Brush skillet or griddle with oil and heat over medium–high heat.

6. When a drop of water dances on the surface of the pan, drop batter onto surface.

7. When edges are golden and a couple of bubbles appear on the surface of the pancake, flip it and continue cooking on the other side.

8. Pancakes are ready when they are cooked through and golden on both sides.

Vanilla Maple Rice Pudding

Serve a scoop of this pudding warmed with some blueberries on the side.

1. Preheat oven to 325°F.

2. Rinse rice.

3. In a small saucepan, bring milk, syrup, and vanilla to a boil.

4. Combine liquid and rice in a covered 2-quart casserole dish.

5. Bake 1 hour.

Vanilla, the Tropical Flower

Vanilla beans come from a member of the orchid family. This plant originated in Mexico, but is widely grown throughout the tropics, especially in Madagascar. The beautiful flavor and aroma of the vanilla bean is used in baked goods, confections, and perfumes around the world.

Yields 4 cups

INGREDIENTS:

1 cup Arborio rice
4 cups milk (dairy or soy)
½ cup maple syrup
2 tablespoons vanilla

Tofu Scramble

*To make this quick entrée even more convenient,
use thawed frozen chopped spinach.*

1. In a large skillet or sauté pan, heat olive oil over medium–high heat.

2. Sauté garlic and onion until soft, golden and fragrant.

3. Add spinach and sauté until wilted.

4. Crumble tofu and add to skillet.

5. Add soy sauce.

6. Cook over medium–high heat until heated through, approximately 7 minutes.

Tropical Fruit Smoothie

This summery treat is loaded with vitamins A and C.

Combine all ingredients in a blender.
Blend all ingredients until smooth.

English Muffins with Cinnamon Butter

Store this butter in your refrigerator in a glass container. It will be easy and handy to use on breads, waffles, and muffins. Try this on the Spicy Pumpkin Muffins on page 127.

1. Blend butter and honey together with a beater.

2. Once blended, add cinnamon and continue to blend.

3. Toast whole-wheat English muffins and spread cinnamon butter on muffins to serve.

Why Store Food in Glass Containers?

Plastic containers contain bisphenol A (BPA) which has been linked to cancer and reproductive abnormalities, and could be causing environmental problems. If you are going to use plastic, avoid plastics with the numbers 3, 6, and 7 on the bottom of the container enclosed in the recycle arrows.

Yields ¾ cup

INGREDIENTS:

½ cup butter or trans fat–free spread, softened

⅓ cup wildflower honey or light agave nectar

¼ teaspoon cinnamon

Whole-wheat English muffins

Breakfast Pizza

Yields 1 pizza

INGREDIENTS:

1 large whole-wheat tortilla

½ teaspoon butter or trans fat–free light spread

1 teaspoon table sugar

⅛ teaspoon cinnamon

⅓ cup whipped cream cheese (dairy or soy)

2 teaspoons honey

¼ cup blueberries

¼ cup strawberries, sliced

½ cup blackberries

¼ cup bananas, sliced

¼ cup kiwi, diced

If you are not going to serve this immediately, dip the bananas in orange, lemon, or lime juice to prevent browning. Bananas and apples turn brown because an enzyme in them reacts with oxygen in the air. Acidic juices stop this enzymatic browning.

1. Preheat oven to 400°F.
2. Place whole-wheat tortilla on an ungreased cookie sheet.
3. Spread butter evenly over tortilla.
4. In a small bowl, combine table sugar and cinnamon. Sprinkle this over the top of the tortilla.
5. Bake tortilla for 3–4 minutes or until edges begin to brown. Remove from oven.
6. In a medium bowl beat cream cheese with honey until well mixed.
7. Spread over the tortilla forming a base for the fruit toppings.
8. Arrange fruit on top of tortilla. Cut into pizza slices and serve.

Quesadilla with Tomato & Avocado

Leftover avocado will turn brown in the refrigerator, but you can sprinkle a bit of lemon juice over it to slow the process. Scoop off the lemony part before feeding, and use the remaining avocado within 1–2 days.

1. Cut avocado, remove pit, and scrape out the insides. Mash avocado flesh with a fork.

2. Add avocado mash on top of 1 tortilla.

3. Dice tomato and layer on top of avocado.

4. Sprinkle cheese on top of this layer and top with second tortilla

5. In medium saucepan, heat canola oil. Place quesadilla in skillet. Heat until cheese begins to melt. Flip and cook to golden brown. Remove from heat and cut into 8 triangles.

6. Top with salsa.

Tortilla Round Up

There are many different types of tortillas. The original tortillas are the corn tortillas, made from corn flour or masa harina. Corn tortillas are a decent source of folate at 7 percent of the daily value. Blue corn tortillas have higher protein than the corn tortillas. Whole-wheat tortillas provide a source of whole grains but are typically larger and higher in calories than corn tortillas.

Yields 1 quesadilla

INGREDIENTS:

1 ripe avocado

2 whole-wheat tortillas

1 ripe tomato

¼ cup shredded Cheddar cheese (dairy or soy)

1 teaspoon canola oil

Salsa for garnish

Burritos

This is a quick and easy dish that can be made for busy nights for dinner. Serve these burritos with a side of Easy Spanish Rice, found on page 210. Rice can be rolled into the burritos or served on the side.

Yields 3 burritos

INGREDIENTS:

1 cup Black Bean & Carrot Mash (page 96)

1 cup cooked and shredded chicken

¾ cup shredded Cheddar cheese

3 whole-wheat tortillas

Salsa for garnish

1. In medium saucepan over medium heat, heat Black Bean & Carrot Mash, shredded chicken, and cheese until heated through.

2. Top each tortilla with ¾ cup of this mixture.

3. Roll up tortillas and top with salsa. Serve.

Easy Spanish Rice

This rice dish is simple but tasty. It is a quick way to make Spanish rice without a lot of prep work. Try it with your favorite salsa.

Yields 2½ cups

INGREDIENTS:

2 cups brown rice

½ cup shredded Cheddar cheese (dairy or soy)

1 cup salsa

1. Cook brown rice according to directions.

2. Remove from heat and mix in cheese to melt.

3. Once melted, mix in salsa. Stir well.

Looking to Spice Up Your Rice?

Adding a prepared salsa, dip, or dressing is an easy way to add some kick to your rice. For your toddlers you can choose a very mild salsa to start. For the rest of the family, you can mix in a hotter salsa or add some hot sauce or fresh serrano or jalapeño peppers to increase the heat.

Tofu Lasagna

For children who can't eat dairy, make sure that soy cheese is casein-free or vegan.

1. Preheat oven to 350°F.
2. In a large stockpot, bring 2½ quarts water and 2 teaspoons olive oil to a boil.
3. Add lasagna noodles, boil 10 minutes.
4. While noodles are cooking, finely chop artichoke hearts.
5. In a large bowl, combine artichoke hearts, spinach, 2 tablespoons olive oil, nutritional yeast, garlic pepper, and tofu.
6. Rinse noodles in cold water.
7. Spread a thin layer of sauce in the bottom of the baking pan.
8. Alternate layers of sauce, noodles, and tofu filling.
9. Finish with sauce and top with mozzarella cheese.
10. Bake for 40 minutes.

Yields 9" square pan

INGREDIENTS:

2 tablespoons plus 2 teaspoons olive oil, divided

6 sheets lasagna noodles

4 artichoke hearts

2 cups chopped spinach

1 tablespoon nutritional yeast

1 teaspoon garlic pepper

8 ounces firm tofu

2 cups pasta sauce (homemade or jarred)

4 ounces mozzarella cheese (dairy or soy)

Mixed Vegetable Kabobs

Serve these kabobs with Quinoa (page 57) and some sliced melon for a complete summertime meal.

Yields 2 kabobs

INGREDIENTS:

1 red bell pepper

4 mushrooms

1 small zucchini

1 green bell pepper

1 carrot, peeled

2 tablespoons olive oil

Salt and pepper to taste

1. Chop all vegetables into 1½" pieces.
2. Toss with olive oil and salt and pepper, if using.
3. Alternate vegetables on a metal or bamboo skewer.
4. Grill or broil, until the vegetables are tender, turning once.

Alternative Pastas

At many well-stocked grocery stores there is a variety of pastas available made from organic grains. These options run the gamut from the traditional semolina to whole wheat, quinoa, corn, and rice. Try them with tomato-based sauces, in soups, or tossed with olive oil and Parmesan cheese.

English Muffin Pizzas

Children who are involved in the preparing and cooking of food are more likely to try new foods. Allow your children to choose and design their own toppings.

1. Preheat the oven to 375°F.

2. Place the English muffin halves cut-side up onto a baking sheet.

3. Combine 2 cups of tomato sauce and ½ cup butternut squash or carrot purée. (For older children, you can use ¼ cup shredded fresh carrots to mix with tomato sauce.)

4. Spoon about ¼ cup of this sauce onto each muffin half.

5. Top each muffin half with ⅛ cup mozzarella cheese and allow your children to add their own toppings and design their own pizzas.

6. Bake for 10 minutes in the preheated oven until the cheese is melted and browned on the edges.

Easy Kid-Friendly Pizza Sauce

Combine 1 can tomato paste, ½ teaspoon garlic powder, ½ teaspoon oregano, ½ teaspoon basil, and ¾ teaspoon agave nectar for a tasty, easy pizza sauce. Store extra sauce in an air-tight container in the refrigerator.

Yields 8 pizza halves

INGREDIENTS:

4 whole-grain English muffins

2 cups tomato sauce

½ cup butternut squash or carrot purée

1 cup mozzarella cheese (dairy or soy)

Topping Options: sliced tomatoes, mushrooms, spinach, peppers, pineapple, nitrate-free ham, olives, or salsa

Beef Brochettes

Yields 10 skewers

INGREDIENTS:

1 cup steak sauce

¼ cup Italian dressing

¼ cup agave nectar

1 garlic clove, minced

1 pound beef sirloin or sirloin steak

1 red bell pepper, cut into squares

1 green bell pepper, cut into squares

1 pineapple, cut into squares

If you are using bamboo skewers, soak them in water for about 1 hour before using to help prevent burning or catching them on fire while grilling.

1. In blender, combine steak sauce, Italian dressing, agave nectar, and garlic. Blend until smooth. Pour into glass baking dish.

2. Cut beef into cubes and place beef in the baking dish, cover, and marinate over night.

3. Use bamboo skewers to grill brochettes. When making the skewers, separate the beef and the vegetables on different skewers for ease of cooking.

4. Grill until done, about 10 minutes for vegetables and approximately 15 minutes for meat. Remove from skewer before giving to children.

Skewer Tips
You can also soak the skewers in beef broth for 1 hour which will provide more flavor while cooking. Coat the skewer lightly with canola oil, which can withstand the high heat of the grill. Instead of putting meat and vegetables on same skewer, separate onto 2 different skewers since they have different cooking times.

Spinach Lasagna

Once your children are older and past the risk of food allergies, sprinkle fresh pine nuts in each layer for a nice flavor and to add a little texture to the lasagna.

1. Preheat oven to 350°F.

2. In a large bowl beat eggs, ricotta, salt, and ¼ cup Parmesan cheese.

3. Lightly grease a 9" × 13" baking dish. Put small amount of spaghetti sauce on bottom.

4. Layer uncooked noodles, ricotta cheese mixture, mozzarella cheese, and about 2–3 cups of fresh spinach per layer. Repeat layers to top of baking dish.

5. Sprinkle top with ½ cup Parmesan cheese.

6. Cover and bake for about 1 hour or until noodles are tender.

Uncooked Noodles in Lasagna?

You do not need to precook the noodles for lasagna and you do not need to purchase special "no-cook" noodles. Most noodles will cook to appropriate tenderness with the high moisture content of the lasagna and long cooking time. One tip: Run the noodles under water before layering in pan to help make sure they cook.

Yields 9" × 13" baking dish

INGREDIENTS:

2 eggs

1 (15-ounce) container of ricotta cheese

½ teaspoon salt

¾ cup Parmesan cheese, divided

1 quart prepared spaghetti sauce

½ pound whole-wheat lasagna noodles, uncooked

½ pound mozzarella cheese, sliced

1 bag fresh spinach

Corn on the Cob with Herbed Butter

Yields ¾ cup butter

INGREDIENTS:

½ cup butter, softened

3 tablespoons grated Parmesan cheese

2 teaspoons chopped fresh parsley

⅛ cup dried oregano

⅛ cup dried Italian seasoning

½ teaspoon garlic powder

Boiled corn on the cob

This herbed butter is versatile. Top garlic bread or pasta with this butter for a fresh twist. Serve this recipe as a side to the Beef Brochettes on page 214.

1. In a small mixing bowl, combine butter, cheese, parsley, oregano, Italian seasoning, and garlic powder and blend with hand mixer until smooth.

2. Serve herbed butter on pre-boiled corn on the cob.

Turkey Cheese Roll-Ups

Yields 12 small wraps

INGREDIENTS:

4 whole-wheat or sun-dried tortillas

½ cup of vegetable cream cheese (dairy or soy)

12 ounces nitrate-free, oven-roasted turkey, sliced

2 cups red cabbage, shredded

1 cucumber, sliced

2 carrots, shredded

Rice wine vinegar

Pack these in picnic lunches or for daycare. Children love to pull apart wraps and sandwiches and eat all the components separately. Playing with food is a great way for children to explore and accept new tastes and textures.

1. Spread out the tortillas.

2. Spread 2 tablespoons of vegetable cream cheese and over each tortilla.

3. Top with 3 ounces of turkey, ½ cup shredded cabbage, slices of cucumber, and shredded carrots.

4. Sprinkle with rice wine vinegar to taste.

5. Roll up tortilla and slice across each tortilla to make 3 smaller wraps.

Shepherd's Pie

*Shepherd's pie is a traditional dish that usually consists of
beef and vegetables topped with mashed potatoes and then baked.
However, any leftover meat would work well in this recipe.*

1. In a large pot bring water to a boil. Cut potatoes and place in boiling water.

2. In large skillet, heat olive oil. Sauté onion and carrots until tender. Add ground beef and flaxseed meal to pan and brown. Drain ground beef and return to hot skillet.

3. Add beef broth, green peas, corn, Worcestershire sauce, ketchup, and mustard to skillet and allow to heat for about 10 minutes.

4. Meanwhile, remove potatoes from boiling water when tender. Mash with milk and butter. Be careful not to make these potatoes too thin.

5. In a 9" × 13" pan, first layer and press meat mixture into the bottom of pan evenly. Then spread mashed potatoes on the top of meat mixture. Use a fork to arrange the potatoes into an even but pointy layer. There should be peaks of potatoes sticking up to get brown.

6. Bake at 400°F for 30 minutes. Broil for 5 minutes at the end to crisp up the top.

Yields 9" × 13" baking dish

INGREDIENTS:

3 large potatoes, peeled

1 tablespoon olive oil

1 red onion, chopped

½ cup diced carrots

1½ pound ground beef

2 tablespoons flaxseed meal

¾ cup beef broth

¾ cup green peas

¾ cup corn

1 teaspoon Worcestershire sauce

1 teaspoon ketchup

1 teaspoon Dijon mustard

½ cup milk (dairy or soy)

2 tablespoons butter or trans fat–free margarine

Veggie Roll-Ups

Yields 2 (3") pieces

This wrap-style sandwich combines textures in a really appealing way.

INGREDIENTS:

2 tablespoons Tofu Avocado Spread (page 109)

1 whole-wheat tortilla

1 tablespoon chopped tomato

1 tablespoons minced red pepper

1 tablespoon chopped cucumber

1. Spread Tofu Avocado Spread across surface of the tortilla.
2. Sprinkle on vegetables.
3. Tightly roll tortilla into a tube.
4. Cut the tube in half.

White Chili

Yields 8 cups

White chili is called white because most of the ingredients are white in color.

INGREDIENTS:

1 tablespoon vegetable oil

1 medium onion, chopped

2 cloves garlic, minced

2 cooked chicken breasts, cubed

1 (12-ounce) can white corn, drained

1 (15-ounce) can cannellini beans, drained

1 (15-ounce) can garbanzo beans, drained

1 (4-ounce) can green chilies

2 (14½-ounce) cans chicken broth

6 ounces shredded Monterey jack cheese (dairy or soy)

1. In a large stock pot, sauté onion and garlic in oil until tender.
2. Add chicken, white corn, cannellini beans, garbanzo beans, green chilies, and chicken broth to pot and simmer for 20–30 minutes or until heated through and beans are tender.
3. Top each serving with Monterey jack cheese.

One-Color Meals

This is an all-white chili, meaning all the ingredients that go into it are the color white. Try this as a way to excite your child about a meal, serve a one-color meal every once and awhile. For instance, an orange meal might be orange slices, mashed sweet potatoes, and cheddar macaroni and cheese with carrot coins.

Sweet Potato Fries

Timesaver tip: Purchase sweet potatoes already peeled and ready to cook.

1. Preheat oven to 450°F.

2. Bring a large pot of water to a boil. Place potatoes in boiling water and cook for 5 minutes. Drain and immediately plunge into bowl of ice water. Dry the potatoes well.

3. Combine egg whites and garlic powder.

4. Toss potatoes with egg white mixture and then dip potatoes in panko bread crumbs.

5. Line baking sheet with parchment paper, place the fries on it and bake for approximately 14 minutes.

6. Turn once, about 7 minutes into cooking.

Why So Many Steps for Sweet Potato Fries?
The moisture content of sweet potatoes is very high and often makes very soggy fries. The blanching, panko coating, and parchment paper all help to prevent soggy fries. One last tip: Make sure to not crowd the baking sheet with too many potatoes. If they are too close, they steam each other and then become soggy.

Yields 4 cups

INGREDIENTS:

4 sweet potatoes, peeled and cut into matchsticks

Large bowl of ice water

2 egg whites

⅛ teaspoon garlic powder

1 cup panko Italian-seasoned bread crumbs

Pinto Bean Burgers

Yields 4–6 burgers

INGREDIENTS:

1 (15-ounce) can of pinto beans (or 2 cups cooked)

½ medium green pepper

½ medium onion

2 garlic cloves

1 tablespoon plus 2 teaspoons olive oil, divided

1 tablespoon flaxseed meal

3 tablespoons water

½ cup bread crumbs

Serve these burgers on a whole-grain bun with a slice of cheese for a filling and nutritious meal.

1. Drain and rinse beans.

2. Mince green pepper, onion, and garlic.

3. In a medium skillet, heat 1 tablespoon olive oil over medium–high heat.

4. Add vegetables and sauté until soft, approximately 3–5 minutes.

5. Add beans, and heat through.

6. Transfer bean mixture into a large bowl.

7. Mash bean mixture with a potato masher or fork.

8. In a small bowl, combine flaxseed meal and water.

9. Combine bean mixture, flaxseed meal mixture, and bread crumbs.

10. Form mixture into patties.

11. Add 2 teaspoons olive oil to skillet. Heat over medium heat.

12. Cook patties, turning occasionally, until browned on both sides, approximately 3–4 minutes per side.

Secret Beef Burgers

No plum purée? A handful of fresh blueberries can also have the same effects on the ground beef and boost the nutrition content of the hamburgers.

1. Combine ground beef, baby food, flaxseed meal, and onions; mix lightly but thoroughly.

2. Shape loosely into 4 (½"-thick) patties. Season with sea salt and pepper to taste.

3. Cook patties immediately for best results. Heat large skillet about 2 minutes over medium heat until hot. Cook patties 10–12 minutes to desired doneness, turning once.

4. Serve burgers on whole-wheat buns with romaine or spinach lettuce, fresh tomatoes, and condiments, if desired.

Prunes in a Burger?

Adding prunes to your burgers may sound surprising, but prunes keep the meat very moist and add a very subtle sweet taste to the burger. Your children will not know that you are providing them a great source of antioxidants that can improve their learning by supplying the brain with needed nutrients.

Yields 4 burgers

INGREDIENTS:

1 pound 95-percent lean ground beef

3 tablespoons store-bought baby food plum purée

1 tablespoon ground flaxseed meal

⅓ cup onions, minced

Sea salt and pepper to taste

4 whole-wheat hamburger buns

Grilled Summer Vegetables

Yields 2½ cups

INGREDIENTS:

1 head broccoli, trimmed into florets

1 yellow summer squash, sliced

3 fresh ripe tomatoes, cut into wedges

1 red onion, sliced

½ cup Italian dressing

¼ teaspoon sea salt

Grill vegetables on the top rack of the grill. Don't choose vegetables with a high water content, like cucumbers. They will not grill well. Stick to heartier vegetables and fruits to grill.

1. Combine all ingredients.
2. Wrap in aluminum foil.
3. Place on top rack of hot grill for 5–7 minutes or until vegetables tender.
4. Remove from heat and transfer to serving bowl.

Asparagus & Swiss Cheese Quiche

Yields a 9" pie

INGREDIENTS:

1½ cups asparagus, trimmed and sliced into ¼" sections

1¾ cups grated Swiss cheese

4 eggs

1½ cups 2-percent milk

1 teaspoon salt

1 teaspoon paprika

½ teaspoon mustard

Any vegetables can be used in this recipe. It is also good with cooked breakfast meat. Make this with nitrate-free bacon and tomatoes or spinach and mushroom.

1. Preheat oven to 375°F.
2. Arrange sliced asparagus on bottom of pie pan.
3. Sprinkle Swiss cheese on top of asparagus.
4. In a small bowl, whisk eggs, milk, salt, paprika, and mustard together.
5. Pour over asparagus and cheese in pie pan. Bake for 30–40 minutes.

Lentil-Stuffed Green Peppers

*This vitamin C– and protein-packed entrée is a
crowd pleaser with family members of all ages.*

1. Preheat oven to 350°F.
2. Spread ⅓ of the pasta sauce in the bottom of 8" × 8" square pan.
3. Remove stems, seeds, and membranes from green peppers.
4. Stuff peppers with Lentils & Brown Rice mixture.
5. Top peppers with cheese.
6. Spread remainder of sauce over peppers.
7. Bake for 40 minutes.

Colorful Bell Peppers

Bell peppers are available in a rainbow of colors from green to red
to purple. All bell peppers start out green, then change color as they
mature. This change in color also indicates a sweeter bell pepper. They
make a sweet and colorful addition to salads, stir-fries, and sauces.

Yields 4 peppers

INGREDIENTS:

*2 cups pasta sauce
(jarred or homemade)*

4 green bell peppers

*1 recipe Lentils & Brown
Rice (page 142)*

*3 ounces mozzarella
cheese (dairy or soy)*

Baja-Style Fish Tacos

Yields 8 fish tacos

INGREDIENTS:

1 teaspoon canola oil

1 pound cod; cut into 2-ounce portions

3 limes, juiced, divided

¾ teaspoon sea salt, divided

½ cup light sour cream

½ cup vegenaise or mayonnaise

½ fresh jalapeño pepper, deseeded, halved, and deribbed

½ teaspoon dried oregano

½ teaspoon dried dill weed

¼ teaspoon ground cumin

¼ teaspoon cayenne

8 corn tortillas

½ medium head cabbage, finely shredded

½ medium head red cabbage, finely shredded

The spice in this dish can be increased by increasing the amount of jalapeño peppers or the cayenne pepper. This sauce is on the low end of the spice range for children.

1. Grease a shallow baking dish with 1 teaspoon canola oil. Arrange fish in dish.

2. Sprinkle fish with juice from 1 lime and ½ teaspoon sea salt. Cover with foil and bake at 400°F for 10–15 minutes. Remove from oven when done.

3. In a blender, combine ¼ teaspoon sea salt with sour cream, vegenaise, juice from the 2 remaining limes, jalapeño, oregano, dill weed, cumin, and cayenne to form sauce for tacos.

4. Heat corn tortillas lightly in skillet on stove, top with portion of cooked fish, drizzle with sauce, and place handful of both types of finely shredded cabbage on top. Serve.

How Hot Is Your Pepper?

The hotness of peppers is measured by the Scoville scale which was developed by Wilbur Scoville in 1912. The range goes from 0 Scoville units to 16,000,000 Scoville units. The bell pepper is a 0 and the habanero is a 200,000. The jalapeño in this recipe scores about 5,000.

Tofu-Stuffed Shells

Use either canned artichoke hearts that have been drained and rinsed or thawed, frozen artichoke hearts for this company-ready entrée.

1. Preheat oven to 350°F.

2. Dice onion, carrots, and zucchini. Set aside.

3. In a large saucepan or sauté pan, heat 1 tablespoon olive oil over medium–high heat.

4. Add carrots, onion, and garlic; sauté 3 minutes.

5. Add sauce and heat through, approximately 8–10 minutes. Set aside.

6. While sauce is cooking, bring 8 cups of water and 2 tablespoons olive oil to boil.

7. Add pasta; cook 10 minutes. Then drain pasta and rinse with cold water.

8. In a medium bowl, combine minced artichoke hearts, tofu, and nutritional yeast. Stir until crumbly.

9. Spread ½ pasta sauce in the bottom of a 9" × 13" pan.

10. Tuck filling inside each pasta shell.

11. Place filled shells on top of sauce.

12. Top with remaining sauce.

13. Bake uncovered for 30 minutes.

Yields 9" x 13" pan

INGREDIENTS:

½ onion, diced

3 medium carrots, peeled and diced

1 medium zucchini, grated

3 tablespoons olive oil, divided

2 garlic cloves, minced

3 cups of pasta sauce (homemade or jarred)

12-ounce box of large pasta shells

4 artichoke hearts, minced

16 ounces firm tofu

1 tablespoon nutritional yeast

Herbed Broccoli

Yields 2½ cups

INGREDIENTS:

1 large head of broccoli

¼ cup vegetable broth

¼ teaspoon basil, dried

¼ teaspoon oregano, dried

⅛ teaspoon thyme, dried

⅛ teaspoon savory, dried

Save the stalks from the broccoli and use them to make vegetable broth.

1. Cut bite-sized florets from the head of broccoli.
2. Toss florets with broth and herbs.
3. Steam in microwave 3 minutes or in a steamer basket until desired tenderness.

Making the Most of Seasonal Vegetables

Whether buying vegetables from the grocery store, farmers' market, or CSA, it's best to buy what is in season.

Guacamole

Yields 2 cups

INGREDIENTS:

2 avocados

½ medium onion

1 medium tomato

2 tablespoons cilantro

1 serrano pepper

1 tablespoon lime juice

Omit the serrano pepper for a more mild guacamole.

1. Slice open avocados, remove pit, and scrape out flesh. Mash avocado flesh with a potato masher or fork.
2. Finely chop onion, tomato, and cilantro.
3. Remove seeds from serrano pepper and finely mince.
4. Mix all ingredients.

Thank You, Aztec Civilization

Guacamole was invented by the Aztec people. It is believed that the higher-fat content of the avocado was an important part of the otherwise relatively low-fat Aztec diet. The mash that we know of today is surprisingly similar to what the Aztecs savored in their day.

Corn Cakes with Black Bean Salsa

*Serve each of these cornmeal pancakes with a dollop of the
black bean salsa for a fun, breakfast-style dinner.*

1. In a medium bowl, combine cornmeal and flour.

2. In a separate bowl, mix flaxseed meal with water. Add room-temperature soup and milk and stir to combine.

3. Slowly mix dry ingredients into wet.

4. Melt 1 teaspoon butter or trans fat–free margarine in a skillet or griddle.

5. Drop batter onto hot pan to form approximately 2" pancakes.

6. When the edges firm up, flip pancake and continue cooking on the other side.

7. While pancakes are cooking, combine salsa and drained and rinsed black beans.

8. Top each pancake with salsa and bean mixture.

Save Those Jars

Organic jarred salsa is good and can be good for the environment in more ways than one. First, as previously mentioned, organic produce means fewer toxins on the plants, in the ground, and in the water. An added bonus is the great storage container that you get when you buy a jar of salsa. The size and shape is perfect for reusing as a food-storage container. Applesauce and pasta sauce jars also hold leftover soup, sauce, smoothies, and more. Reduce, reuse, and recycle has never been tastier!

Yields 6 small pancakes

INGREDIENTS:

¼ cup cornmeal

½ cup white whole-wheat flour

1 tablespoon flaxseed meal

2 tablespoons water

½ cup creamy corn soup

¼ cup milk (dairy or soy)

2 teaspoons butter or trans fat–free margarine

1 cup mild salsa

¼ cup cooked black beans

Spinach- & Ricotta-Stuffed Shells

These stuffed shells are great paired with the Green Salad with Mock Caesar Dressing on page 198 and followed with the Blueberry Sorbet on page 232.

...on page 198 and followed with the Blueberry Sorbet on page 232.

Yields 9" × 13" baking dish

INGREDIENTS:

1 pound whole-wheat jumbo shell pasta

2 pounds spinach

1¼ cup ricotta cheese

2 egg yolks

¾ cup Parmesan cheese

Pinch nutmeg

⅛ teaspoon salt

⅛ teaspoon pepper

1 (26-ounce) jar marinara sauce

1. Preheat oven to 350°F.

2. Bring large pot of water to a boil. Cook jumbo shells until al dente and remove, drain.

3. Steam spinach, drain, and chop.

4. Using hand mixer, combine ricotta, egg yolks, cheese, nutmeg, salt, and pepper.

5. Using washed hands, combine spinach into mixture.

6. Fill shells with above mixture. Lay in baking dish. Top with marinara sauce.

7. Bake for 30–45 minutes.

Timesaver Tip

In order to make filling the shells easier, put the ricotta cheese and spinach mixture in a gallon-size plastic bag. Cut off lower edge of bag on a diagonal and squeeze mixture into shells. This technique can be used for filling cannelloni pasta or any stuffed pasta dish.

Vegetable Lasagna

A lasagna this hearty is often the only course of a family meal. Follow this with a Lemon Raspberry Ice Pop found on page 232 for a refreshing end to the meal.

1. Preheat oven to 350°F.

2. In a large saucepan, heat oil and garlic until clear.

3. Add onion, broccoli, carrots, red peppers, and zucchini, and cook until tender. Remove from heat and set aside.

4. In a large bowl, beat eggs, ricotta, salt, and ¼ cup Parmesan cheese.

5. Lightly grease a 9" × 13" baking dish. Put small amount of marinara sauce on bottom.

6. Layer uncooked noodles, ricotta cheese mixture, mozzarella cheese, and vegetable mixture. Repeat layers to top of baking dish.

7. Sprinkle top with remaining ½ cup Parmesan cheese and Italian seasoning.

8. Cover and bake for about 1 hour or until noodles are tender.

Yields 9" × 13" baking dish

INGREDIENTS:

1 tablespoon canola oil

2 cloves garlic

½ red onion, chopped

2 heads broccoli, chopped

2 carrots, peeled and diced

2 red peppers, chopped

2 small zucchini, chopped

2 eggs

1 (15-ounce) container of ricotta cheese

½ teaspoon salt

¾ cup Parmesan cheese, divided

1 quart prepared marinara sauce

½ pound lasagna noodles, uncooked

½ pound mozzarella cheese, sliced

3 tablespoons Italian seasoning

Baked Tortilla Chips

Yields 40 chips

INGREDIENTS:

5 corn tortillas

Sprinkle of sea salt

⅛ cup canola oil put into spray pump

Use whole-wheat tortillas instead of corn for an interesting variation.

1. Preheat oven to 350°F.
2. Cut tortillas into 8 wedges each.
3. Spray a large cookie sheet with canola oil.
4. Spread tortilla wedges on a cookie sheet in a single layer.
5. Spray tops of tortilla wedges with oil and sprinkle with salt.
6. Bake 13–15 minutes until golden and crispy.

Some Snacking Ideas

Not every morsel that goes into your baby's mouth is likely to be home-made. There are some great organic snacks that can make being out and about with your baby a little easier. Here are some ideas: fruit cups, pretzels, dry cereal, and applesauce cups.

Roasted Red Pepper Hummus

Using jarred red peppers adds vitamin C and convenience.

1. If using canned garbanzo beans, drain and rinse beans.

2. Combine all ingredients in a food processor or blender.

3. Process until smooth.

How to Roast a Red Pepper

An easy way to roast a red pepper is to broil a whole red pepper until the skin starts to blister and blacken, approximately 5 minutes. Remove pepper from the oven and place in a closed paper bag, until the skin loosens from the pepper (approximately 5 minutes). Remove pepper from the bag, then remove the skin by sliding it from the pepper with either your fingers or a knife. Slice and remove seeds and membranes.

Yields 2¼ cups

INGREDIENTS:

2 cups cooked garbanzo beans (homemade or canned)

1 tablespoon tahini

¼ cup roasted red peppers

2 teaspoons lemon juice

3 tablespoons olive oil

1 clove garlic

¼ teaspoon cumin

⅛ teaspoon salt

Blueberry Sorbet

Yields 2¼ cups

This all-fruit sorbet is a great way to provide vitamin C in a fun way.

INGREDIENTS:

1½ cups blueberries
½ cup lemonade
2 tablespoons apple juice concentrate

1. Combine all ingredients in a blender. Blend all ingredients until smooth.
2. Pour into a freezer-safe container.
3. Freeze for 2 hours, then fluff with a fork.
4. Return to freezer.
5. Continue fluffing every 1½–2 hours until serving.

Lemon Raspberry Ice Pops

Yields 3 ice pops

Vitamin C takes a refreshing turn in this sweet treat.

INGREDIENTS:

½ cup lemonade
½ cup raspberry purée

1. Combine lemonade and raspberry purée.
2. Pour into a clean, empty ice cube tray.
3. Cover ice cube tray with aluminum foil or plastic wrap.
4. Poke a craft stick through a slit in each of the filled ice cube spots.
5. Freeze until solid, and remove foil or plastic wrap.
6. If it is difficult to get the pops out of the tray, run the bottom of the ice-cube tray under warm water to loosen.

Avocado Yogurt Dip

This sweet and creamy dip can also be used as a dressing for a green salad.

1. Mash avocado.
2. Add remaining ingredients.
3. Stir until smooth.

Yields 1 cup

INGREDIENTS:

½ ripe avocado

¼ cup plain yogurt

1 teaspoon agave nectar

2 tablespoons orange juice

Hot Chocolate

Add an ice cube or two to make hot chocolate "not quite so hot" for tender mouths.

1. In an empty coffee cup, combine agave nectar, cocoa, and vanilla.
2. In a small saucepan, heat milk until hot, but not boiling.
3. Add warm milk to chocolate mixture.
4. Stir thoroughly.

Yields 1 cup

INGREDIENTS:

1 tablespoon agave nectar

2 teaspoons cocoa

½ teaspoon vanilla

1 cup milk (dairy or soy)

Appendix A

Weekly Organic Menus for Each Age Group

Four to Six Months Menus

Breast milk or Formula: 24 to 32 ounces per day

Day 1 to 4

Baby's First Rice Cereal
***Watch for signs of allergies for 4 to 7 days and then introduce a new food.

Day 5 to 8

Baby's First Rice Cereal
Apple Purée
***Watch for signs of allergies for 4 to 7 days and then introduce a new food.

Day 8 to 12

Baby's First Rice Cereal mixed with Apple Purée
Apricot Purée
***Watch for signs of allergies for 4 to 7 days and then introduce a new food.

Six to Nine Months Menus

Always introduce new foods separately to watch for signs of allergies. Once your baby has shown no reaction to the foods alone, you can introduce mixtures of foods.

Every Day

Breast Milk or Formula: 24 to 32 ounces per day
Iron-Fortified Infant Cereal: ¼ cup per day

Monday

Rice Cereal
Black Bean Mash
Apricot Pear Purée

Tuesday

Rice Cereal
Pumpkin Peach Oatmeal Cereal
Spinach & Potato Purée

Wednesday

Rice Cereal
Potato & Plum Purée
Peach & Raspberry Purée

Six to Nine Months Menus
(continued)

Thursday

Rice Cereal
Sweet Potato & Carrot Purée
Chicken Purée & Parsnip

Friday

Rice Cereal
Refried Pinto Beans
Fall Harvest Purée

Saturday

Rice Cereal
Apple & Carrot Mash
Chicken, Papaya, & Nutmeg Mash

Sunday

Rice Cereal
Rutabaga & Pear Purée
Beef & Barley

Nine to Twelve Months Menus

Every Day

Breast Milk or Formula: 24 to 32 ounces per day

Monday

Blueberry Mini Muffins
Lentil Soup
Quinoa and Tofu Bites

Tuesday

Yogurt Berry Parfait
Organic Farmer's Pie
Whole-Wheat Shells with Marinara Sauce

Wednesday

Oatmeal with Sautéed Plantains
Chickpea, Carrot, & Cauliflower Mash
Turkey Chili

Thursday

Whole-Grain Waffles with Blueberry Syrup
Split Pea Curry
Roast Lamb, Rice, & Tomato Compote

Nine to Twelve Months Menus
(continued)

Friday

Oatmeal with Cinnamon Apples
Cauliflower & Potato Mash
Couscous with Grated Zucchini & Carrots
Hummus

Saturday

Zucchini Corn Muffins
Lentils with Spinach & Quinoa
Black Bean & Carrot Mash and Mango & Brown Rice

Sunday

Banana Bread
Chicken Vegetable Soup
Vegetable Barley Casserole and Mashed Sweet Potatoes

Twelve to Eighteen Months Menus

Every Day

Whole Milk (dairy or soy): 16 ounces per day
Typical Pattern: 3 meals plus 1 to 3 snacks

Monday

Zucchini Corn Muffins with scrambled eggs
Creamy Pasta Salad
Lentils & Brown Rice
Snack: Mangosteen Cereal Mix

Tuesday

Maple Barley Breakfast with whole milk (dairy or soy)
Broccoli Cheese Soup and whole-wheat crackers
Baked Honey Pescado with Lemony Rice & Asparagus Salad
Snack: Fruit Kabobs

Wednesday

French Toast with side of fresh fruit
Easy Baked Chicken and Honeyed Carrots
Broccoli with Meat & Rigatoni
Snack: Tropical Pudding Pie Dip with organic vanilla wafers or fresh fruit

Twelve to Eighteen Months Menus
(continued)

Thursday

Spicy Pumpkin Muffins and 6 ounces yogurt (dairy or soy)
Chicken Salad and whole-wheat crackers
Spaghetti Squash with Italian Herbs
Snack: Take Along Cereal Snack

Friday

Cantaloupe Papaya Smoothie
Chicken Pot Pie
Macaroni and Cheese with side of steamed broccoli
Snack: Creamy Salsa Dip with blue corn tortilla chips

Saturday

Blueberry Pancakes
Mushroom Barley Casserole
Vegetable Tofu Pot Pie and Creamy Cauliflower Soup
Snack: Pink Milk

Sunday

Spinach Tomato Scramble with slice whole wheat toast
Roasted Potato Salad and Turkey Divan Muffins
Caribbean Baked Risotto
Snack: Vanilla & Raspberry Sorbet

Eighteen to Twenty-Four Months Menus

Every Day

Whole Milk (dairy or soy): 16 ounces per day
Typical Pattern: 3 meals plus 1 to 3 snacks

Monday

Breakfast Burrito
Pumpkin Risotto
Hummus & Mango Sandwich with side of Cucumber Tomato Salad
Snack: Green Boats

Tuesday

Blueberry & Banana Yogurt with Crispy Rice
Bean & Avocado Quesadilla
Barbecue Meatloaf Muffins and Frosted Cauliflower
Snack: Caribbean Dream Boat

Wednesday

Mixed Berry Yogurt Smoothie
Grilled Cheese Squares with Butternut Squash and Corn Purée with side of steamed peas
Tabouli Salad and Hummus Yogurt Dipping Sauce with Pita Chips
Snack: Yogurt Applesauce Dip

Eighteen to Twenty-Four Months Menus
(continued)

Thursday

Sweet Potato Biscuits and vegetarian sausage
Taco Dinner
Chicken & Udon Noodles with Roasted Carrots
Snack: Limeade Sorbet

Friday

Sunflower Seed Butter & Banana Smoothie
Mixed Vegetable Stir-Fry and brown rice
BBQ Chicken Pizza
Snack: Eggy Boats

Saturday

Cherry Apple Coconut Rice Pudding
Cheesy Polenta with Roasted Vegetables
Quinoa Primavera with grilled chicken or tofu
Snack: Chocolate Pomegranate Dip with fresh berries

Sunday

Raspberry Strawberry Muffins and 6 ounces yogurt
Mango Cole Slaw and Pinto Bean Roll-Ups
Black Bean Cakes with Pineapple Salsa
Snack: Strawberry Shortcake

Twenty-Four to Thirty-Six Months Menus

Every Day

1-percent or 2-percent milk (dairy or soy): 16 ounces per day
Typical Pattern: 3 meals plus 1 to 3 snacks

Monday

Vanilla Maple Rice Pudding
English Muffin Pizza
Asparagus & Swiss Cheese Quiche
Snack: Apple Pear Crisp

Tuesday

Whole-Grain English Muffin with Cinnamon Butter
Lentil-Stuffed Green Peppers with Carrot Pineapple Salad
Spinach & Ricotta-Stuffed Shells with Green Salad with Mock Caesar Dressing
Snack: Fruit Salad and Oatmeal Cookies

Wednesday

Coconut Chocolate Chip Muffins
Quesadilla with Tomato & Avocado with Easy Spanish Rice
Shepherd's Pie
Snack: Blueberry Sorbet

Twenty-Four to Thirty-Six Months Menus
(continued)

Thursday

Tropical Smoothie
Burritos
Pinto Bean Burgers or Secret Beef Burgers with Sweet Potato Fries
Snack: Lemon Raspberry Ice Pop

Friday

Whole-wheat waffles with Strawberry Syrup
Turkey Cheese Roll-Up
Spinach Lasagna
Snack: Avocado Yogurt Dip with Baked Tortilla Chips

Saturday

Breakfast Pizza
Baja Style Fish Taco
Beef Brochettes or Mixed Vegetable Kabobs with Corn on the Cob with Herbed Butter
Snack: Sunflower Seed Butter Cookies and milk (dairy or soy)

Sunday

Moist Yogurt Pancakes
Minestrone Soup with Veggie Roll-Ups
White Chili with Corn Muffins
Snack: Hot Chocolate and Citrus Fruit Salad

Appendix B

Resources for More Information

Organic food is becoming more readily available. Most large grocery stores, including Target and Wal-Mart, now carry some organic options. The Internet is also a great resource for learning more about organics, finding farmer's markets and CSAs, and connecting with other people who are interested in pursuing an organic lifestyle.

Organic Information

The National Organic Program
www.ams.usda.gov/NOP

The Organic Trade Association
www.ota.com

The Organic Trade Association's O'Mama Report
www.theorganicreport.com

The Environmental Working Group
www.foodnews.org

Organic Consumers Association
www.organicconsumers.org

Farmers' Market and Organic Store Finder

Organic.org
www.organic.org

The Alternative Farming Systems Information Center
http://afsic.nal.usda.gov

National Sustainable Agriculture Information Service
http://attra.ncat.org/attra-pub/localfood_dir.php

Pick Your Own Fruits and Vegetables
www.pickyourown.org

Nutrition and Medical Information

Breastfeeding support through La Leche League
www.llli.org

Books about Child Nutrition by Ellyn Satter
www.ellynsatter.com

American Academy of Pediatrics
www.aap.org

Food Allergy and Anaphylaxis Network
www.foodallergy.org

Handbook of Pediatric Nutrition, 2005, Jones and Bartlett Publishers, Inc.

These are just a few ideas to get you started in learning about how to best provide a balanced, organic diet for your baby and toddler. Other resources include your local chamber of commerce, local hospital, parent support groups, and your local health-food store or grocery store. Once you start looking, you'll see that information on organics is all around you!

Appendix C

Nutritional Information for Common Baby Foods

The number of calories that a baby or toddler needs to stay healthy depends on your child's individual metabolism, how active she is, and how quickly she is growing. In general, you can figure out how many calories per day your child should be eating based on either her weight (for less than 12 months) or her height (for ages 1–3 years).

For infants, the basic calorie requirement is about 50 calories per pound. Of course, if your baby is growing particularly fast, he might need more food—some babies need as few as 35 calories per pound or as many as 75 calories per pound. As long as his height and weight are increasing and are following his particular curve on a growth chart, you don't need to worry. Remember that breast milk or iron-fortified formula will remain your child's primary source of nutrition in his first year—solid foods are just a supplement.

The phenomenal growth of your baby's first year will slow down once she hits the toddler years, and her calorie requirements also begin to slow down. The average toddler needs about 40 calories per day for every inch of height. In addition to calories, your child will also need the required amounts of other vitamins and minerals to stay healthy. Providing a multi-vitamin is certainly an option, but most vitamins are absorbed best from natural sources. The following list details the vitamins and other nutrients found in a number of fruits, vegetables, and other foods liked by many babies. Experiment and find your child's favorites!

Acorn Squash

Typical serving size . . . . ½ cup
Calories 75
Potassium . . . . 450 mg
Vitamin A . . . . 450 IU
Vitamin C . . . . 12 mg
Dietary Fiber. . . . . .3.2 g

Apples

Typical serving size . . . . ½ medium
Calories 50
Potassium . . . . 79 mg
Vitamin A . . . . 37 IU
Vitamin C . . . . 3 mg
Dietary Fiber . . . . .1.7 g

Avocados

Typical serving size . . . . ¼ cup
Calories 60
Potassium . . . . .110 mg
Vitamin A . . . . 25 IU
Vitamin C . . . . 1 mg
Dietary Fiber . . . . .1.8 g

Brown Rice

Serving size . . . . ⅛ cup dry
Calories 85
Potassium . . . . 50 mg
Vitamin A 0
Vitamin C 0
Dietary Fiber . . . . 1 g

Carrots

Typical serving size . . . . ¼ cup cooked
Calories 15
Potassium . . . . .115 mg
Vitamin A . . . . 7350 IU
Vitamin C . . . . 6 mg
Dietary Fiber . . . . .1.5 g

Corn

Typical serving size . . . . ¼ cup
Calories 45
Potassium . . . . .115 mg
Vitamin A . . . . 1 IU
Vitamin C . . . . 3 mg
Dietary Fiber . . . . .1.1 g

Green Beans

Typical serving size . . . . ¼ cup cooked
Calories 12
Potassium . . . . 65 mg
Vitamin A . . . . 200 IU
Vitamin C . . . . 3 mg
Dietary Fiber . . . . 1 g

Oatmeal

Typical serving size . . . . ¼ cup dry
Calories 60
Potassium . . . . 50 mg
Vitamin A 0
Vitamin C 0
Dietary Fiber . . . . 1 g

Pasta, Enriched

Typical serving size . . . . ⅛ cup dry
Calories 55
Potassium 0
Vitamin A 0
Vitamin C 0
Dietary Fiber . . . . .0.5 g

Peaches

Typical serving size . . . . ½ medium
Calories 25
Potassium . . . . 94 mg
Vitamin A . . . . 100 IU
Vitamin C . . . . 4 mg
Dietary Fiber . . . . .1 g

Pearl Barley

Typical serving size . . . . ⅛ cup dry
Calories 90
Potassium . . . . 36 mg
Vitamin A 0
Vitamin C 0
Dietary Fiber . . . . 4 g

Pears

Typical serving size . . . . ½ medium
Calories 48
Potassium . . . . 100 mg
Vitamin A . . . . 23 IU
Vitamin C . . . . 3 mg
Dietary Fiber . . . . .2.5 g

Peas

Typical serving size . . . . ¼ cup cooked
Calories 11
Potassium . . . . 45 mg
Vitamin A . . . . 500 IU
Vitamin C . . . . 21 mg
Dietary Fiber . . . . .1.3 g

Plums

Typical serving size . . . . ½ medium
Calories 20
Potassium . . . . 90 mg
Vitamin A . . . . 350 IU
Vitamin C . . . . 4 mg
Dietary Fiber . . . . 1 g

Spinach

Typical serving size . . . . ¼ cup
Calories 12
Potassium . . . . 248 mg
Vitamin A . . . . 4710 IU
Vitamin C . . . . 4 mg
Dietary Fiber . . . . 1.1 g

Sweet Potatoes

Typical serving size . . . . ¼ cup
Calories 45
Potassium . . . . 190 mg
Vitamin A . . . . 8100 IU
Vitamin C . . . . 6.1 mg
Dietary Fiber . . . . 1.8 g

Appendix D

Glossary of Basic Cooking Terms

Active dry yeast

This is a small plant that has been preserved by drying. When rehydrated, the yeast activates and begins producing carbon dioxide and alcohols.

Al dente

A term used in Italian cooking that refers to the texture of cooked pasta. When cooked "al dente," the pasta is tender, but still firm in the middle. The term literally means "to the tooth."

Bake

To cook in dry heat, usually in an oven, until proteins denature, starches gelatinize, and water evaporates to form a structure.

Beat

To combine two mixtures and to incorporate air by manipulating with a spoon or an electric mixer until fluffy.

Blanch

Blanching is a means of cooking food by immersing it in boiling water. After blanching, the cooked food is immediately placed in cold water to stop the cooking process. Always drain blanched foods thoroughly before adding to a dish.

Butter

A natural fat obtained by churning heavy cream to consolidate and remove some of the butterfat.

Calorie

A unit of measurement in nutrition, a calorie is the amount of energy needed to raise the temperature of 1 gram of water by 1 degree Celsius. The number of calories in a food is measured by chemically analyzing the food.

Cholesterol

Cholesterol is not a fat, but a sterol, an alcohol and fatty acid, a soft, waxy substance used by your body to make hormones. Your body makes cholesterol and you eat foods containing cholesterol. Only animal fats have cholesterol.

Chop

Chopping consists of cutting food into small pieces. While chopped food doesn't need to be perfectly uniform, the pieces should be roughly the same size.

Confectioner's sugar

This sugar is finely ground and mixed with cornstarch to prevent lumping; it is used mostly in icings and frostings. It is also known as powdered sugar and 10X sugar.

Corn oil

An oil obtained from the germ of the corn kernel. It has a high smoke point and contains a small amount of artificial trans fat.

Cornmeal

Coarsely ground corn, used to make polenta, also to coat foods to make a crisp crust.

Cornstarch

Very finely ground powder made from the starch in the endosperm of corn; used as a thickener.

Deep-fry

To fry in a large amount of oil or melted shortening, lard, or butter so the food is completely covered. In this dry-heat method of cooking, about 10 percent of the fat is absorbed into the food.

Dice

Dicing consists of cutting food into small cubes, usually ¼ inch in size or less. Unlike chopping, the food should be cut into even-sized pieces.

Dissolve

To immerse a solid in a liquid and heat or manipulate to form a solution in which none of the solid remains.

Drain

Draining consists of drawing off the liquid from a food. Either a colander (a perforated bowl made of metal or plastic) or paper towels can be used to drain food.

Dredge

To dip a food into another mixture, usually made of flour, bread crumbs, or cheese, to completely coat.

Edamame

The word for edible soybeans, a green pea encased in a pod.

Emulsify

To combine an oil and a liquid, either through manipulation or the addition of another ingredient, so they remain suspended in each other.

Fatty acids

A fatty acid is a long chain of carbon molecules bonded to each other and to hydrogen molecules, attached to an alcohol or glycerol molecule. They are short-chain, medium-chain, and long-chain, always with an even number of carbon molecules.

Flaky

A word describing food texture, usually a pie crust or crust on meat, which breaks apart into flat layers.

Flax seed

This small oil-rich seed is used primarily to make linseed oil, but is also a valuable source of nutrients like calcium, iron, and omega-3 fatty acids.

Fry

To cook food in hot oil, a dry heat environment.

Gluten

A protein in flour made by combining glutenin and gliadin with a liquid and physical manipulation.

Golden

The color of food when it is browned or quickly sautéed.

HDL

High-density lipoproteins, the "good" type of cholesterol that carries fat away from the bloodstream.

Herbs

The aromatic leafy part of an edible plant; herbs include basil, parsley, chives, thyme, tarragon, oregano, and mint.

Hummus

A combination of puréed chickpeas with garlic, lemon juice, and usually tahini; used as an appetizer or sandwich spread.

Hydrogenation

The process of adding hydrogen molecules to carbon chains in fats and fatty acids.

Italian salad dressing

A dressing made of olive oil and vinegar or lemon juice, combined into an emulsion, usually with herbs like basil, oregano, and thyme.

Jelly

A congealed mixture made from fruit juice, sugar, and pectin.

Julienne

To julienne food (also called matchstick cutting) consists of cutting it into very thin strips about 1½–2 inches long, with a width and thickness of about ⅛ inch. Both meat and vegetables can be julienned.

Kebab

Meats, fruits, and/or vegetables threaded onto skewers, usually barbecued over a wood or coal fire.

Kidney bean

A legume, either white or dark red, used for making chili and soups.

Knead

To manipulate a dough, usually a bread dough, to help develop the gluten in the flour so the bread has the proper texture.

Lard

The fat from pork, used to fry foods and as a substitute for margarine or butter.

LDL

Low-density lipoproteins, the "bad" cholesterol, which carries fat from the liver and intestines to the bloodstream.

Lecithin

A fatty substance that is a natural emulsifier, found in eggs and legumes.

Lipid

Lipids are organic molecules insoluble in water, consisting of a chain of hydrophobic carbon and hydrogen molecules and an alcohol or glycerol molecule. They include fats, oil, waxes, steroids, and cholesterol.

Long-chain fatty acids

These fatty acids have 12 to 24 carbon molecules bonded to hydrogen molecules and to a glycerol molecule.

Margarine

A fat made by hydrogenating polyunsaturated oils, colored with yellow food coloring to resemble butter.

Marinate

To coat foods in an acidic liquid or dry mixture to help break down protein bonds and tenderize the food.

Mayonnaise

An emulsification of egg yolks, lemon juice or vinegar, and oil, blended into a thick white creamy dressing.

Meat thermometer

A thermometer specially labeled to read the internal temperature of meat.

Medium-chain fatty acids

These fatty acids have 6 to 12 carbon molecules bonded to each other and to hydrogen molecules. Coconut and palm oils contain these fatty acids and they are used in infant formulas.

Mince

Mincing consists of cutting food into very small pieces. In general, minced food is cut into smaller pieces than chopped food.

Monounsaturated oil

A fatty acid that has two carbons double-bonded to each other, missing two hydrogen molecules. These very stable oils are good for frying, but can have low smoke points. Examples include olive, almond, avocado, canola, and peanut oils.

Mortar and pestle

A mortar is a bowl-shaped tool, sometimes made of stone or marble, and a pestle is the round instrument used to grind ingredients in the mortar.

Mouthfeel

A food science term that describes the action of food in the mouth; descriptors range from gummy to dry to slippery to smooth to chewy to tender.

Nuts

The edible fruit of some trees, consisting of a kernel in a hard shell. Most edible nuts are actually seeds and are a good source of monounsaturated fats.

Omega-3 fatty acids

A polyunsaturated fat named for the position of the first double bond. The body cannot make Omega-3 fatty acids; they must be consumed.

Omega-6 fatty acids

A polyunsaturated fat name for the position of the first double bond. Too much of this fatty acid in the body can cause heart disease. Like HDL with LDL cholesterol, works in concert with Omega-3 fatty acids.

Organic food

Food that has been grown and processed without pesticides, herbicides, insecticides, fertilizers, artificial coloring, artificial flavoring, or additives.

Pan-fry

To quickly fry in a small amount of oil in a saucepan or skillet.

Polyunsaturated oil

A fatty acid that has more than two carbon molecules double-bonded to each other; it is missing at least four hydrogen molecules. Examples include corn, soybean, safflower, and sunflower oils.

Processed food

Any food that has been manipulated by chemicals or otherwise treated, such as frozen food, canned food, enriched foods, and dehydrated foods.

Rancid

Fats can become rancid over time and through exposure to oxygen. The fats oxidize, or break down, and free radicals form, which then exacerbate the process. Rancid fats smell and taste unpleasant.

Reduction

Quickly boiling or simmering liquid to evaporate the water and concentrate the flavor.

Risotto

An Italian rice dish made by slowly cooking rice in broth, stirring to help release starch that thickens the mixture.

Roast

To cook food at relatively high heat in an oven. This is a dry-cooking method, usually used for vegetables and meats.

Roux

A mixture of flour and oil or fat, cooked until the starches in the flour can absorb liquid. It is used to thicken sauces, from white sauce to gumbo.

Saturated fat

A fatty acid that has no double-bonded carbons, but has all the carbons bonded to hydrogen molecules. Butter, coconut oil, and palm oil are all high in saturated fats.

Sauté

To quickly cook food in a small amount of fat over relatively high heat.

Sear

Searing meat consists of quickly browning it over high heat before finishing cooking it by another method. Searing meat browns the surface and seals in the juices.

Season

To change the flavor of food by adding ingredients like salt, pepper, herbs, and spices.

Short-chain fatty acid

A fat that contains 2 to 6 carbon molecules; examples include lauric and octanoic acids.

Shortening

A partially hydrogenated oil that is solid at room temperature, used to make everything from frostings to cakes to pastries and breads.

Shred

Shredding food consists of cutting it into thin strips that are usually thicker than a julienne cut. Meat, poultry, cabbage, lettuce, and cheese can all be shredded.

Simmer

Simmering food consists of cooking it in liquid at a temperature just below the boiling point.

Smoke point

The temperature at which fats begin to break down under heat. The higher the smoke point, the more stable the fat will be while frying and cooking. Butter's smoke point is 350°F, olive oil 375°F, and refined oils around 440°F.

Spices

Aromatic seasonings from seeds, bark, roots, and stems of edible plants. Spices include cinnamon, cumin, turmeric, ginger, and pepper, among others.

Trans

Latin word means "across," referring to the positioning of the hydrogen molecules on the carbon chain of a fatty acid.

Trans fat

A specific form of fatty acid, where hydrogen molecules are positioned across from each other, in the "trans" position, as opposed to the "cis" position.

Tropical oils

Oils from plants grown in the tropic region; the most common are coconut oil and palm oil. These oils are usually fully saturated and are solid at room temperature.

Unsalted butter

Sometimes known as "sweet butter," this is butter that contains no salt or sodium chloride. It's used for greasing pans, since salt in butter will make batter or dough stick.

Unsaturated fat

Fatty acids that have two more carbon molecules double-bonded to each other; an unsaturated fat is missing at least two hydrogen molecules.

Vanilla

The highly aromatic seeds contained in a long pod, or fruit, of the vanilla plant, a member of the orchid family.

Vegetable oil

Oils made by pressing or chemically extracting lipids from a vegetable source, whether seeds, nuts, or fruits of a plant.

Vitamins

Vitamins are molecules that are used to promote and facilitate chemical reactions in the body. Most vitamins must be ingested as your body cannot make them.

Index

Note: Page numbers in **bold** indicate itemized recipe lists,
and page numbers in *italics* indicate menus.

Age groups
  4 to 6 months, 18, **31**–54, *236*
  9 to 12 months, 19, **83**–117, *239–40*
  12 to 18 months, 20, **119**–52, *241–42*
  18 to 24 months, 20–21, **153**–94,
    243–44
  24 to 36 months, 20–21, **195**–233,
    245–46
Allergy prevention, 23–24
Apples
  about: apple juice, 44; applesauce for
    baking, 64; frozen apple pops, 35;
    locally grown, 43; nutritional value
    of, 253; organic jarred applesauce,
    46
  Apple, Pumpkin, & Barley Cereal, 46
  Apple, Sweet Potato, & Cinnamon
    Purée, 62
  Apple & Banana Oatmeal Cereal, 75
  Apple & Carrot Mash, 64
  Apple & Oatmeal Cereal, 43
  Apple & Pear Purée, 61
  Apple & Plum Compote, 70
  Apple & Sweet Potato Mini Muffins,
    90
  Apple Pear Crisp, 203
  Apple Purée, 35
  Apple-Roasted Carrots, 112
  Apricot & Apple Purée, 70
  Butternut Squash with Apples &
    Pears, 71
  Cherry Apple Coconut Rice Pudding,
    164
  Fall Harvest Purée, 63
  Homemade Applesauce, 64

Minced Pork Chop with Applesauce,
    81
  Oatmeal with Cinnamon Apples, 91
  Papaya, Apple, & Oatmeal Cereal, 44
  Pinto Beans, Apples, & Barley, 76
  Strawberry Applesauce, 115
  Sweet Pea & Apple Purée, 49
  Take-Along Cereal Snack, 149
  Yogurt Applesauce Dip, 191
Apricots
  about: vitamin A in, 38
  Apricot, Dried Plum, & Barley Cereal,
    46
  Apricot, Pear, & Barley Cereal, 61
  Apricot & Apple Purée, 70
  Apricot & Banana Mash, 69
  Apricot Pear Purée, 48
  Apricot Purée, 38
  Banana, Apricot, & Oatmeal Cereal,
    42
  Mango & Apricot Purée, 50
Asparagus
  about, 125
  Asparagus & Swiss Cheese Quiche,
    222
  Cheesy Polenta with Roasted
    Vegetables, 178
  Lemony Rice & Asparagus Salad, 125
Avocados
  about: nutritional value of, 253;
    ripeness of, 109; storing, 35
  Avocado & Barley Cereal, 45
  Avocado & Black Beans, 73
  Avocado Banana Mash, 47
  Avocado Mash, 35

Avocado Pumpkin Mash, 50
  Avocado Summer Salad, 197
  Avocado Yogurt Dip, 233
  Bean & Avocado Quesadilla, 176
  Green Beans & Avocado Mash, 53
  Guacamole, 226
  Peach & Avocado Mash, 49
  Tofu Avocado Spread, 109

Bananas
  about: freezing purée, 66; plantains
    vs., 94; ripening, 47
  Apple & Banana Oatmeal Cereal, 75
  Apricot & Banana Mash, 69
  Avocado Banana Mash, 47
  Banana, Apricot, & Oatmeal Cereal,
    42
  Banana, Sweet Pea, & Rice Cereal,
    41
  Banana & Blueberry Purée, 62
  Banana & Oatmeal Cereal, 42
  Banana Bread, 89
  Banana Mash, 36
  Banana Pumpkin Mash, 52
  Banana Yogurt Milkshake, 133
  Barley with Bananas & Blueberries,
    161
  Blueberry & Banana Yogurt, 163
  Chicken, Banana, & Coconut, 78
  Mango Banana Purée, 65
  Oatmeal with Sautéed Plantains, 94
  Papaya & Banana Mash, 48, 66
  Strawberry, Blueberry, & Banana
    Smoothie, 130
  Strawberry Banana Yogurt, 92

Bananas—*continued*
 Sunflower Seed Butter & Banana
  Smoothie, 163
Barley
 about: nutritional value of, 255
 Apple, Pumpkin, & Barley Cereal, 46
 Apricot, Dried Plum, & Barley Cereal,
  46
 Apricot, Pear, & Barley Cereal, 61
 Avocado & Barley Cereal, 45
 Barley with Bananas & Blueberries,
  161
 Basic Barley, 56
 Beef & Barley, 81
 Dried Plum & Barley Cereal, 45
 Island Breakfast Cereal, 76
 Italian Beans & Barley, 145
 Maple Barley Breakfast, 132
 Mushroom Barley Casserole, 134
 Pinto Beans, Apples, & Barley, 76
 Summer Barley Salad, 154
 Vegetable Barley Casserole, 103
Beans
 about: black beans, 96; canned, 10;
  cannellini beans, 196
 Arrounce Verde con Frijoles Negro,
  137
 Avocado & Black Beans, 73
 Bean & Avocado Quesadilla, 176
 Black Bean & Carrot Mash, 96
 Black Bean Cakes, 179
 Black Bean Mash, 60
 Black Bean Roll-Ups, 177
 Breakfast Burrito, 161
 Burritos, 210
 Italian Beans & Barley, 145
 Minestrone Soup, 196
 Pinto Bean Burgers, 220
 Pinto Bean Roll-Ups, 173
 Pinto Beans, Apples, & Barley, 76
 Pinto Beans & Brown Rice, 75
 Pork & Beans, 175

 Quinoa Bean Salad, 124
 Red Beans & Rice, 147
 Refried Pinto Beans, 60
Beef
 Barbecue Meatloaf Muffins, 182
 Beef & Barley, 81
 Beef Brochettes, 214
 Beef Stew Mash, 80
 Broccoli with Meat & Rigatoni, 135
 Secret Beef Burgers, 221
 Taco Dinner, 185
Beets, Orange, 180
Blackberries, about, 150
Blackberry Frozen Yogurt, 114
Blackstrap molasses, 127
Blueberries
 about, 161; freezing, 93
 Banana & Blueberry Purée, 62
 Barley with Bananas & Blueberries,
  161
 Blueberry & Banana Yogurt, 163
 Blueberry Mini Muffins, 88
 Blueberry Pancakes, 129
 Blueberry Sorbet, 232
 Blueberry Syrup, 93
 Citrus Fruit Salad, 197
 Strawberry, Blueberry, & Banana
  Smoothie, 130
Breast milk and breastfeeding, 12–14,
 18–19
Broccoli
 Broccoli & Quinoa Casserole, 106
 Broccoli Cheese Soup, 120
 Broccoli with Meat & Rigatoni, 135
 Chicken & Broccoli Stir Fry, 166
 Herbed Broccoli, 226
Burgers, 220, 221
Burritos, 161, 210

Cakes, 116, 192
Canned foods, 10
Cantaloupe. *See* Melons

Carrots
 about: nutritional value of, 253
 Apple & Carrot Mash, 64
 Apple-Roasted Carrots, 112
 Black Bean & Carrot Mash, 96
 Butternut Squash with Carrots, 71
 Carrot & Zucchini Mini Muffins, 91
 Carrot Pineapple Salad, 199
 Chicken, Carrot, & Sweet Onion
  Mash, 80
 Chickpea, Carrot, & Cauliflower
  Mash, 106
 Couscous with Grated Zucchini &
  Carrots, 108
 Happy Second Birthday Carrot Cake,
  192
 Honeyed Carrots, 135
 Poached Fish & Carrots, 82
 Roasted Carrots, 170
 Sweet Potato & Carrot Purée, 69
 Vegetable Barley Casserole, 103
Cauliflower
 about: colors of, 98; nutritional value
  of, 122
 Cauliflower & Potato Mash, 98
 Chickpea, Carrot, & Cauliflower
  Mash, 106
 Creamy Cauliflower Soup, 122
 Frosted Cauliflower, 169
Celery boats, 187, 188
Cereals, **31**, **55**, **119**
Cheese
 Asparagus & Swiss Cheese Quiche,
  222
 Broccoli Cheese Soup, 120
 Cheesy Grits, 138
 Cheesy Polenta with Roasted
  Vegetables, 178
 Cream Cheese Frosting, 193
 Egg & Cheese Strata, 162
 Grilled Cheese with Squash & Corn
  Purée, 174

Macaroni & Cheese, 138
Spinach- & Ricotta-Stuffed Shells, 228
Turkey Cheese Roll-Ups, 216
Cherries
    Cherry Apple Coconut Rice Pudding, 164
    Chicken with Cherries & Brown Rice, 77
Chicken
    Barbecue Chicken Pizza, 165
    Chicken, Banana, & Coconut, 78
    Chicken, Carrot, & Sweet Onion Mash, 80
    Chicken, Papaya, & Nutmeg Mash, 79
    Chicken, Sweet Pea, & Sweet Potato Dinner, 107
    Chicken & Broccoli Stir Fry, 166
    Chicken & Mango Purée, 78
    Chicken & Parsnip Purée, 79
    Chicken & Udon Noodles, 168
    Chicken Enchiladas, 184
    Chicken Noodle Soup, 87
    Chicken Pot Pie Muffins, 136
    Chicken Salad, 123
    Chicken with Cherries & Brown Rice, 77
    Easy Baked Chicken, 140
    Parsnip & Chicken Purée, 113
Chickpea, Carrot, & Cauliflower Mash, 106
Chili, 110, 218
Chocolate
    Chocolate Pomegranate Dip, 194
    Coconut Chocolate Chip Muffins, 201
    Hot Chocolate, 233
Choking, 22–23
Cinnamon
    Apple, Sweet Potato, & Cinnamon Purée, 62
    Cinnamon Yogurt Fruit Dip, 152
    English Muffins with Cinnamon Butter, 207

Oatmeal with Cinnamon Apples, 91
Coconut
    Cherry Apple Coconut Rice Pudding, 164
    Chicken, Banana, & Coconut, 78
    Coconut Chocolate Chip Muffins, 201
    Coconut Pineapple Rice Pudding, 99
    Orange Coconut Sorbet, 117
Coconut oil, about, 97
Collard greens, 156
Community-supported agriculture (CSA), 8
Containers, 27, 207, 227
Convenience foods, 169
Cookies, 159, 200, 202
Corn
    about: cornbread, 128; nutritional value of, 254
    Butternut Squash & Corn Purée, 63, 174
    Corn Cakes with Black Bean Salsa, 227
    Corn Muffins, 128
    Corn on the Cob with Herbed Butter, 216
    Zucchini Corn Muffins, 126
Couscous with Grated Zucchini & Carrots, 108
Cucumber Tomato Salad, 155

Eating out, 70
Eggplant, Italian, 148
Eggs
    about: protein in, 162; substitute for, 182
    Asparagus & Swiss Cheese Quiche, 222
    Breakfast Burrito, 161
    Egg & Cheese Strata, 162
    Eggy Boats, 187
    French Toast, 130
    Spinach Tomato Scramble, 132

Fat intake, 85
Feeding basics, 11–30
    breast milk/breastfeeding, 12–14, 18–19
    formulas, 14–16, 18–19
    quantity/serving guidelines by age, 18–21
    safety considerations, 22–26, 64, 71, 207
    self-feeding, 17, 19
    solid food readiness, 16–17
Fish
    about: white sea bass, 134
    Baja-Style Fish Tacos, 224
    Baked Honey Pescado, 134
    Poached Fish & Carrots, 82
Flaxseeds, 88, 108, 182
Formulas, 14–16, 18–19
Freezing/thawing tips, 32, 66, 72, 76, 93
French Toast, 130
Frosting, Cream Cheese, 193
Frozen organics, 9–10
Fruits. See also specific fruits
    about: canned, 10; roasting, 170
    Fresh Fruit Slush, 194
    Fruit Kabobs, 150
    Fruit Salad, 199
    Mixed Fruit Yogurt Smoothie, 164
    Tropical Fruit Smoothie, 206
    Yogurt Berry Parfait, 92

Garbanzo beans
    Hummus, 107
    Hummus & Mango Sandwich, 173
    Hummus Yogurt Dipping Sauce, 191
    Roasted Red Pepper Hummus, 231
Genetically modified organisms (GMOs), 6
Glossary of terms, 257–68
Green beans
    about: nutritional value of, 254; snapping, 33

Green beans—*continued*
    Green Bean Purée, 33
    Green Beans, Mango, & Rice Cereal, 41
    Green Beans & Avocado Mash, 53
    Green Beans & Rice Cereal, 40
Grits, 58, 138

Honey, 64

Italian diets, 111

Kasha (roasted buckwheat), 58
Kasha with Peach & Pear Purée, 77
Kitchen equipment, tools, gadgets, 27–28, 113

Lamb
    Lamb & Pumpkin Mash, 82
    Roast Lamb, Rice, & Tomato Compote, 99
Lasagna, 211, 215, 229
Lemon Raspberry Ice Pops, 232
Lentils, 59
    about: cooking, 104
    Lentils & Brown Rice, 142
    Lentil Soup, 84
    Lentil-Stuffed Green Peppers, 223
    Lentils with Spinach & Quinoa, 104
Limeade Sorbet, 190

Mangos
    about, 41
    Chicken & Mango Purée, 78
    Green Beans, Mango, & Rice Cereal, 41
    Hummus & Mango Sandwich, 173
    Island Breakfast Cereal, 76
    Mango, Peach, & Rice Cereal, 40
    Mango & Apricot Purée, 50
    Mango & Brown Rice, 97
    Mango Banana Purée, 65

Mango Coleslaw, 156
Mango Honeydew Sorbet, 115
Mango Purée, 39
Pear Mango Purée, 47
Sweet Pea & Mango Purée, 53
Mangosteen Cereal Mix, 149
Mashes, **31**, **55**, **83**
Melons
    about: watermelon baskets, 199
    Cantaloupe Papaya Smoothie, 131
    Mango Honeydew Sorbet, 115
    Strawberry Cantaloupe Sorbet, 113
Menus by age group, *235–46*
Milk. *See also* Breast milk and breastfeeding
    Banana Yogurt Milkshake, 133
    organic, 5
    Pink Milk, 152
Muffins, **83**, **119**, **153**, **195**
Mushroom Barley Casserole, 134

Nitrates, 24–25
Nutritional information summary, 251–56

Oat flour, making, 116
Oatmeal, 57
    about: nutritional value of, 254
    Apple & Banana Oatmeal Cereal, 75
    Apple & Oatmeal Cereal, 43
    Banana, Apricot, & Oatmeal Cereal, 42
    Banana & Oatmeal Cereal, 42
    Oatmeal Cookies, 202
    Oatmeal with Cinnamon Apples, 91
    Oatmeal with Sautéed Plantains, 94
    Papaya, Apple, & Oatmeal Cereal, 44
    Papaya, Pear, & Oatmeal Cereal, 42
    Pumpkin, Peach, & Oatmeal Cereal, 44
Olive oil, 155
Oranges

Citrus Fruit Salad, 197
Citrusy Rice Salad, 121
Orange Beets, 180
Orange Coconut Sorbet, 117
Orange Pineapple Smoothie, 133
Organics, 1–10
    additional resources on, 247–49
    benefits of, 3–4
    canned, 10
    choosing produce, 4–5, 7–10
    defined, 1–10
    food pyramid guidelines and, 6–7
    fresh, seasonal produce, 7–9
    frozen, 9–10
    GMOs and, 6
    importance of, 3–4
    levels of/labeling program, 2
    pantry items, 28–30
    top twenty, 4–5
Orzo
    about: as rice substitute, 73
    Orzo & Sweet Pea Purée, 73
    Orzo with Creamy Tomato Spinach Sauce, 112
    Tomato & Orzo Soup, 85

Pancakes, 129, 204, 227
Pantry items, 28–30
Papayas
    about: ripeness of, 37; ripening, 79
    Cantaloupe Papaya Smoothie, 131
    Chicken, Papaya, & Nutmeg Mash, 79
    Island Breakfast Cereal, 76
    Papaya, Apple, & Oatmeal Cereal, 44
    Papaya, Pear, & Oatmeal Cereal, 42
    Papaya & Banana Mash, 48, 66
    Papaya Purée, 37
Parsnips
    about, 95
    Chicken & Parsnip Purée, 79
    Mashed Potatoes & Parsnips, 95
    Parsnip & Chicken Purée, 113

Pumpkin & Parsnip Purée, 67
Roasted Winter Vegetables, 165
Party food, 177
Pasta. *See also* Lasagna; Orzo
    about: alternative types, 212;
        nutritional value of, 254
    Alphabet Noodle Soup, 86
    Broccoli with Meat & Rigatoni, 135
    Chicken & Udon Noodles, 168
    Chicken Noodle Soup, 87
    Creamy Pasta Salad, 123
    Macaroni & Cheese, 138
    Spinach- & Ricotta-Stuffed Shells, 228
    Tofu-Stuffed Shells, 225
    Whole-Wheat Rotini with Bolognese
        Sauce, 111
    Whole-Wheat Shells with Marinara
        Sauce, 105
Peaches
    about, 74; nutritional value of, 255
    Kasha with Peach & Pear Purée, 77
    Mango, Peach, & Rice Cereal, 40
    Peach & Avocado Mash, 49
    Peaches & Quinoa, 72
    Peach Pear Purée, 51
    Peach Purée, 38
    Peach Raspberry Compote, 131
    Peach Raspberry Purée, 66
    Pumpkin, Peach, & Oatmeal Cereal,
        44
    Rice Cereal & Peach Purée, 74
Pears
    about: baked, 51; nutritional value
        of, 255
    Apple & Pear Purée, 61
    Apple Pear Crisp, 203
    Apricot, Pear, & Barley Cereal, 61
    Apricot Pear Purée, 48
    Butternut Squash with Apples &
        Pears, 71
    Dried Plum & Pear Purée, 51
    Kasha with Peach & Pear Purée, 77

Papaya, Pear, & Oatmeal Cereal, 42
Peach Pear Purée, 51
Pear Mango Purée, 47
Pear Purée, 36
Pumpkin Pear Rice Cereal, 39
Rutabaga & Pear Purée, 68
Peas
    about: nutritional value of, 255; split
        peas (green or yellow), 59
    Banana, Sweet Pea, & Rice Cereal, 41
    Chicken, Sweet Pea, & Sweet Potato
        Dinner, 107
    Orzo & Sweet Pea Purée, 73
    Split Pea Curry, 86
    Split Peas, 59
    Split Pea Soup, 84
    Sweet Pea & Apple Purée, 49
    Sweet Pea & Mango Purée, 53
    Sweet Pea Purée, 32
Peppers
    about, 223; hotness of, 224; roasting,
        231
    Lentil-Stuffed Green Peppers, 223
    Roasted Red Pepper Hummus, 231
Pesticides, 3, 4–5, 16
Pineapple
    about: making purée, 192
    Broiled Pineapple with Frozen
        Yogurt, 181
    Carrot Pineapple Salad, 199
    Citrus Fruit Salad, 197
    Citrusy Rice Salad, 121
    Coconut Pineapple Rice Pudding, 99
    Orange Pineapple Smoothie, 133
    Pineapple Salsa, 179
Pita Chips, Baked, 186
Pizzas, 165, 183, 208, 213
Plantains, Oatmeal with, 94
Plums
    about: nutritional value of, 256;
        prunes, 37
    Apple & Plum Compote, 70

Apricot, Dried Plum, & Barley Cereal,
    46
Dried Plum & Barley Cereal, 45
Dried Plum & Pear Purée, 51
Dried Plum Purée, 37
Potato & Plum Purée, 67
Polenta, Cheesy, withy Roasted
    Vegetables, 178
Pork
    about: iron content, 81
    Minced Pork Chop with Applesauce,
        81
    Pork & Beans, 175
Potatoes
    Cauliflower & Potato Mash, 98
    Cream of Potato Soup, 121
    Mashed Potatoes & Parsnips, 95
    Organic Farmer's Pie, 101
    Potato & Plum Purée, 67
    Potato Smash Up, 181
    Roasted Potato Rounds, 100
    Roasted Potato Salad, 144
    Shepherd's Pie, 217
    Spinach & Potato Purée, 68
    Sweet Potato Spread, 114
    Traditional Potato Salad, 158
    Two-Potato Mash, 65
Produce, pesticide-free organic, 4–5,
    7–10
Prunes. *See* Plums
Pumpkin
    about: canned, 10; cooking, 54; types
        of, 171
    Apple, Pumpkin, & Barley Cereal, 46
    Avocado Pumpkin Mash, 50
    Banana Pumpkin Mash, 52
    Fall Harvest Purée, 63
    Lamb & Pumpkin Mash, 82
    Pumpkin, Peach, & Oatmeal Cereal,
        44
    Pumpkin & Parsnip Purée, 67
    Pumpkin Pear Rice Cereal, 39

Pumpkin—*continued*
   Pumpkin Purée, 54
   Pumpkin Risotto, 171
   Spicy Pumpkin Muffins, 127
Puréeing, 70, 107, 192
Purées, **31**, **55**, **83**, **153**

Quesadillas, 176, 209
Quinoa, 57
   about, 72, 106, 124
   Barbecue Tofu & Quinoa, 100
   Broccoli & Quinoa Casserole, 106
   Lentils with Spinach & Quinoa, 104
   Peaches & Quinoa, 72
   Quinoa Bean Salad, 124
   Quinoa Primavera, 172
   Tabouli Salad, 157

Raspberries
   about: antioxidant value of, 150
   Lemon Raspberry Ice Pops, 232
   Peach Raspberry Compote, 131
   Peach Raspberry Purée, 66
   Raspberry Strawberry Muffins, 160
   Vanilla Raspberry Sorbet, 150
Red wine vinaigrette, 154
Resources, 247–49
Rice
   about: nutritional value of, 253;
     spicing up, 210; substitute for, 73
   Arrounce Verde con Frijoles Negro,
     137
   Baby's First Rice Cereal, 32
   Banana, Sweet Pea, & Rice Cereal, 41
   Brown Rice, 56
   Caribbean Baked Risotto, 146
   Cherry Apple Coconut Rice Pudding,
     164
   Chicken with Cherries & Brown Rice,
     77
   Citrusy Rice Salad, 121
   Coconut Pineapple Rice Pudding, 99

   Easy Spanish Rice, 210
   Green Beans, Mango, & Rice Cereal,
     41
   Green Beans & Rice Cereal, 40
   Lemony Rice & Asparagus Salad, 125
   Lentils & Brown Rice, 142
   Mango, Peach, & Rice Cereal, 40
   Mango & Brown Rice, 97
   Pinto Beans & Brown Rice, 75
   Pumpkin Pear Rice Cereal, 39
   Pumpkin Risotto, 171
   Red Beans & Rice, 147
   Rice Cereal & Peach Purée, 74
   Roast Lamb, Rice, & Tomato
     Compote, 99
   Vanilla Maple Rice Pudding, 205
   Vegetable Baked Risotto, 144
   Vegetable Rice Soup, 85
   Zucchini & Rice Cereal, 74
Rice wine vinegar, 172
Roll-ups, 173, 177, 216, 218
Rutabaga & Pear Purée, 68

Safety considerations, 22–26, 64, 71, 207
Salads, **119**, **153**, **195**
Salt intake, 89
Sauces and dips
   about, 102
   Avocado Yogurt Dip, 233
   Chocolate Pomegranate Dip, 194
   Cinnamon Yogurt Fruit Dip, 152
   Creamy Salsa Dip, 146
   Easy Gravy, 102
   Hummus Yogurt Dipping Sauce, 191
   Marinara Sauce, 105
   Pineapple Salsa, 179
   Sunflower Seed Butter Dip, 151
   Tomato Spinach Sauce, 112
   Yogurt Applesauce Dip, 191
Self-feeding, 17, 19
Six to nine months, 18–19, **55–82**,
   237–38

Skewer tips, 214
Slow cookers, 81
Smoothies, 130, 131, 133, 163, 164, 206
Snacking ideas, 230
Solid foods
   baby being ready for, 16–17
   quantity/serving guidelines by age,
     19–21
Sorbets, 113, 115, 117, 150, 190, 232
Soups, **83**, 87, **119**, **195**
Spinach
   about: nutritional value of, 256
   Arrounce Verde con Frijoles Negro,
     137
   Creamed Spinach, 145
   Creamy Spinach Pita Pizza, 183
   Lentils with Spinach & Quinoa, 104
   Spinach & Potato Purée, 68
   Spinach- & Ricotta-Stuffed Shells, 228
   Spinach Lasagna, 215
   Spinach Tomato Scramble, 132
   Tomato Spinach Sauce, 112
Squash
   about: cooking, 71; nutritional value
     of, 252; summer and winter, 174;
     zucchini vessels, 189
   Butternut Squash & Corn Purée, 63,
     174
   Butternut Squash with Apples &
     Pears, 71
   Butternut Squash with Carrots, 71
   Carrot & Zucchini Mini Muffins, 91
   Couscous with Grated Zucchini &
     Carrots, 108
   Maple Acorn Squash, 142
   Roasted Winter Vegetables, 165
   Spaghetti Squash with Italian Herbs,
     143
   Squash Purée, 34
   Zucchini & Rice Cereal, 74
   Zucchini Corn Muffins, 126
   Zucchini Yachts, 189

Stir-frying, about, 166
Strawberries
    Pink Milk, 152
    Raspberry Strawberry Muffins, 160
    Strawberry, Blueberry, & Banana
        Smoothie, 130
    Strawberry Applesauce, 115
    Strawberry Banana Yogurt, 92
    Strawberry Cantaloupe Sorbet, 113
    Strawberry Topping, 203
Stuffing, Homestyle, 141
Sunflower seed butter, 52
    Sunflower Seed Butter & Banana
        Smoothie, 163
    Sunflower Seed Butter Cookies, 200
    Sunflower Seed Butter Dip, 151
Sweeteners, 64, 89, 127
Sweet peas. See Peas
Sweet potatoes
    about: nutritional value of, 256;
        potatoes vs., 158
    Apple, Sweet Potato, & Cinnamon
        Purée, 62
    Apple & Sweet Potato Mini Muffins,
        90
    Chicken, Sweet Pea, & Sweet Potato
        Dinner, 107
    Fall Harvest Purée, 63
    Hawaiian Sweet Potatoes, 109
    Mashed Sweet Potatoes, 105
    Mashed Turnip & Sweet Potato, 72
    Roasted Winter Vegetables, 165
    Sweet Potato & Carrot Purée, 69
    Sweet Potato Biscuits, 157
    Sweet Potato Fries, 219
    Sweet Potato Purée, 34

Two-Potato Mash, 65

Tacos, 185, 224
Tastes and textures, 84
Tofu
    about, 112, 198
    Barbecue Tofu & Quinoa, 100
    Green Salad with Mock Caesar
        Dressing, 198
    Tofu Avocado Spread, 109
    Tofu Bites, 97
    Tofu Lasagna, 211
    Tofu Salad, 155
    Tofu Scramble, 206
    Tofu-Stuffed Shells, 225
    Vegetable Tofu Pot Pie, 139
Tomatoes. See also Sauces and dips
    about: canned, 10
    Cucumber Tomato Salad, 155
    Quesadilla with Tomato & Avocado,
        209
    Roast Lamb, Rice, & Tomato
        Compote, 99
    Spinach Tomato Scramble, 132
    Tomato & Orzo Soup, 85
Tortilla Chips, Baked, 230
Turkey
    Turkey Cheese Roll-Ups, 216
    Turkey Chili, 110
    Turkey Divan Muffins, 143
Turnip & Sweet Potato, Mashed, 72

Vanilla
    about, 205
    Happy Birthday Vanilla Cake, 116
    Vanilla Maple Rice Pudding, 205

Vanilla Raspberry Sorbet, 150
Vegetables. See also Salads
    about: canned, 10; freezing, 32
    Alphabet Noodle Soup, 86
    Grilled Summer Vegetables, 222
    Minestrone Soup, 196
    Mixed Vegetable Kabobs, 212
    Mixed-Vegetable Stir Fry, 167
    Organic Farmer's Pie, 101
    Roasted Winter Vegetables, 165
    Vegetable Baked Risotto, 144
    Vegetable Lasagna, 229
    Vegetable Rice Soup, 85. See also
        specific vegetables
    Vegetable Tofu Pot Pie, 139
    Veggie Roll-Ups, 218

Whole-wheat flour (white), 159

Yeast, nutritional, 139
Yogurt. See also Smoothies
    about: types of, 140
    Avocado Yogurt Dip, 233
    Banana Yogurt Milkshake, 133
    Blackberry Frozen Yogurt, 114
    Blueberry & Banana Yogurt, 163
    Broiled Pineapple with Frozen
        Yogurt, 181
    Cinnamon Yogurt Fruit Dip, 152
    Hummus Yogurt Dipping Sauce, 191
    Moist Yogurt Pancakes, 204
    Strawberry Banana Yogurt, 92
    Yogurt Applesauce Dip, 191
    Yogurt Berry Parfait, 92

Zucchini. See Squash

THE EVERYTHING SERIES!

BUSINESS & PERSONAL FINANCE

Everything® Accounting Book
Everything® Budgeting Book, 2nd Ed.
Everything® Business Planning Book
Everything® Coaching and Mentoring Book, 2nd Ed.
Everything® Fundraising Book
Everything® Get Out of Debt Book
Everything® Grant Writing Book, 2nd Ed.
Everything® Guide to Buying Foreclosures
Everything® Guide to Fundraising, $15.95
Everything® Guide to Mortgages
Everything® Guide to Personal Finance for Single Mothers
Everything® Home-Based Business Book, 2nd Ed.
Everything® Homebuying Book, 3rd Ed., $15.95
Everything® Homeselling Book, 2nd Ed.
Everything® Human Resource Management Book
Everything® Improve Your Credit Book
Everything® Investing Book, 2nd Ed.
Everything® Landlording Book
Everything® Leadership Book, 2nd Ed.
Everything® Managing People Book, 2nd Ed.
Everything® Negotiating Book
Everything® Online Auctions Book
Everything® Online Business Book
Everything® Personal Finance Book
Everything® Personal Finance in Your 20s & 30s Book, 2nd Ed.
Everything® Personal Finance in Your 40s & 50s Book, $15.95
Everything® Project Management Book, 2nd Ed.
Everything® Real Estate Investing Book
Everything® Retirement Planning Book
Everything® Robert's Rules Book, $7.95
Everything® Selling Book
Everything® Start Your Own Business Book, 2nd Ed.
Everything® Wills & Estate Planning Book

COOKING

Everything® Barbecue Cookbook
Everything® Bartender's Book, 2nd Ed., $9.95
Everything® Calorie Counting Cookbook
Everything® Cheese Book
Everything® Chinese Cookbook
Everything® Classic Recipes Book
Everything® Cocktail Parties & Drinks Book
Everything® College Cookbook
Everything® Cooking for Baby and Toddler Book
Everything® Diabetes Cookbook
Everything® Easy Gourmet Cookbook
Everything® Fondue Cookbook
Everything® Food Allergy Cookbook, $15.95
Everything® Fondue Party Book
Everything® Gluten-Free Cookbook
Everything® Glycemic Index Cookbook
Everything® Grilling Cookbook
Everything® Healthy Cooking for Parties Book, $15.95
Everything® Holiday Cookbook
Everything® Indian Cookbook
Everything® Lactose-Free Cookbook
Everything® Low-Cholesterol Cookbook

Everything® Low-Fat High-Flavor Cookbook, 2nd Ed., $15.95
Everything® Low-Salt Cookbook
Everything® Meals for a Month Cookbook
Everything® Meals on a Budget Cookbook
Everything® Mediterranean Cookbook
Everything® Mexican Cookbook
Everything® No Trans Fat Cookbook
Everything® One-Pot Cookbook, 2nd Ed., $15.95
Everything® Organic Cooking for Baby & Toddler Book, $15.95
Everything® Pizza Cookbook
Everything® Quick Meals Cookbook, 2nd Ed., $15.95
Everything® Slow Cooker Cookbook
Everything® Slow Cooking for a Crowd Cookbook
Everything® Soup Cookbook
Everything® Stir-Fry Cookbook
Everything® Sugar-Free Cookbook
Everything® Tapas and Small Plates Cookbook
Everything® Tex-Mex Cookbook
Everything® Thai Cookbook
Everything® Vegetarian Cookbook
Everything® Whole-Grain, High-Fiber Cookbook
Everything® Wild Game Cookbook
Everything® Wine Book, 2nd Ed.

GAMES

Everything® 15-Minute Sudoku Book, $9.95
Everything® 30-Minute Sudoku Book, $9.95
Everything® Bible Crosswords Book, $9.95
Everything® Blackjack Strategy Book
Everything® Brain Strain Book, $9.95
Everything® Bridge Book
Everything® Card Games Book
Everything® Card Tricks Book, $9.95
Everything® Casino Gambling Book, 2nd Ed.
Everything® Chess Basics Book
Everything® Christmas Crosswords Book, $9.95
Everything® Craps Strategy Book
Everything® Crossword and Puzzle Book
Everything® Crosswords and Puzzles for Quote Lovers Book, $9.95
Everything® Crossword Challenge Book
Everything® Crosswords for the Beach Book, $9.95
Everything® Cryptic Crosswords Book, $9.95
Everything® Cryptograms Book, $9.95
Everything® Easy Crosswords Book
Everything® Easy Kakuro Book, $9.95
Everything® Easy Large-Print Crosswords Book
Everything® Games Book, 2nd Ed.
Everything® Giant Book of Crosswords
Everything® Giant Sudoku Book, $9.95
Everything® Giant Word Search Book
Everything® Kakuro Challenge Book, $9.95
Everything® Large-Print Crossword Challenge Book
Everything® Large-Print Crosswords Book
Everything® Large-Print Travel Crosswords Book
Everything® Lateral Thinking Puzzles Book, $9.95
Everything® Literary Crosswords Book, $9.95
Everything® Mazes Book
Everything® Memory Booster Puzzles Book, $9.95

Everything® Movie Crosswords Book, $9.95
Everything® Music Crosswords Book, $9.95
Everything® Online Poker Book
Everything® Pencil Puzzles Book, $9.95
Everything® Poker Strategy Book
Everything® Pool & Billiards Book
Everything® Puzzles for Commuters Book, $9.95
Everything® Puzzles for Dog Lovers Book, $9.95
Everything® Sports Crosswords Book, $9.95
Everything® Test Your IQ Book, $9.95
Everything® Texas Hold 'Em Book, $9.95
Everything® Travel Crosswords Book, $9.95
Everything® Travel Mazes Book, $9.95
Everything® Travel Word Search Book, $9.95
Everything® TV Crosswords Book, $9.95
Everything® Word Games Challenge Book
Everything® Word Scramble Book
Everything® Word Search Book

HEALTH

Everything® Alzheimer's Book
Everything® Diabetes Book
Everything® First Aid Book, $9.95
Everything® Green Living Book
Everything® Health Guide to Addiction and Recovery
Everything® Health Guide to Adult Bipolar Disorder
Everything® Health Guide to Arthritis
Everything® Health Guide to Controlling Anxiety
Everything® Health Guide to Depression
Everything® Health Guide to Diabetes, 2nd Ed.
Everything® Health Guide to Fibromyalgia
Everything® Health Guide to Menopause, 2nd Ed.
Everything® Health Guide to Migraines
Everything® Health Guide to Multiple Sclerosis
Everything® Health Guide to OCD
Everything® Health Guide to PMS
Everything® Health Guide to Postpartum Care
Everything® Health Guide to Thyroid Disease
Everything® Hypnosis Book
Everything® Low Cholesterol Book
Everything® Menopause Book
Everything® Nutrition Book
Everything® Reflexology Book
Everything® Stress Management Book
Everything® Superfoods Book, $15.95

HISTORY

Everything® American Government Book
Everything® American History Book, 2nd Ed.
Everything® American Revolution Book, $15.95
Everything® Civil War Book
Everything® Freemasons Book
Everything® Irish History & Heritage Book
Everything® World War II Book, 2nd Ed.

HOBBIES

Everything® Candlemaking Book
Everything® Cartooning Book
Everything® Coin Collecting Book
Everything® Digital Photography Book, 2nd Ed.

Everything® Drawing Book
Everything® Family Tree Book, 2nd Ed.
Everything® Guide to Online Genealogy, $15.95
Everything® Knitting Book
Everything® Knots Book
Everything® Photography Book
Everything® Quilting Book
Everything® Sewing Book
Everything® Soapmaking Book, 2nd Ed.
Everything® Woodworking Book

HOME IMPROVEMENT

Everything® Feng Shui Book
Everything® Feng Shui Decluttering Book, $9.95
Everything® Fix-It Book
Everything® Green Living Book
Everything® Home Decorating Book
Everything® Home Storage Solutions Book
Everything® Homebuilding Book
Everything® Organize Your Home Book, 2nd Ed.

KIDS' BOOKS

All titles are $7.95
Everything® Fairy Tales Book, $14.95
Everything® Kids' Animal Puzzle & Activity Book
Everything® Kids' Astronomy Book
Everything® Kids' Baseball Book, 5th Ed.
Everything® Kids' Bible Trivia Book
Everything® Kids' Bugs Book
Everything® Kids' Cars and Trucks Puzzle and Activity Book
Everything® Kids' Christmas Puzzle & Activity Book
Everything® Kids' Connect the Dots
    Puzzle and Activity Book
Everything® Kids' Cookbook, 2nd Ed.
Everything® Kids' Crazy Puzzles Book
Everything® Kids' Dinosaurs Book
Everything® Kids' Dragons Puzzle and Activity Book
Everything® Kids' Environment Book $7.95
Everything® Kids' Fairies Puzzle and Activity Book
Everything® Kids' First Spanish Puzzle and Activity Book
Everything® Kids' Football Book
Everything® Kids' Geography Book
Everything® Kids' Gross Cookbook
Everything® Kids' Gross Hidden Pictures Book
Everything® Kids' Gross Jokes Book
Everything® Kids' Gross Mazes Book
Everything® Kids' Gross Puzzle & Activity Book
Everything® Kids' Halloween Puzzle & Activity Book
Everything® Kids' Hanukkah Puzzle and Activity Book
Everything® Kids' Hidden Pictures Book
Everything® Kids' Horses Book
Everything® Kids' Joke Book
Everything® Kids' Knock Knock Book
Everything® Kids' Learning French Book
Everything® Kids' Learning Spanish Book
Everything® Kids' Magical Science Experiments Book
Everything® Kids' Math Puzzles Book
Everything® Kids' Mazes Book
Everything® Kids' Money Book, 2nd Ed.
Everything® Kids' Mummies, Pharaoh's, and Pyramids
    Puzzle and Activity Book
Everything® Kids' Nature Book
Everything® Kids' Pirates Puzzle and Activity Book
Everything® Kids' Presidents Book
Everything® Kids' Princess Puzzle and Activity Book
Everything® Kids' Puzzle Book

Everything® Kids' Racecars Puzzle and Activity Book
Everything® Kids' Riddles & Brain Teasers Book
Everything® Kids' Science Experiments Book
Everything® Kids' Sharks Book
Everything® Kids' Soccer Book
Everything® Kids' Spelling Book
Everything® Kids' Spies Puzzle and Activity Book
Everything® Kids' States Book
Everything® Kids' Travel Activity Book
Everything® Kids' Word Search Puzzle and Activity Book

LANGUAGE

Everything® Conversational Japanese Book with CD, $19.95
Everything® French Grammar Book
Everything® French Phrase Book, $9.95
Everything® French Verb Book, $9.95
Everything® German Phrase Book, $9.95
Everything® German Practice Book with CD, $19.95
Everything® Inglés Book
Everything® Intermediate Spanish Book with CD, $19.95
Everything® Italian Phrase Book, $9.95
Everything® Italian Practice Book with CD, $19.95
Everything® Learning Brazilian Portuguese Book with CD, $19.95
Everything® Learning French Book with CD, 2nd Ed., $19.95
Everything® Learning German Book
Everything® Learning Italian Book
Everything® Learning Latin Book
Everything® Learning Russian Book with CD, $19.95
Everything® Learning Spanish Book
Everything® Learning Spanish Book with CD, 2nd Ed., $19.95
Everything® Russian Practice Book with CD, $19.95
Everything® Sign Language Book, $15.95
Everything® Spanish Grammar Book
Everything® Spanish Phrase Book, $9.95
Everything® Spanish Practice Book with CD, $19.95
Everything® Spanish Verb Book, $9.95
Everything® Speaking Mandarin Chinese Book with CD, $19.95

MUSIC

Everything® Bass Guitar Book with CD, $19.95
Everything® Drums Book with CD, $19.95
Everything® Guitar Book with CD, 2nd Ed., $19.95
Everything® Guitar Chords Book with CD, $19.95
Everything® Guitar Scales Book with CD, $19.95
Everything® Harmonica Book with CD, $15.95
Everything® Home Recording Book
Everything® Music Theory Book with CD, $19.95
Everything® Reading Music Book with CD, $19.95
Everything® Rock & Blues Guitar Book with CD, $19.95
Everything® Rock & Blues Piano Book with CD, $19.95
Everything® Rock Drums Book with CD, $19.95
Everything® Singing Book with CD, $19.95
Everything® Songwriting Book

NEW AGE

Everything® Astrology Book, 2nd Ed.
Everything® Birthday Personology Book
Everything® Celtic Wisdom Book, $15.95
Everything® Dreams Book, 2nd Ed.
Everything® Law of Attraction Book, $15.95
Everything® Love Signs Book, $9.95
Everything® Love Spells Book, $9.95
Everything® Palmistry Book
Everything® Psychic Book
Everything® Reiki Book

Everything® Sex Signs Book, $9.95
Everything® Spells & Charms Book, 2nd Ed.
Everything® Tarot Book, 2nd Ed.
Everything® Toltec Wisdom Book
Everything® Wicca & Witchcraft Book, 2nd Ed.

PARENTING

Everything® Baby Names Book, 2nd Ed.
Everything® Baby Shower Book, 2nd Ed.
Everything® Baby Sign Language Book with DVD
Everything® Baby's First Year Book
Everything® Birthing Book
Everything® Breastfeeding Book
Everything® Father-to-Be Book
Everything® Father's First Year Book
Everything® Get Ready for Baby Book, 2nd Ed.
Everything® Get Your Baby to Sleep Book, $9.95
Everything® Getting Pregnant Book
Everything® Guide to Pregnancy Over 35
Everything® Guide to Raising a One-Year-Old
Everything® Guide to Raising a Two-Year-Old
Everything® Guide to Raising Adolescent Boys
Everything® Guide to Raising Adolescent Girls
Everything® Mother's First Year Book
Everything® Parent's Guide to Childhood Illnesses
Everything® Parent's Guide to Children and Divorce
Everything® Parent's Guide to Children with ADD/ADHD
Everything® Parent's Guide to Children with Asperger's
    Syndrome
Everything® Parent's Guide to Children with Anxiety
Everything® Parent's Guide to Children with Asthma
Everything® Parent's Guide to Children with Autism
Everything® Parent's Guide to Children with Bipolar Disorder
Everything® Parent's Guide to Children with Depression
Everything® Parent's Guide to Children with Dyslexia
Everything® Parent's Guide to Children with Juvenile Diabetes
Everything® Parent's Guide to Children with OCD
Everything® Parent's Guide to Positive Discipline
Everything® Parent's Guide to Raising Boys
Everything® Parent's Guide to Raising Girls
Everything® Parent's Guide to Raising Siblings
Everything® Parent's Guide to Raising Your
    Adopted Child
Everything® Parent's Guide to Sensory Integration Disorder
Everything® Parent's Guide to Tantrums
Everything® Parent's Guide to the Strong-Willed Child
Everything® Parenting a Teenager Book
Everything® Potty Training Book, $9.95
Everything® Pregnancy Book, 3rd Ed.
Everything® Pregnancy Fitness Book
Everything® Pregnancy Nutrition Book
Everything® Pregnancy Organizer, 2nd Ed., $16.95
Everything® Toddler Activities Book
Everything® Toddler Book
Everything® Tween Book
Everything® Twins, Triplets, and More Book

PETS

Everything® Aquarium Book
Everything® Boxer Book
Everything® Cat Book, 2nd Ed.
Everything® Chihuahua Book
Everything® Cooking for Dogs Book
Everything® Dachshund Book
Everything® Dog Book, 2nd Ed.
Everything® Dog Grooming Book

Everything® Dog Obedience Book
Everything® Dog Owner's Organizer, $16.95
Everything® Dog Training and Tricks Book
Everything® German Shepherd Book
Everything® Golden Retriever Book
Everything® Horse Book, 2nd Ed., $15.95
Everything® Horse Care Book
Everything® Horseback Riding Book
Everything® Labrador Retriever Book
Everything® Poodle Book
Everything® Pug Book
Everything® Puppy Book
Everything® Small Dogs Book
Everything® Tropical Fish Book
Everything® Yorkshire Terrier Book

REFERENCE

Everything® American Presidents Book
Everything® Blogging Book
Everything® Build Your Vocabulary Book, $9.95
Everything® Car Care Book
Everything® Classical Mythology Book
Everything® Da Vinci Book
Everything® Einstein Book
Everything® Enneagram Book
Everything® Etiquette Book, 2nd Ed.
Everything® Family Christmas Book, $15.95
Everything® Guide to C. S. Lewis & Narnia
Everything® Guide to Divorce, 2nd Ed., $15.95
Everything® Guide to Edgar Allan Poe
Everything® Guide to Understanding Philosophy
Everything® Inventions and Patents Book
Everything® Jacqueline Kennedy Onassis Book
Everything® John F. Kennedy Book
Everything® Mafia Book
Everything® Martin Luther King Jr. Book
Everything® Pirates Book
Everything® Private Investigation Book
Everything® Psychology Book
Everything® Public Speaking Book, $9.95
Everything® Shakespeare Book, 2nd Ed.

RELIGION

Everything® Angels Book
Everything® Bible Book
Everything® Bible Study Book with CD, $19.95
Everything® Buddhism Book
Everything® Catholicism Book
Everything® Christianity Book
Everything® Gnostic Gospels Book
Everything® Hinduism Book, $15.95
Everything® History of the Bible Book
Everything® Jesus Book
Everything® Jewish History & Heritage Book
Everything® Judaism Book
Everything® Kabbalah Book
Everything® Koran Book
Everything® Mary Book
Everything® Mary Magdalene Book
Everything® Prayer Book

Everything® Saints Book, 2nd Ed.
Everything® Torah Book
Everything® Understanding Islam Book
Everything® Women of the Bible Book
Everything® World's Religions Book

SCHOOL & CAREERS

Everything® Career Tests Book
Everything® College Major Test Book
Everything® College Survival Book, 2nd Ed.
Everything® Cover Letter Book, 2nd Ed.
Everything® Filmmaking Book
Everything® Get-a-Job Book, 2nd Ed.
Everything® Guide to Being a Paralegal
Everything® Guide to Being a Personal Trainer
Everything® Guide to Being a Real Estate Agent
Everything® Guide to Being a Sales Rep
Everything® Guide to Being an Event Planner
Everything® Guide to Careers in Health Care
Everything® Guide to Careers in Law Enforcement
Everything® Guide to Government Jobs
Everything® Guide to Starting and Running a Catering
    Business
Everything® Guide to Starting and Running a Restaurant
**Everything® Guide to Starting and Running
    a Retail Store**
Everything® Job Interview Book, 2nd Ed.
Everything® New Nurse Book
Everything® New Teacher Book
Everything® Paying for College Book
Everything® Practice Interview Book
Everything® Resume Book, 3rd Ed.
Everything® Study Book

SELF-HELP

Everything® Body Language Book
Everything® Dating Book, 2nd Ed.
Everything® Great Sex Book
**Everything® Guide to Caring for Aging Parents,
    $15.95**
Everything® Self-Esteem Book
Everything® Self-Hypnosis Book, $9.95
Everything® Tantric Sex Book

SPORTS & FITNESS

Everything® Easy Fitness Book
Everything® Fishing Book
Everything® Guide to Weight Training, $15.95
Everything® Krav Maga for Fitness Book
Everything® Running Book, 2nd Ed.
Everything® Triathlon Training Book, $15.95

TRAVEL

Everything® Family Guide to Coastal Florida
Everything® Family Guide to Cruise Vacations
Everything® Family Guide to Hawaii
Everything® Family Guide to Las Vegas, 2nd Ed.
Everything® Family Guide to Mexico
Everything® Family Guide to New England, 2nd Ed.

Everything® Family Guide to New York City, 3rd Ed.
**Everything® Family Guide to Northern California
    and Lake Tahoe**
Everything® Family Guide to RV Travel & Campgrounds
Everything® Family Guide to the Caribbean
Everything® Family Guide to the Disneyland® Resort, California
    Adventure®, Universal Studios®, and the Anaheim
    Area, 2nd Ed.
Everything® Family Guide to the Walt Disney World Resort®,
    Universal Studios®, and Greater Orlando, 5th Ed.
Everything® Family Guide to Timeshares
Everything® Family Guide to Washington D.C., 2nd Ed.

WEDDINGS

Everything® Bachelorette Party Book, $9.95
Everything® Bridesmaid Book, $9.95
Everything® Destination Wedding Book
Everything® Father of the Bride Book, $9.95
Everything® Green Wedding Book, $15.95
Everything® Groom Book, $9.95
Everything® Jewish Wedding Book, 2nd Ed., $15.95
Everything® Mother of the Bride Book, $9.95
Everything® Outdoor Wedding Book
Everything® Wedding Book, 3rd Ed.
Everything® Wedding Checklist, $9.95
Everything® Wedding Etiquette Book, $9.95
Everything® Wedding Organizer, 2nd Ed., $16.95
Everything® Wedding Shower Book, $9.95
Everything® Wedding Vows Book, 3rd Ed., $9.95
Everything® Wedding Workout Book
Everything® Weddings on a Budget Book, 2nd Ed., $9.95

WRITING

Everything® Creative Writing Book
Everything® Get Published Book, 2nd Ed.
Everything® Grammar and Style Book, 2nd Ed.
Everything® Guide to Magazine Writing
Everything® Guide to Writing a Book Proposal
Everything® Guide to Writing a Novel
Everything® Guide to Writing Children's Books
Everything® Guide to Writing Copy
Everything® Guide to Writing Graphic Novels
Everything® Guide to Writing Research Papers
Everything® Guide to Writing a Romance Novel, $15.95
Everything® Improve Your Writing Book, 2nd Ed.
Everything® Writing Poetry Book

Available wherever books are sold! To order, call 800-258-0929, or visit us at *www.adamsmedia.com*.
Everything® and everything.com® are registered trademarks of F+W Publications, Inc.
Bolded titles are new additions to the series.
All Everything® books are priced at $12.95 or $14.95, unless otherwise stated. Prices subject to change without notice.